THE SWORD AND THE CIRCLE

Suddenly Arthur's head was clear and his heart strong within him; and he knew that whatever he had to do in this new life, he could do it . . .

   'I am your King! You and I together, let us make this a good land, where men do not rule only because they are strong, but where men are strong for the Right . . .'

A vivid and haunting new retelling of the legendary exploits of King Arthur of Britain, his Knights of the Round Table and Merlin the magician, and their ceaseless fight for the good and glory of Britain.

'The imagery is fresh, vivid, robust; the characters memorable; the echoes potent.'

The Times

Cover illustration by Shirley Felts

The Sword and the Circle

King Arthur and the Knights of the Round Table

Rosemary Sutcliff

Decorations by Shirley Felts

KNIGHT BOOKS
Hodder and Stoughton

First published 1981 by The Bodley
Head Ltd

Knight Books edition 1983
Fifth impression 1987

Printed and bound in Great Britain
for Hodder and Stoughton
Paperbacks, a division of Hodder
and Stoughton Ltd., Mill Road,
Dunton Green, Sevenoaks, Kent.
TN13 2YA.
(Editorial Office: 47 Bedford
Square, London WC1B 3DP) by
Cox & Wyman Ltd., Reading.

British Library C.I.P.

Sutcliff, Rosemary
  The sword and the circle.
  I. Title
  823'.914[J]   PZ7

  ISBN 0 340 28562 1

CONTENTS

AUTHOR'S NOTE

Some time early in the fifth century A.D. – history books used to say A.D. 410, but now the experts think that probably there were a few auxiliary troops left in Britain a good deal later than that – the last Roman legions were withdrawn from Britain to defend Rome itself, and the British were left to hold off the invading Saxons as best they could. In the end they failed, but they put up such a fight that it took the Saxons around two hundred and fifty years to complete their occupation; and they never did take over all of the Western country. But none the less, the withdrawal of Rome was the beginning of what we call 'the Dark Ages' chiefly because so little record of them has survived.

It is to some time early in these Dark Ages that King Arthur belongs.

Many people believe, as I do, that behind the legends of King Arthur as we know them today, there stands a real man. No king in shining armour, no Round Table, no fairy-tale palace at Camelot, but a Roman–British war leader, who when the dark tide of the barbarians came flooding in, did all that a great leader could do to hold them back and save something of civilisation. In *The Lantern Bearers* and *Sword at Sunset*, I have written about this war leader, trying to get back through the hero-tale and the high romance to the real man and the world he lived in.

But if the hero-tale had never grown up, and gathered to itself the mass of Celtic myth and folklore and the medieval splendours that we know now as the legends of King Arthur, we should have lost something beautiful and mysterious and magical out of our heritage. All down the ages, the stories have been told and told again, most splendidly of all by Sir Thomas Malory in *Morte d'Arthur*.

In *The Sword and the Circle* I have followed Malory in the main, but I have not followed him slavishly – no minstrel ever follows exactly the songs that have come down to him from the time before. Always he adds and leaves out and embroiders and puts something of himself into each retelling. And some of the stories in this retelling of mine are not to be found in Malory at all.

So – I have based the first story, of Vortigern and Merlin, Utha and Igraine and the dragon-light in the sky, upon Geoffrey of Monmouth's *British History*.

Sir Gawain and the Green Knight comes from a Middle English poem.

For *Tristan and Iseult* I have turned back to a much earlier version, which Malory doesn't seem to have known, by Godfrey of Strasburg. But this story is in outline the same as the still older Irish tragedies of *Deirdre and the Sons of Usna* and *Diarmid and Grania*.

Geraint and Enid is from the ancient Welsh book, *The Mabinogion*.

Sir Gawain and the Loathely Lady is based on a Middle English ballad.

The early part of Sir Percival's adventures are loosely based on another Early English poem with a few incidents from the *Conte de Graal*, but the end is largely my own invention – and why not, when the story of *Beaumains, the Kitchen Knight* seems to have come entirely out of Malory's own head?

Two things I should like to explain. The first, that in medieval times dinner was at about ten o'clock in the morning and supper at about six o'clock in the evening.

The second, that a tilt or joust was a trial of strength and skill between two knights at a time, a form of sport, though a dangerous one; while a tournament was a kind of sham battle between any number of knights, which often got out of hand and ended in a lot of people being killed.

1

THE COMING OF ARTHUR

In the dark years after Rome was gone from Britain, Vortigern of the narrow eyes and the thin red beard came down from the mountains of Wales, and by treachery slew Constantine of the old royal house and seized the High Kingship of Britain in his place.

But his blood-smirched kingship was little joy to him, for his realm was beset by the wild hordes of Picts and Scots pouring down from the North, and the Saxons, the Sea Wolves, harrying the eastern and southern shores. And he was not a strong man, as Constantine had been, to hold them back.

At last, not knowing what else to do, he sent for two Saxon warchiefs, Hengest and Horsa, and gave them land and gold to bring over their fighting men and drive back the Picts and the Scots and their own sea-raiding brothers. And that was the worst of all things in the world that he could have done. For Hengest and Horsa saw that the land was rich; and at home in Denmark and Germany there were many younger sons, and not enough land nor rich enough harvests to feed them all; and after that Britain was never free of the Saxon-kind again.

They pushed further and further in from the coasts, sacking the towns and laying waste the country through which they passed, harrying the people as wolves harry the sheep in a famine winter; and many a farmer died on his own threshold and many a priest before his altar, and ever the wind carried the smell of burning where the Saxons went by.

Then, seeing what he had done, Vortigern drew back into the dark fastnesses of Wales and summoned his wise men, his seers and wonder-workers and begged them tell him what he should do.

'Build yourself a mighty tower and lie close in it. There is nothing else left to you,' said the foremost of the seers.

So Vortigern sent out men skilled in such matters to find the best place for building such a stronghold, and when he had listened to their reports, his choice fell upon Eriri, the Place of the Eagles, high in the mountains of Gwynedd. And there he gathered together workmen from the North and the South and the East and the West, and bade them build him a tower stronger than any tower that ever had stood in Britain before then. The men set to work, cutting great blocks of stone from quarries in the hillsides; and the straining teams of men and horses dragged them up to the chosen place. And there, on the cloudy crest of Eriri, they began to set the mighty foundations that should carry such a stronghold as had never been seen in Britain until that time.

But then came a strange thing. Every morning when they went to start work, they found the stones that they had raised and set in place the day before cast down and scattered all abroad. And day by day it was the same, so that the stronghold on the Place of the Eagles never grew beyond its first day's building.

Then Vortigern sent again for his seers and magicians and demanded to know the cause of the thing, and what they should do about it.

And the seers and magicians looked into the stars by night and the Seeing-Bowl of black oak-water by day, and said, 'Lord King, there is need of a sacrifice.'

'Then bring a black goat,' said Vortigern.

'A black goat will not serve.'

'A white stallion, then.'

'Nor a white stallion.'

'A man?'

'Not even a man who is as other men.'

'What, then, in the Devil's name?' shouted the High King, and flung down the wine-cup that was in his hand, so that the wine spattered like blood into the moorland heather.

And the chief of the wise men looked at the stain of it, and smiled. 'Let you seek out a youth who never had a mortal father, and cause him to be slain in the old way, the sacred way, and his blood sprinkled upon the stones, and so you shall have a sure foundation for your stronghold.'

So Vortigern sent out his messengers to seek for such a youth. And after long searching they came to the city of Caermerddyn; and in that city they found a youth whose mother was a princess of Demetia, but whose father no man knew. The princess had long since entered a nunnery, but before that, when she was young, she had been visited, as though in a dream, by one of those who the Christian folk call fallen angels, fair and fiery, and lost between Heaven and Earth. And of his coming to her, she had borne a son and called him Merlin.

All this she told freely to the High King's messengers when they asked her, thinking no harm. But when they had heard all that she told, they seized the boy Merlin and brought him to Vortigern in the fine timber hall that he had caused to be set up in the safety of the mountains hard by Eriri. And Vortigern sat in his great seat spread with finely dressed wolfskins and cloth of crimson and purple, and pulled at his meagre beard and looked at the boy through the smoke tendrils of the hearth fire. And the boy stood before him, lean and whippy as a hazel wand, with dark hair like the ruffled feathers of a hawk, and stared back at him out of eyes that were yellow as a hawk, also, and demanded, as a man demanding of an equal, to know why he had been brought there.

The High King was not used to being spoken to in that tone, and in his surprise he told Merlin what he asked, instead of merely ordering him to be killed at once.

And the boy listened; and when it was told, he said, 'And so my blood is to be shed that your tower may stand. It is a fine story that your magicians have told you, my Lord King, but there is no truth in it.'

'As to that,' said Vortigern, 'the matter is easily put to the proof.'

'By scattering my blood upon the stones of your stronghold? Nay now, do you send for your magicians, and bid them stand before me, and easily enough I will prove them liars.'

Vortigern tugged at his beard and his narrow eyes grew narrower yet. But in the end he sent for his wise men, and they came and stood before the boy Merlin. And Merlin looked them over from one to another, and said, 'The Sight and the Power have grown weak in you and your like in the long years since the passing of the true Druid kind. Therefore, because you are darkened to the truth, you have told the King that my blood shed upon these stones shall make his tower stand. But I tell you that it is not the need for my blood that causes his stones to fall, but some strange happening beneath the ground which every night engulfs the work of the day. Let you tell me then in your wisdom, what thing that is!'

The magicians were silent, for their powers had indeed grown dim.

Then Merlin turned from them to Vortigern. 'My Lord the High King, let your men dig beneath the foundations until they come to the deep pool that they will find there.'

So the King gave his orders and the men set to work, and in a while they broke in through the roof of a vast cave; and all the floor of the cave was one deep, dark pool, from the depth of which slow bubbles rose to the surface as though some great creature lay asleep and breathing deeply far below.

Then Merlin turned to Vortigern who had come from his hall to look on, and to his magicians behind him, and said, 'Tell me, oh workers of wonders and walkers in secret ways, what lies at the bottom of this pool?'

And again they could not answer.

And Merlin said to the King, 'My Lord Vortigern, now let you give orders that this pool be drained, for at the bottom of it you shall find two dragons lying asleep.'

And when the pool was drained, there, far down among the rocks, lay the two dragons, sleeping; and one of them was white as frost and the other was red as fire. And the King and all those who stood about the pool were struck with amazement. But the magicians had slipped away.

'By day,' said the boy Merlin, 'these creatures sleep as you see them now; but every night they wake and fight together, and their battle lasts until the sunrise gives them sleep again; and their battling shakes the mountain crest, and the earth gapes and closes and the waters of the pool are lashed to tempest; and it is so that the tower that you would build above them does not stand.'

Now the end of the day had come, and the dusk was deepening fast, and even as he spoke the sleeping dragons began to rouse. Fire-red and frost-white coils rippled and stirred and the great heads reared up, and the jaws gaped and began to breathe out thin jets of fire that grew and strengthened to rolling clouds of flame; and with a waking roar that made the very ground thrum beneath the watcher's feet, the two monsters sprang together.

All night long, by the levin-light of their own breath that filled the great chasm and played like summer lightning upon the whipped-up shallows remaining of the pool, the two fought. And first the white dragon had the advantage and drove the red to the far end of the pool; and then the red dragon rallied and turned the fight again; and the water boiled about their lashing coils, and all the crest of the mountain shuddered with the tumult of their battle. And slowly the red dragon drove the white back until he in his turn was at the end of the pool. And then when it seemed that all was over, the white dragon gathered himself and hurled himself yet once more upon the red . . .

But the first light of day was waking in the sky, and the fire of the dragons sank and their movements grew slower, and little by little the great coils relaxed, and they sank to sleep.

Then Vortigern demanded of the boy Merlin the meaning of what he had seen; and Merlin told him that the red dragon was Britain and the white dragon was the Saxon kind, and that every night they fought out the conflict between the two.

'Then surely the red dragon had the victory,' Vortigern said, 'and I and my realm have nothing to fear.'

'But the white dragon was gathering his fighting power again when this new day laid sleep once more upon them both,' said Merlin. And he looked as though into a great distance; but a distance that was within himself. Three strains of power ran deep within Merlin; from his mother who was of the Demetii he had the herb-skills and the ancient half-lost wisdoms of the Old People, the Little Dark People; and from the old Druid, almost the last of his kind, who had taken and reared and trained him after his mother entered her nunnery, he had star-knowledge and the skills of shape-shifting and art-magic; and both these he could use at will. But from his father he had the power to look into the future as other men look into the past; and this came not at his own will but at the will of the power itself, that was like a great wind that snatched him up into some place where past and future were one. So now he began to shake like a young aspen tree in the wind. And he began to prophesy in a high clear voice many things concerning the red dragon and the white.

And when at last the high wind of prophecy forsook him and he ceased to shake, and looked again out of his own golden eyes and spoke again in his own voice, he said, 'But all these things will be after your time, my Lord the King.'

And a pang of fear shot through Vortigern, and he said, 'Then how can they concern me? Tell me now of *my* time!'

'Your time?' said Merlin. 'Your time is short, and ends in fire at the hands of the sons of the dead High

King Constantine, Ambrosius and Utha. They have gathered many fighting men in Less Britain, which some call Brittany, that gave them shelter when you slew their sire; and already their ships are fitted out, already they spread their sails to the wind that shall carry them across the Narrow Seas. They will drive back the Saxon hordes; but you they will burn shut up in your strongest tower, in vengeance for their father's murder. Then Ambrosius shall be crowned High King; and he shall do great things for this realm of Greater Britain; but he shall die at the Saxons' hands; and after him Utha shall take the crown; but his days, too, shall be cut short, by poison. Yet after him, to Britain in her need, shall come another, greater than they.'

Then between fear and rage, Vortigern cried out to his guards, 'Seize him! Stop his mouth with your swords!'

But the rim of the sun was lifting above the rim of the mountains eastward, and the first rays shone level into the eyes of King and court and guards, making them blink; and when the dazzle cleared from their sight, the dark gape of the dragon-pool had closed over, and only the mountain grasses shivered in the dawn wind where it had been. And of the boy Merlin nothing remained but a kind of shimmer in the air that was gone almost before they saw it; and a voice that lingered after the rest was gone, 'There shall come another . . . another . . . greater than they . . .' and was lost in the soughing of the wind through the grasses.

Within three days Ambrosius and Utha his brother landed on the coast of Britain with a great war host behind them. They marched upon the stronghold to which Vortigern had fled, and sought to beat down the walls; and when the walls proved too strong for them they piled timber and brushwood all round the place and kindled it, and shot fire arrows into the thatch of the tall roof; and the flames leapt up day and night until the stones cracked and flew apart, and the great timbers roared up and crumbled into ash, and the whole tower was eaten by the flames as by a dragon, and Vortigern with it; and so their father Constantine was avenged.

Then Ambrosius was crowned High King, and with Utha his brother he turned upon the Saxons, and by long and desperate fighting drove them back from the lands that they had overrun.

But the time came when Utha, leading his troops up through Wales to meet a Scottish thrust from the north-west, saw a great star blazing in the night sky above his camp fires. And from the star shone a beam of light which became a dragon all of misty fire as though the star-trace that men call the Milky Way had gathered itself into the shape of a great winged beast. And from the dragon's mouth shone two more rays that bestrode the whole of Greater and Less Britain. Then Utha sent for Merlin, who had been with one brother or the other from the time they landed, and asked him the meaning of the strange lights in the sky. And Merlin said, 'Grief upon me! Grief upon us all! For Ambrosius your brother is dead! Yet the light foretells also great things to come, for in the battle that lies before you the victory shall be yours, and you shall be High King of Britain, for the star and the dragon beneath it are yourself, and the two rays from the dragon's mouth foretell that you shall have a son greater than his sire whose power shall reach over all the lands that the rays bestride.'

So Utha grieved for his brother, and rode on against the men of the North and West. And when he was crowned High King of Britain in Ambrosius's place, he took the name of Utha Pendragon, which in the British tongue means Utha Dragon's-Head.

And in battle after battle he fought and defeated the

Saxons and the Picts and the men from over the Irish Sea, until all the southern part of Britain was free of fire and sword; and then he drew a breath of quiet and set his mind to keep Easter in London, and make a great thanksgiving feast. And he bade all his lesser kings and nobles with their wives to come and join him there. Now among those who gathered to him in London that Eastertide were Gorloise, Duke of Cornwall, and his wife, the Duchess Igraine. And Igraine was the fairest of all the ladies about the court, and as soon as he saw her, the King's whole heart fixed itself upon her as it had never done upon any woman before, for all his life since he came to manhood had been too full of fighting to have room for love. He sent gifts to her chamber, gold cups and jewels for her neck; and whenever she sat at table or walked abroad she had but to look up to find his hungry gaze upon her.

Then the Duchess Igraine went to her husband and said, 'The King sends me overmany gifts and his eyes are always upon me. Therefore let us leave here quickly and go back to our own place.'

So the Duke gave his orders, and with the Lady Igraine and all their following, left the King's court before he knew it and set the horses' heads towards Cornwall.

And when the King found them gone, he was fiercely angry, and sent after them demanding that they should return. And when they did not return, he gathered his fighting men and marched after them and made war on the Duke of Cornwall.

Duke Gorloise set his lady in Tintagel Castle, which was the strongest hold in all Cornwall, being set on a headland above the pounding sea, with but one causeway leading to it from the mainland, and that so narrow that it could be held by three men against an army. And he pitched his war camp in another strong place inland of the castle and barring the way to the King. Then Utha Pendragon came up, and made his own camp opposite to where Duke Gorloise was. So the fighting began between them and lasted many days. And all the while his hot and hungry love for Igraine tore at the King, giving him no peace, whether in the red heart of the battle by day or in his lonely tent at night. At last, when a week had gone by, he called to him Merlin, who was with the camp. And Merlin came and stood like a tall shadow in the entrance to the tent, with the flicker of the camp fires behind him, not asking why he had been sent for, for he had been watching the great star hanging in the green twilight sky over Tintagel, and he already knew.

'I am sick with my heart's longing for Igraine,' said the King, 'and no nearer to her than I was seven nights ago. You who have the wisdom of the Old Ones, tell me what I must do to come to her.'

Merlin never moved. He knew that the time was come for the beginning of Utha's son, who should be greater than ever his father was. And he said, 'If you will give yourself up to my skills, I can give you the outer-seeming of Duke Gorloise for one night, and take upon myself the outer-seeming of Brastius, one of his household, that I may accompany you. And so you may go to Igraine in Tintagel Castle this night, none stopping you. But there is a price to pay.'

'Anything!' said Utha Pendragon. 'Anything under the sky.'

'Swear,' said Merlin.

'On the cross of my sword, I swear.'

Then Merlin came in and stood beside the brazier, looking at him across the little licking flames. 'If you go to the Lady Igraine tonight, your son will be born at Christmas; the son I told you of, when we saw the great lights in the sky on the night that Ambrosius died. And within the hour of his birth you shall give him into my keeping, that I may take and rear him for his destiny.'

Silence came down between them; and in the silence Utha said, 'It will be from Duke Gorloise that you must claim that.'

And back across the small licking birch flames in the brazier he looked at Merlin, with a frown-line deepening like a sword-cut between his brows. He had not thought until that moment that any child of his begun as this one was to be, would seem ever after, in the eyes of all men, even in the eyes of the Lady Igraine, to be Duke Gorloise's and not the High King's.

'No,' said Merlin, seeing the thought. 'It will be from you that I must claim it.'

And the King believed him. But he asked, 'Why do you ask this price?'

'Because you may have other sons. That could mean danger to this one, this chosen one, with a cloud lying over his birth, and because your way of life is not a safe one, and if you die before he is of an age to take the crown, in the struggle for power among your nobles he will be trampled underfoot.'

And Utha saw the truth in this; and he was bound by his blindly taken oath; but more than either of these things, he was driven by his love for Igraine. And he agreed the price.

So Merlin went away, and in a short while returned to the King's tent with many things hidden under his cloak; and he cast a powder on to the brazier that filled the tent with a strange-smelling smoke; and he called up figures in the smoke, and made a magic that was older than the Druid kind. And at moonrise, two who to all outward seeming were Duke Gorloise and Sir Brastius of his household knights slipped out of the camp, and away, skirting the Duke's camp, by secret ways to the gates of Tintagel high on its rocks above the crooning sea.

The gate-guard passed them through, thinking only that the Lord of Cornwall had snatched a few hours to come home to his wife; and they crossed the narrow courts of the castle and climbed the outside stair to the Duchess's chambers. And down below in the walled shelter of the castle garden, a whitethroat was singing as though it were already dawn.

And the Duchess's ladies gave him entrance, thinking only as the men of the gate-guard had done, and as the Lady Igraine thought also when he stood within her chamber, that her lord was come home.

And that night, in the great chamber high above the crooning of the western tide, with the whitethroat singing in the castle garden and Merlin standing with a drawn sword before the door, Arthur of Britain was conceived.

But meanwhile Duke Gorloise had made a night attack on the royal camp, and in the desperate fighting had met his death before ever the King came to the door of Igraine's chamber.

Before dawn the High King took his leave of Igraine, saying that he must return to his men by daybreak; and so, with Merlin, slipped away.

And when soon after, news was brought to her of the night attack and her husband's death, Igraine was struck with grief, and also with a great wonder as to who and what it was that had come to her in his likeness that night. But she kept the matter in her own heart, and did not speak of it even to the nearest of her ladies.

By and by King Utha Pendragon came into Tintagel in his own seeming and as a conqueror, but a gentle conqueror, for truly he was grieved at the death of Duke Gorloise, though glad that now Igraine was free. And when enough time was passed, he began to pay court to her; and though for a while she fought her own heart, it seemed to her that there was something about him that she remembered, and the something was sweet. And so after six months they were married with great rejoicing.

Later, when it was not far short of the time for the Queen's child to be born, Utha asked her one night when they were alone in their chamber to tell him the truth of the strange story he had heard concerning the father of the babe she carried. And at first she was afraid, but then she gathered her courage and told him. 'Truly I do not know, for the night that my lord died, at the very hour of his death, as his knights told it to me, one came to my chamber who seemed to be my lord, and in the dawn he went away again. And in the night that he was with me, the child was begun. There was a whitethroat singing in the castle garden. I noticed it because we so seldom have any birds but gulls and ravens here.'

'I remember the whitethroat,' said the King.

'You?' said the Queen.

And in his turn he told her all the truth.

Then she wept afresh for Gorloise her first lord. But it was on Utha's shoulder that she wept.

At Christmas time the Queen bore her child; a fine manchild. But within an hour of his birth a message was brought to the King that a poor man stood at the postern gate and sent word to him to remember the vow taken on the cross of his sword.

And the King gave orders to two knights and two ladies to take the babe and wrap him in cloth-of-gold and then in warm skins for a winter journey, and to give him to the poor man they would find waiting at the postern gate.

So all was done as he ordered, and the child handed over to Merlin in his beggar's guise. And Merlin took him to a certain good knight called Sir Ector, who lived far away from the court, to be brought up along with his own son in all the ways of knightly valour and courtesy. And when Ector would have known whose son it was that he was to foster with his own, Merlin told him, 'His name is Arthur, and whose son he is, you shall know when the time comes for knowing.' And Sir Ector asked no more.

And Utha, with his own heart sore within him, was left to comfort the Queen in her grieving.

2

THE SWORD IN THE STONE

Now Igraine had borne three daughters to Gorloise her first lord, before ever she became Utha's Queen, and two of them being above twelve years old were already married, Margawse the eldest to King Lot of Orkney, and Elaine the next to King Nantres of Garlot; but the youngest, Morgan La Fay, was still a child and at school in a nunnery. And in all three of the Cornish princesses the blood of the Old People, the Little Dark People, was strong, and with it the old wisdom and the old skills, so that all of them had something of magic power; but in Morgan La Fay it ran strongest of all, and she was a witch and of dark kinship with the Faery Kind before

16

ever she left her nunnery to become wife to King Uriens of Gore.

But after Arthur, Utha and Igraine had no more children. And in two years the Saxon wars broke out again, and though the High King flung them back as strongly as he had done before, the Saxons and the men of the North sent spies into his war camp, who poisoned his wine-cup so that on the very night of his victory over them, he died.

Then Britain fell upon dark days indeed, for with no strong-handed heir to take up the High King's sword when he laid it down, the lesser kings and the great lords fought among themselves as to who should be High King after him; and the Saxon kind, seeing the realm without a leader, came thrusting in again, deeper and deeper, until the greater part of all that Ambrosius and Utha Pendragon had won back from the barbarians was lost once more. And from his retreat in the mountains of Gwynedd, Merlin watched with a sorry heart the sorrows of Britain, but knew that the time was not yet come for the strong hand that should save the realm.

And in the castle of Sir Ector, in the dark country bordering Wales that men called the Wild Forest, Arthur grew from a child to a boy, along with Kay, Sir Ector's son and his foster brother, learning those lessons of honour and courage and gentleness and self-discipline, and the weapon-skill and the patience with hawk and hound and horse that would fit him one day to be a knight – and fit him also to be a king. But this he did not know, any more than he knew that the wandering harper or travelling smith or wounded soldier making his way home from the wars who would appear at the castle from time to time were all Merlin in one guise or another, come to see how it went with the future High King of Britain.

So the dark years went by, until at last Merlin judged

that the time and the new High King were both ready. And then he betook him to the City of London, which was still in British hands, and spoke with Dubricius the Archbishop. Merlin held by an older faith than the Archbishop's, and followed the patterns laid down by other gods. But Dubricius was a wise man, wise enough to allow for other wisdoms and other patterns beside his own. And he listened to what Merlin had to say; and he called a great gathering of knights and nobles and lesser kings for Christmas Day, promising that Jesus Christ who was born upon that day would show them by some miracle who was the rightful High King, and so put an end to all their struggling among themselves.

Christmas came, and with it a great gathering who thronged the abbey church, while those for whom there was no room inside crowded the churchyard to watch the distant glimmer of candles and hear the singing and share in the Mass as best they could through the great West door which stood open wide. And when Mass was done, and they turned to go, and those within the church began to come out, suddenly there began a murmur of wonder which spread out and out through the throng like the ripples spreading when a trout leaps in a pool.

For there in the midst of the churchyard, none having seen it come, was a great block of marble, and rooted in the block, an anvil; and standing with its point bedded in the anvil and through into the marble beneath, a naked sword. And round the block was written in letters of gold, clear in the winter sunshine, '*Who so pulleth out this sword from this stone and anvil is true-born King of all Britain.*'

Then one after another the lesser kings and the lords and at last even the simple knights of their followings began to try to draw the sword from the stone. But none succeeded; and far on towards evening when the last

18

had tried, there stood the sword, as firmly set as it had been at the first moment of its appearing; and the crowd stood around, weary and baffled, with their breath smoking in the cold air.

'He is not here, who shall draw this blade,' said the Archbishop, 'but God shall send him in good time. Hear now my counsel: let messengers be sent out the length and breadth of the land, telling of this wonder, and bidding all who would seek to win the sword and with it the kingdom come to a great tournament to be held here in London upon Candlemas Day. And meanwhile let a silken pavilion be set up to shelter the wonder, and let ten knights be chosen to stand guard over it night and day. And so maybe God shall send us our King that day.'

So the messengers rode out on the fastest horses that could be found, carrying the word far and wide through the land, as though it had been a flaming torch. And at last it came to the castle of Sir Ector in the Wild Forest on the fringes of Wales.

Now Sir Ector was a quiet man, and growing old; but his son Kay had been made a knight at the feast of Hallowmas only a few months before, and felt his knighthood bright and untried upon him, and longed like every other young knight in the kingdom to try his fortune at drawing the wonderful sword.

His father laughed at him, but kindly. 'Do you think, then, that you are the rightful High King of all Britain?'

Kay, who could not bear to be laughed at, flushed scarlet. 'I am not such a fool as that, Father; but this will be the greatest and most splendid tournament that has ever been seen, and it would be a fine thing to prove myself there.'

'It would so,' said Sir Ector. 'Well, I remember when my knighthood was three months old I would have felt the same.'

Now Arthur, who was but just turned fifteen, was standing by and listening to the talk of his foster kin; a tall big-boned lad with a brown skin and mouse-fair hair and eyes that would be kind and quiet when he was older but just now were full of eager lights at the thought of the great tournament and the magic sword. And Kay turned on him impatiently: 'You heard! We're going to London for the tournament! Oh, don't just stand there like a shock of wet barley! You're my squire – go and get my armour ready or we'll never be in London by Candlemas!'

Arthur looked at him for a moment as though he would have liked to hit him. But then he thought, It is only because his knighthood is so new upon him. When he has had time to grow used to it, he will be different. He was used to making excuses to himself for Kay. And he went to see to his foster brother's armour, although he knew that Candlemas was as yet a long way off and there was plenty of time.

They reached London on a snowy Candlemas Eve, and found the city buzzing like a hive of bees about to swarm, so full of nobles and knights and their squires and trains of servants that at first it did not seem that they would be able to find lodgings for the night. But they found a corner in an inn at last; and next morning set out through the crowded streets to the tournament ground. All the world seemed going the same way, and it was as though they were carried along by a river in spate. The snow had been swept from the tournament field outside the city walls, so that it was like a green lake in the white-bound countryside; and all round the margin of the lake were the painted stands for the onlookers and the pavilions of those who were to take part; blue and emerald and vermilion, chequered and striped; and the crowds were gathering thicker every moment, and all among them horses were being walked up and down, their breath steaming on the cold air. And it all seemed to Arthur, fresh from his forest country, to be as beautiful and confusing as some kind of dream.

But just as they reached the tournament ground, Kay discovered that, with too much eagerness and too much anxiety, he had left his sword behind him at the inn.

'That is my blame,' Arthur said quickly. 'I am your squire, I should have seen that you were properly armed.'

And Kay, who had been going to say that same thing himself, could only say, 'It's over late to be worrying as to whose blame it is. Ride back quickly and fetch it and come on after us.'

So Arthur turned his cob and began to ride back the way they had come. But now he was going against the flow of the people, and when at last he managed to reach the inn, it was fast locked and shuttered, and all the people of the house were gone to watch the jousting.

Now what am I to do? thought Arthur. There will be jests and laughter if Kay comes to the tournament without a sword – and yet how am I to get one for him in this strange city and with so little time to spare?

And as if in answer, there came clearly into his mind the picture of a sword that he had seen earlier that morning, standing upright in a stone in the garth of the great abbey church close by. I wonder what it is there for, and if it lifts out of the stone? he thought, and found that he was already urging his cob that way.

For the strange thing was that in the moment that he thought of the sword in the stone, he forgot its meaning and why the tournament had been called. Maybe that had something to do with the passing beggarman whose strange golden eyes had met his for an instant as he turned his cob from the locked door of the inn; for assuredly if he had not forgotten, he would never have thought of trying to get it out of the stone, even for Kay

21

his foster brother . . .

When he reached the garth of the abbey church he dismounted and hitched his cob to the gate and went in. The fresh snow lay among the tombstones, and in the midst of the tall black sentinel towers of the yew trees the pavilion glowed crimson as a rose at Midsummer; and the sword stood lonely in its anvil on the great stone, for even the ten knights were gone to the jousting.

Then Arthur took the sword two-handed by its quillions. There was golden writing on the stone, but he did not stop to read it. The sword seemed to thrill under his touch as a harp thrills in response to its master's hand. He felt strange, as though he were on the point of learning some truth that he had forgotten before he was born. The thin winter sunlight was so piercing-bright that he seemed to hear it; a high white music in his blood.

He drew the sword from the anvil in one familiar-seeming movement as though from a well-oiled sheath. And he ran back to the gate where his cob waited, and made all haste back towards the tournament field. The crowds in the streets were thinning now, and in only a short while he reached the place where Sir Kay had turned aside, sitting his horse in a fret, to wait for him.

'This is not my sword,' Kay said, as Arthur thrust it into his hand.

'I could not get in, the place was locked up – I came on this one by chance, in the abbey garth, sticking in a great stone –'

Kay looked at the sword again. He was suddenly very white. Then he wheeled his horse and began thrusting through the crowd towards Sir Ector, who had ridden on ahead. Arthur followed hard behind.

'Sir,' said Kay, when he reached his father, 'here is the sword out of the stone; here in my hand. It must be that I am the true High King of Britain.'

But Sir Ector looked at his son steadily and kindly, and from him to Arthur and back again, and said, 'Let us go back to the church.'

And when the three of them had dismounted and gone into the great echoing church, all glimmering with tapers for Candlemas, he made Kay put his hand on the Bible and said, 'Now tell me in all truth, how you came by this sword.'

And Kay turned from white to red, and said, 'My brother Arthur brought it to me.'

Sir Ector turned to his foster son, and asked, 'How came you by this sword?'

Arthur, troubled because he could not think what Kay had meant when he said that he must be High King of Britain, but still not remembering, said, 'Kay sent me to fetch his sword, but the lodging was empty and locked up, and I could not think what to do – and then I thought me of this sword in the church garth, and it was serving no useful purpose there, while Kay needed a sword, so I pulled it out and brought it to him.'

'Were there any knights standing by, who saw you do the thing?' asked Sir Ector.

Arthur shook his head. 'No one.'

'Then,' said Sir Ector, 'put the sword back in its place.' And when Arthur had done so, Sir Ector tried to draw it out again, and could not shift it. And then at his order Kay tried, but with no better success. 'Now do you draw it forth again, Fosterling,' he said. And Arthur, greatly wondering what all the to-do was about, drew the sword again, as easily as he had done the first time.

Then Sir Ector knelt down before him, and bowed his head, and Kay also, though more slowly; and Arthur, beginning to remember and trying not to, and suddenly more afraid than ever he had been in his life before, cried out, 'Father – Kay – why do you kneel to me?'

'Because you have drawn the sword from the stone, and it is ordained by God himself that none shall do that save he who is rightfully High King of Britain.'

'Not me!' Arthur said. 'Oh, not me!'

'I never knew whose son you were when Merlin brought you to me for fostering,' said Sir Ector. 'But I know now that you were of higher blood than I thought you.'

'Get up!' said Arthur. 'Oh sir, get up! I cannot bear that you should kneel to me, you who have been my father all these years!' And when Sir Ector would not, he dropped on to his knees also, to be on a level with the old man again.

'I kneel to my liege lord,' said Sir Ector. 'I will serve you in all things and keep true faith with you. Only be a gentle lord to me, and to Kay your foster brother.'

'Kay shall be Seneschal of all my lands, if I be King indeed,' said Arthur. 'And how could I be any but a gentle lord to you whom I love. And for the rest – I will serve God and the realm of Britain with the best that is in me. Only get up now, for indeed I cannot bear it!' And he covered his face with his hands and wept as though his heart would break.

Then Sir Ector and Sir Kay got up, and Arthur himself last of all; and they went to the Archbishop and told him of what had happened, and as the word spread, knights and nobles came pouring up from the tournament ground, demanding that they should also try for the sword, as was their right; and Arthur set it back into the stone, and one after another, they tried without avail.

Yet they would not accept that a boy not yet come to his knighthood, and with no proof of his fathering, should be king over them. And so the Archbishop ordained another gathering at Easter, and then yet another at Pentecost, and to each of these the great lords swarmed in to try again; but none could draw the sword save Arthur. And at last the people cried that they were weary of this striving, and would have Arthur for their king.

Then Arthur took his sword across both hands and offered it before the altar in the abbey church, and received his knighthood of the Archbishop. And that same day the Archbishop set the crown upon his head.

The royal circlet pressed down upon his forehead with all the weight of the fear and bewilderment that had been with him ever since he had first drawn the sword from the stone; so that it was all he could do to hold his head high as he turned to confront the knights and nobles who crowded the body of the great church. And then he became aware that as the Archbishop Dubricius stood beside him on his right, somebody else was with him on his left – a tall man in a dark mantle, with hair on his head like black ruffled feathers. Arthur did not know who he was; but it was clear that the Archbishop knew, and Sir Ector his foster father standing close by, and many others in the church, and that even those who did not know felt the power that flowed from him like light from a torch or the spreading quiver in the air from a lightly tapped drum.

There was faint stirring and shifting among the crowd, and a whisper began to go round, 'Merlin! It is Merlin!' 'He was with Utha and Ambrosius; often I saw him!' 'It is Merlin, the magician!'

And one of the great lords, leader of many fighting men, who had had high hopes of his own claim to the crown, shouted, 'It is Merlin and not God who has chosen for us this beardless boy to be our new king!'

And another joined him, as hound bays after hound, 'Aye, it is naught but Merlin's dream-weaving, this magic of a sword in a stone!'

Standing so still that save for his back-falling sleeve, not a fold of his dark mantle stirred, Merlin raised his arm, and silence flowed out from him the length and breadth of the church. Only a faint murmur seemed to hang between the pillars and in the emptiness under the high arched roof like the echo of the sea in a shell. And into the silence, Merlin lifted up his voice and spoke.

'Listen now, oh people of Britain, and you shall know the truth. Truth that has been hidden from you many years until the time should come for you to hear it. Here stands your High King, true and rightful son of Utha Pendragon and his Queen Igraine; born to be the greatest king that Britain has ever known, born to drive back the enemies of the realm further even than the Pendragon drove them in his day. Born to bring that brightness between the Dark and the Dark that men shall remember beyond the mists of time and call the Kingdom of Logres. He was God's choice, not mine, but it was given to me to know him, before he was born, before even his king-star hung in the sky, and to do what must be done to bring him safely to this day!'

And standing still with his hand raised, he told the whole story of the dragon in the sky, and of Arthur's birth, and how he had taken the child and given him to Sir Ector's fosterage to be brought up in safety from the troubles that followed his father's death, until the time came for him to take the crown and the sword.

When he had done, he lowered his hand, and, as though it was a signal, the uproar broke out again, but now it swelled into a roar of acclamation; and men were shouting, 'Utha's son! Utha's son!'

And in the midst of the shouting the tall man in the dark cloak turned his head and looked at the boy beside him; and Arthur found himself looking back, into strange golden eyes that were not like the eyes of any

mortal man that he had met before. And yet as he
looked into them he seemed to remember for a moment
a beggar by the inn doorway that Candlemas morning
that now seemed a lifetime ago, and a stray harper
playing by the fire in the hall of his old home, and a
travelling tinker, and a wounded soldier making his way
home from the wars. The rags of memory were gone
before he could lay hold of them. But with them, all the
fear and bewilderment went from his mind. The sorrow
for the loss of his old life remained, but it no longer
mattered. Suddenly his head was clear and his heart
strong within him; and he knew that whatever he had to
do in this new life, he could do it.

'Speak to them,' said Merlin, beside him.

And Arthur spoke, lifting up his voice clear for all the
knights and nobles in the great church, and the people
thronging beyond the open door, and for all the people
of Britain. 'I am your King! I will keep faith with you.
Do you keep faith with me! When this feast of Pentecost
is over let us gather our forces, and together we will
drive back the Sea-wolves and the men of the North
who ravage these lands! We will free the realm of the
strife and the fire and the sword that have torn it apart in
the years since my father's death. You and I together,
let us make this a good land, where men do not rule only
because they are strong, but where men are strong for
the Right, none the less! Give me your love and your
faithkeeping, oh people of Britain, and I will give you
mine through all the days of my life!'

And there was no more shouting and acclamation;
only a deep silence in the great church. But it was a good
silence; and the tall man with the golden eyes smiled, as
one that is well content.

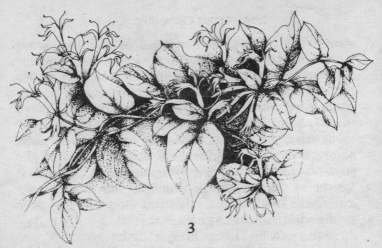

3

THE SWORD FROM THE LAKE

From the day of his crowning, Merlin was always beside
the new High King, as he had been with his father Utha
before him. And with Merlin to advise and council him,
Arthur Pendragon gathered his war hosts and thrust
back the Saxons and the Picts and the men from over
the Irish Sea. And he led his men also across the Narrow
Seas to Less Britain to aid King Ban and King Bors of
Benwick, who had sheltered Ambrosius and Utha after
their father was slain, when they in their turn were beset
by enemies on their borders.

And when all this was done, and it seemed as though
there might be peace for a while, he made his capital at
Camelot. And some people say the place where Camelot
once stood is now the city of Winchester, and some that
Cadbury Hill is what remains of it today; but no man
knows for sure where the towers of Camelot once rose,
just as no man knows for sure the last sleeping-place of
Arthur the King.

But wherever his capital might be, neither Arthur nor
his knights were left long to be at peace in it. For the

dust of the fighting was scarcely sunk and the wounds were scarcely healed, when eleven lesser kings from the outland and mountain places along the fringes of Britain gathered each their war hosts and came against the new High King. King Lot of Orkney and King Nantres of Garlot, King Anguish of Ireland and King Idris of Far Cornwall and King Uriens of Gore and six more beside, they gathered to the great forest that furred all the mid-lands of Britain, and there laid siege to the great Castle of Bedegraine which was one of Arthur's chiefmost strongholds, meaning to make it their headquarters against him.

Then, by the advice of Merlin, Arthur sent word into Less Britain, to King Bors and King Ban of Benwick; and they in their turn came with their fighting men; and together they raised the siege of Bedegraine, and overthrew the eleven kings and drove them back into their own mountains and away over the Irish Seas, all save those who sued for peace and swore their fealty to the High King.

But no sooner was that done with, and Bors and Ban were away to their own lands once more, than word came from King Leodegraunce of Camelaird who was of Arthur's following, that Rience of North Wales made war upon him and pressed him sore. And again Arthur gathered his war hosts and marched to the aid of his vassal.

Six days they were on the march, and when he heard that they were coming, Rience laughed, and swirled about him his great war-cloak that was fur-bordered with the beards of kings and princelings that he had overcome; and he made ready to meet them upon the skirts of Snowdon and make an end of them.

But when they came together, it was the war host of Rience the tyrant which broke and scattered; and Arthur rode victorious into Camelaird town.

And when, in a few days, his men being rested, he rode south again, he carried with him not only another victory, but something that went deeper with him, though he did not know it, and was to remain with him all his days. For in the high-walled garden of the castle there, he saw Guenever, King Leodegraunce's daughter, for the first time. She was sitting with her ladies, and all of them weaving garlands of honeysuckle and columbine and the little loose-petalled Four-Seasons roses to braid into their hair. The Princess's hair was black with a shimmer of copper where the sun caught it, and her eyes, when she looked up from the flowers in her lap, were grey-green as willow leaves and full of cool shadows.

And Arthur saw all this; but she was scarcely more than a child, and though he was but eighteen himself, he was feeling very old, old and weary with his hard-won victories and the deaths of men. And though they gave each other one long grave look before her father swept him on his way, he thought no more of that first encounter after he rode south again, than that he had seen a girl making a flower-chain in the King's garden.

Yet something of him was changed from that moment. Something in him that had been asleep before, began to stir and to ache, longing for – he did not know what. Almost he forgot, as time went by, but never quite, until the time came for him to remember fully once again.

Arthur rode south to his great castle of Caerleon. And while he was there, Margawse his half-sister, she who was Queen to King Lot of Orkney, came to spy out for her husband the secrets and the strengths and weaknesses of his realm. She came, no man knowing who she was, as a noble lady on a journey, seeking a night's shelter for herself and her ladies and escorting men-at-arms. And Arthur, who had never seen her before, did not know her either, and gave her courteous welcome.

Merlin could have warned him, but for once Merlin was not at his side but had gone north on a visit to his old master who had reared and trained him. Cabal, Arthur's favourite hunting dog, growled and raised the hackles on his neck when she came near, but Arthur paid no heed, only thrust him back with his heel and ordered him from the Great Hall lest he frighten their guest.

That evening they made merry in the Great Hall in honour of the lady's coming, and when supper was over, the harpers made their music that was as sweet as the music of the Hollow Hills. But the night was heavy, full of thunder in the air, and the torches in their wall-sconces burned tall and unwavering; and by and by, the lady said, 'My Lord King, the night is over-heavy within doors, and there is no air to breathe; is there a garden in this castle?'

'There is a garden behind the keep,' Arthur said, 'it will be cooler there.'

'Then by your leave, I and my maidens will walk alone there in the dusk.'

And so the lady and her maidens went out to the garden; and in the Great Hall the harpers played on, and the pages set out the boards for chess, and cleared the floor for the games that the young knights and the squires played after supper.

But in a while one of the pages came to Arthur and whispered, 'Sir, the lady asks that you go to her in the garden, for she bears a message for you which she says cannot be spoken here in the crowded Hall.'

So Arthur got up and went quietly from the Hall, and down the narrow stairway in the wall and through the postern door that gave on to the castle garden. The air was like warm milk, and the scent of honeysuckle and sweet briar hung heavy between the high walls, and the full moon was pale and blurred in the hazy sky. And in the entrance to the vine-trained arbour at the far end, the lady waited for him, quite alone, for all her maidens it seemed were gone.

Queen Margawse was twice as old as he was; she had borne four sons to the King of Orkney, and the eldest of them, Gawain, was not much younger than Arthur himself; but he neither knew nor cared for that. Something to do with another garden was stirring at the back of his heart, waking an old longing and loneliness in him. And she was very beautiful. He had seen how beautiful in the light of the Hall torches, and he saw it still more now in the blurred lily-light of the moon; beautiful with a warm richness like ripe fruit, and the scent of musk and rose-oil came from the folds of her gown and her unbraided hair.

Her hands were held out to him; and Arthur took them, and never remembered to ask her what was the message she brought, that could not be told in the crowded Hall.

Why she did it, there can never be any knowing; for she knew, though he did not, what kin they were to each other (but for herself, she had never cared for any law save the law of her own will). Maybe she thought to have a son to one day claim the High Kingship of Britain. Maybe it was just revenge; the revenge of the Dark People, the Old Ones, whose blood ran strong in her, upon the Lords of Bronze and Iron, and the People of Rome, who had dispossessed them. Maybe it was because she had never loved King Lot and dreaded growing old, and Arthur was young and good to look upon. Maybe she thought it might help her in her spying. Maybe it was all these things mingled together . . .

Nine months later, far away in the North, Queen Margawse bore a fifth son, and his father was not Lot of Orkney, but Arthur the High King. And she sent word to Arthur that she had borne him a son and would name him Mordred, and that one day she would send him south to be a knight of his father's court.

And she told him who she was.

Then Arthur knew that he had done one of the forbidden things. He had done it all unknowing, but he had done it, and no tears or prayers or penance could undo it again. He had let loose his own doom, and in the end, as night gives place to day and day turns to night again, his doom would return upon him. He spent three wakeful nights wrestling with certain horrors within himself. Then, seeing that he had a life to lead and a kingdom to rule as best he might, meanwhile, he put the thing from him until the appointed time the web of things should bring it back again. And he called for horses and hounds, and rode hunting. And if, during the day's hunting, it seemed to the High King that he, and not the fleeting red deer, was the quarry, no one knew.

Only those who were closest to him knew that suddenly the last of his boyhood was gone from the High King.

But all that was still nine months in the future, and the lady had scarcely gone her way northward from Caerleon, when one day a young squire rode into the castle courtyard, leading a second horse, across whose back his knight lay newly slain. And dropping wearily from the saddle, he cried out, 'Vengeance, my Lord King! Christian burial for my master, as good a knight as ever set lance in rest, and vengeance upon his slayer!'

'The one you shall have without question,' said Arthur. 'The other if it be deserved. Who is the slayer?'

'King Pellinore,' said the squire. 'Not many leagues

from here he has set up his pavilion close to a well beside the high road; and there he challenges all comers to joust with him; and there he slew my master. Pray you let one of your knights ride out to take up the challenge and avenge my master's death!'

Now there was a squire at court called Gryflet, of about the same age as Arthur himself; and when he heard this he came and knelt before the King, and begged to be given his knighthood, that he might take the challenge upon himself.

And Arthur looked down at him, and knew that he had been a good squire, and would be a good knight also if he lived. But, 'You are over young to be taking up such a challenge,' he said, 'not yet come to your full strength, while King Pellinore of Wales is one of the strongest and most skilful fighters of any in this world.'

'Yet pray you give me my knighthood,' said the boy. 'It was I who spoke up first for the taking of this challenge.'

And Arthur sighed, and gave him the light blow between neck and shoulder that made him a knight. 'And now, Sir Gryflet, since I have given you what you ask for, I claim something of you in exchange.'

'Anything that is mine to give.'

'A promise,' said Arthur. 'Promise me that when you have ridden one course against King Pellinore, whether you be still in the saddle or unhorsed and on foot, you will let the thing rest there, and return to me without more ado.'

'That I promise,' said the young knight. And since he had as yet no squire of his own, he fetched his horse and spear for himself; and hitched his shield on his shoulder and was away with one stirrup still flying.

He followed the summer-dry road in a cloud of his own dust, out of the sunlight into the forest shade, until he came to the well beside the way. And there he saw a rich pavilion and close by a fine horse ready saddled and bridled; and hanging from the lowest branch of an oak tree, a shield blazoned with many colours and beside it a great spear. Reining up and standing in his stirrups he hammered on the shield with the butt of his own spear as was the custom when taking up such a challenge, until the forest rang and the splendid shield came crashing to the ground.

Then King Pellinore, fully armed, came out from his pavilion, and asked, as was the proper custom also, 'Fair knight, why smote you down my shield?'

'For that I would joust with you,' said Sir Gryflet.

Then King Pellinore left the proper custom, and said, 'It were better you do not, for you are but young, and as I judge a newly made knight, and have not yet come to your full strength to match with mine.'

'For all that, I would still joust with you,' said Gryflet.

'It is by no wish of mine. But if you take up my challenge I cannot refuse. Yet if we are to fight, tell me first whose knight you are.'

'I am King Arthur's knight,' said the boy.

And King Pellinore took his spear and shield and mounted his horse, and they drew apart the proper distance, and turning, set their spears in rest and rode full tilt upon each other.

Gryflet took King Pellinore in mid-shield, and shattered it to pieces; but Pellinore's point went clean through Gryflet's shield and deep into his left flank and there broke off short, the point lodging in his body, and horse and rider were brought crashing down.

Then Pellinore dismounted, and bending over the wounded knight unloosed his helm to give him air. 'This is a boy with a lion's heart,' he said, 'and if he lives, shall be among the best of knights.' And with the spearhead still in his flank, he helped him into the saddle, and turned the horse's head towards Caerleon, and set it to find its own way home.

Arthur was crossing the outer courtyard with a falcon on his fist when the horse and his sore-wounded rider returned. 'I rode but the one course as you bade me,' said Sir Gryflet, and fell out of the saddle at the King's feet.

Then the King was deeply angry, not only with King Pellinore, but with himself, that he had listened to the boy, and let him go upon a man's business (forgetting that he himself was no older) and when he had seen Gryflet carried away to be tended, he called for his squires to arm him and bring his best warhorse, and taking no companion, though many begged to ride with him, he set off along the track into the forest, to take up the challenge himself, and avenge the hurt to his youngest knight. And he rode with his vizor closed and the cover still upon his shield that no man might know him by the blood-red dragon upon it.

By and by he came to the rich pavilion beside the well. A new shield hung from the branch of the oak tree, and he beat upon it in a fury until all the forest rang with the clamour of it like a flawed bell; and out from the pavilion came the knight he knew must be King Pellinore.

'Fair knight,' said Pellinore, 'why do you beat upon my shield?'

'Sir Knight,' returned Arthur, 'why do you bide here, letting no man to pass this way unless he joust with you?'

'It is my custom,' said Pellinore. 'If any man would make me change it, let him try.'

'I am come to make you change it,' said Arthur.

'And I stand here to defend my custom,' said King Pellinore, quiet in his helmet; and took up his new shield and his spear and mounted his horse which a squire had brought to him. And they rode apart the proper distance, then turned and spurred their mounts to full gallop, and so came thundering to meet each other. And each took the other in the centre of the shield, and their spears were splintered all to pieces.

Then Arthur made to draw his sword, but King Pellinore said, 'It is not yet time for swords. Let us try another course with spears.'

'I would be willing enough,' said Arthur, 'if I had another spear.'

King Pellinore flicked a finger at his squire, and the squire brought two more good spears and offered the first choice to Arthur; and when Arthur had chosen, King Pellinore took the other; and again they spurred their horses together; and again the spears shattered, and again Arthur would have drawn his sword.

'Nay,' said King Pellinore, 'let us ride one more course with the spears, for the love of the high order of knighthood, for you are such a jouster as my heart warms to.'

So the squire brought two more spears, and a third time they spurred against each other. But though Arthur's spear splintered yet again, this time King Pellinore's took him so hard on the right spot that both he and his horse were brought crashing to the ground.

Then Arthur sprang clear and drew his sword indeed, and Pellinore swung down from the saddle, drawing his own blade. And there began a great fight between them, and they hacked and hewed at each other until their armour was split and dinted and the blood ran down to slake the dust of the trackway like a crimson rain. At last their blades crashed together with such force that Arthur's sword flew to pieces, and he was left with the hilt and a jagged stump of the fine blue blade in his hand.

Then Pellinore let out a deep cry of triumph. 'Now

you are mine to slay or spare as I will! Kneel to me and ask mercy as a beaten knight, and it may be that I will let you live!'

'There are two words as to that,' said Arthur. 'Death I will take when it comes, but I yield on my knees to no man!' And flinging aside his useless sword hilt, he leapt at Pellinore, diving low under his guard, and got him round the waist in a wrestler's grip and flung him down. So they wrestled upon the ground, a slow hard struggle in their armour; but King Pellinore was a big and powerful man, and Arthur, even as he had said to Sir Gryflet, was not yet come to his full strength; and in a while King Pellinore came uppermost, and tore off the young King's helmet and reached for his sword . . .

And in that moment something stirred among the tree-shadows around the well, as though one of the ancient thorns were moving; and out from among them stepped a tall dark man with golden eyes, and his black mantle powdered almost white about the hem with the dust of a long journey.

His shadow in the long evening light fell across the two figures, and Pellinore checked his hand and looked up.

'Nay, leave your sword where it lies,' Merlin said. 'If you slay this man you slay all hope for Britain.'

'Why, then, who is he?' asked Pellinore in a sudden quiet.

'He is Arthur, the High King.'

Then for the first time fear came upon Pellinore, for men who seek to slay a king, and fail, often themselves die ugly deaths; and again for an instant his hand moved towards his sword.

'Nay,' said Merlin, 'no need for that,' and he raised his hand and pointed a long forefinger at Pellinore; and Pellinore gave a deep sigh and folded gently on to the grass, and lay still.

Then Merlin turned to Arthur, who could scarcely stand for his wounds, and helped him to remount his horse which stood nearby, and led him away.

But Arthur looked back at the still figure beside the well, and said, 'Merlin, what have you done? You have killed this good knight by your crafts; a strong and valiant knight, and I would give a year of my kingship that he should be whole and alive again!'

'Cease to trouble,' Merlin said, 'you are more like to die than he is, for you are sore wounded, while his hurts are less deep than yours, and he only sleeps, and will wake again in three hours. Aye, and you shall meet this King Pellinore many times in friendship, for he shall be a valiant knight of yours, and his son after him.'

So Merlin brought the King to a hermitage in the forest, where the hermit was a man of great skill with healing herbs, and within three days his wounds were so well knit together that he could ride again. And they set out for Caerleon once more.

But Arthur rode with his head on his breast. 'I am ashamed,' he said. 'I have no sword.'

'No need to be troubled as to that,' Merlin told him. 'Your old sword has served its purpose. It gave proof of your right to the High Kingship and it served you well through the battles that won back your kingdom, but now it is time for you to take your own sword; time for Excalibur, that shall go with you the rest of your days.'

So they went on deep and deeper into the forest, following ways that no man might know but only the light-foot deer; until at last the great hills rose about them and the trees fell back, and they came to the reedy margin of a lake. And though the light evening wind hushed through the branches of the trees behind them, no breath of moving air stirred the rushes, nor the surface of the water, nor the faint mist that scarfed its sky-reflecting brightness and hid the further shore.

Almost, Arthur thought, it was as though there were no further shore, though he could see the hills that rose above it into the western sky. And there was no crying and calling of lake birds as there should have been; only a stillness such as, it seemed to him, he had never heard before. 'What place is this?' he asked at half breath as though he were afraid to break the silence.

'It is the Lake,' Merlin said, 'it is the Lake of the Lordly Ones, who have their palace in its midst, unseen by the eyes of men. Away over yonder – away to the West – there lies Ynys Witrin, the Glass Island; Avalon of the Apple Trees, that is the threshold between the world of men and the Land of the Living that is also the Land of the Dead . . .'

His voice seemed to come and go, so that Arthur was not sure whether he heard the words or if it was only the faint wind-song in the trees behind them.

'A strange place indeed,' he said.

'And not far off is Camlann,' said Merlin beside him, and his voice came back out of the faint wind-song and sounded heavy and old.

'Camlann?' Arthur said, feeling a sudden coldness between his shoulders, as men do when a grey goose flies over the place of their grave.

'Camlann, the place of the last battle . . . Nay, but that is another story, for another day as yet far off.' Merlin's voice lost its heaviness, 'See, there is your sword as I promised.'

And looking where he pointed, Arthur saw an arm rise from the midst of the lake, clad in a sleeve of white samite and holding in its hand a mighty sword. And even as he looked, he saw a maiden whose dark gown and hair seemed to float about her like the mists come walking towards him across the water, her feet leaving no ripple-track upon its brightness.

'Who is that?' whispered Arthur.

'That is the Lady among all the Ladies of the Lake. Speak to her courteously and she will give you the sword.'

So when the maiden came to the lake shore and stood before them swan-proud among the reeds, Arthur dismounted and saluted her in all courtesy and asked her, 'Damosel, pray you tell me what sword it is that yonder arm holds above the water.'

'It is a sword that I have guarded for a long time. Do you wish to take it?'

'Indeed I do,' said Arthur, looking out across the lake with longing eyes. 'For I have no sword of my own.'

'Then promise me never to foul the blade with an unjust cause, but keep it always as befits the Sword of Logres, and it is yours.'

'That I swear,' Arthur said.

'So,' said the Lady of the Lake, 'then step you into the barge that waits for you.'

And for the first time, Arthur saw a boat lying close by among the reeds.

He stepped aboard, and instantly the boat began to move, slipping through the water of its own accord and leaving no wake behind, until it checked like a well-gentled steed beside the arm where it rose from the lake depths.

Then Arthur reached out and said, 'By your leave,' and took the sword into his own hands, seeing how the milky water-light played on the finely wrought gold and gems of the hilt and on the richly worked sheath. And as he did so, the arm in its white samite sleeve slipped quietly beneath the water.

And the boat returned as quietly to the nearby shore.

Of the Lady there was no sign, and it was as though she had never been; but Merlin stood where he had left him, holding the horse's bridle. And Arthur buckled on his sword, and mounted and they set forth once more towards Caerleon.

And as he rode, Arthur drew his sword, and looked at it, letting the evening light play with the silken surface of the blade. 'Excalibur,' he said softly; and then, 'Excalibur,' again.

Merlin looked at him sideways, and asked, 'Which do you love better, the sword or the sheath?'

And Arthur laughed at the seeming foolishness of the question. 'It is a pretty sheath, fair to see, with all these gold threads on the crimson leather; but the sword is a sword, and I would rather a hundred times have that!'

'Nevertheless, have a care to that scabbard, and keep it always, for while it is safely buckled to your sword-belt, by the strength of the magic in it, however sore you may be wounded it battle, you shall lose not one drop of blood.'

'I will have a care,' said Arthur, sheathing his blade. 'But still I like the sword best.'

4

THE ROUND TABLE

It was not long before the High King had need of his
new sword; for in the spring of the next year, word came
to him that Rience of North Wales was once more
gathering a war host; and wild-riding bands of his
followers were already harrying the lands of Arthur's
subject kings across his borders. And when Arthur sent
word to him to cease his wolf-pack ways, all he received
in reply was a message from King Rience that he had
conquered more kings in his time than he could count
on the fingers of both hands, and cut off their beards to
make a border for his mantle, but that he would spare
King Arthur if he sent his own beard to add to their
number.

'This is the ugliest message that ever I received,' said Arthur to the messenger. 'Go now back to your lord, and tell him that it is unwise to send such messages to the High King of Britain. Tell him also that unless he ceases from his pillaging and comes in to swear fealty to me, as better men than he have done, I will come against him as I did before; but this time I shall do more than drive him back to his mountains. This time I shall take this kingly mantle of his, and not only his beard but his head to go with it!' And he felt the young man's down on his own chin, and added, with the laughter breaking through his wrath, 'Tell him also that in any case, I fear my beard would be of little use to him as yet.'

So the messenger returned to his lord. And Arthur gathered his war hosts yet again and marched into the mountains of North Wales. And there he found Rience and many rebel knights and war leaders waiting for him; and among them King Lot of Orkney, which grieved him, for he knew in his heart that it was Queen Margawse and not her husband who was truly his enemy, and that it was by her will rather than his own that he was there.

All one long summer's day they fought; and sometimes the battle swung this way and sometimes that; but as the day drew on, the tide of the fighting set more and more against the rebels, until, when the shadows of men and horses and spears grew long at evening, Rience and all his leaders lay dead, save for King Lot, who still fought on, stubborn as a boar at bay, with his body-guard close about him.

Now King Pellinore of Wales was fated at times to ride questing after a strange beast which had the head of a serpent and the body of a leopard and the feet of a hart, and which made in its belly a noise as of thirty couple of hounds giving tongue. And it so happened that on that day the quest had led him into the hills among which the battle was being fought. And hearing the outcry and the ring of weapons, and seeing the red and golden standard of Britain above the dust of the struggle, he turned aside from the quest for a while to join his High King. He came just as Arthur was leading in another charge against the men of Orkney, and riding with him and his household knights, while all around them sounded the cry of thirty couple of hounds giving tongue on a hot scent, he drove deep into the enemy mass until he reached King Lot himself and in the close-locked struggle all around dealt him such a crashing blow that the sword blade bit through helm and bone, and King Lot pitched from the saddle and was dead before he hit the ground.

And the heart went out of the men of Orkney, and they fled away into the gathering dusk, that still seemed full of fading hound music.

So peace came to Britain for a while; and the men of the North and West were quiet again in their mountains and the Sea-wolves fled away overseas. There were stray war bands still loose in the land, and evil knights and wild men lurking in the forests, ripe for any ill-doing that came their way. And the men in the mountains told stories of ancient wrongs around the fires at night to keep their hate alive. Yet even so there was more of peace in Britain than there had been since long before the Romans left.

Now there was time for men to draw breath and think how they would choose to live their lives. And the best knights in the kingdom, many of whom had shared in the past fighting, gathered to Arthur in Camelot. Old knights such as Sir Ulpius and Sir Bleoberis the standard-bearer, who had served with King Utha Pendragon; young knights seeking glory and a shining cause to fight for, such as Sir Bedivere and Sir Lucan and Sir Gryflet le Fise de Dieu and Lamorack, who was the son of King Pellinore by his first love, before ever he wedded his queen; and unfledged squires eager for knighthood at the hands of the greatest king in Christendom. Even Gawain, the eldest son of King Lot and Queen Margawse, and with him Gaheris his younger brother (for all the sons of Margawse left home as soon as might be, until it came to the turn of Mordred, the last son of all. But that was another matter.)

Never, the harpers said, had such a court flowered about such a king.

Then, in a while, Arthur sent one evening for Merlin to come to him in the great chamber above the hall, and said to him, 'My lords and nobles are hounding me that I should take a wife. Give me your counsel, for always your council has been good for me to hear.'

'It is right that you should take a wife,' said Merlin. 'For now you are past twenty and the greatest king in all Christendom. Is there any maiden who comes close to your heart?'

And Arthur thought. And his thoughts touched in passing upon the fair faces of many maidens, and upon the dark ripe beauty of Queen Margawse, and flinched away from that memory to that which lay beyond. And so his thoughts came to rest upon a girl with smooth dark hair and shadowy grey-green eyes, making a garland of honeysuckle and columbine and Four-Seasons roses in a high-walled castle garden. And he said, 'Guenever, the daughter of Leodegraunce of Camelaird.'

Merlin was silent a moment, and then he said, 'You are sure of this?'

And Arthur was silent also. A big soft-winged moth hovered in through the window and began to flutter about and about the candles on the carved cloak-chest. Then he said, 'I am very sure. I love the Princess

Guenever, though I did not know it until now; and my heart feels good and quiet and at rest when I think of her.'

Merlin, knowing what he knew of the future, could have said, 'Grief upon me! Look elsewhere! For if you marry the Princess Guenever, sorrow and darkness and war and death will come of it by and by, to you and her and your dearest friend and to all the kingdom.' But he knew that no man may escape what is written on his forehead, and he knew what was written upon Arthur's as surely as he knew what was written on his own. So he said, 'Sir, if you were not so sure, I could find you a score of maidens as beautiful and as good as she, who could gladden your heart just as sweetly. But I know you, and I know that when your heart has gone out of your breast it will not lightly return to you again.'

'That is so,' said the King.

And the moth blundered into the sea-blue heart of a candle flame, and fell with singed wings.

Then Merlin set out next day for Camelaird, and stood before King Leodegraunce, and told him that the High King of Britain would have the Princess Guenever for his Queen.

When he heard this, Leodegraunce was overjoyed, and said, 'This is the best tidings that ever I heard. Assuredly the High King shall have my daughter to wife.' And then he thought, What shall I give him for her dowry, for of lands he has already all that he can wish for? And the answer came to him, and he said aloud, 'And her dowry shall be a thing that will mean more to him than lands of gold, for I will give him the great Round Table that belonged to Utha his father, and that Utha gave to me, and with it a hundred knights of my best and bravest!' he sighed. 'There's room at that table for a hundred and fifty; but after the wars of my lifetime I can spare no more.'

'The hundred will be enough, for Arthur has good knights of his own. He will be glad of your gift, and glad of the lady who you send to him to be his Queen,' said Merlin, with a small inward-turning smile, for he himself had fashioned the Round Table for Utha Pendragon, long years ago when he was young, and he knew its powers.

So the Round Table was taken apart for its journey, and loaded into great ox-carts. And the Princess also was made ready. No one had asked her wishes in the matter; but she remembered the young man with the tired face, and the long look that had passed between them in the castle garden, and how, after he had passed on, she had found that she had broken the garland in her lap; and though her heart made no singing within her, she was well content.

So, riding among her maidens, with Merlin beside her and the hundred knights following after, and last of all the great ox-carts lumbering along the summer-dusty tracks, Guenever set forth on her marriage journey; and three days before Pentecost, she came to Camelot, where Arthur waited for her. Across the three-arched bridge that spanned the river she went, and up through the steep streets of the town where the people crowded to see her pass, and the swallows swooped among the eaves and gables overhead. And in the outer courtyard of the palace Arthur stood to help her dismount and lead her into his Great Hall.

All things were made ready for their wedding in three days' time; and on the morning of that day – which was also the Feast of Pentecost – Gawain the son of King Lot and Lamorack the son of King Pellinore came to Arthur to beg the honour of knighthood; and both of them he knighted most gladly; and so when the High King went to his wedding in the tall church of Saint Stephen, they were among the knights who followed him.

Then came Guenever in robes of white and gold for her wedding and her coronation. And when two bishops had joined her hand and Arthur's, they took off the garland of white briar roses from her hair and set in its place the gold circlet of a queen. And hand in hand, under the golden canopy which four kings upheld on spear-points above their heads, they paced back through the crowded streets; and all the people shouted for joy that the High King had got him so fair a queen.

Guenever walked with her head held very high, for the crown was much heavier than the white rose garland had been. But she was proud that Arthur had chosen her to be his lady; and there was a great fondness for him growing within her, that she thought at that time was love.

In the Great Hall the Round Table had been set up; a table like the rim of a mighty wheel with all the space in the middle clear for the pages and serving squires to come and go. And about it were ranged tall-backed seats for a hundred and fifty knights, and on the back of each seat, written in fair gold, the name of the knight who should sit therein.

'Surely no king under Heaven ever had so fair a wedding gift as this!' said Arthur. And he and all his knights went to take their places, while the Queen and her ladies went apart to feast in another chamber, for such was still the custom of the British people at that time, that the men and women did not sit down to meat together upon state occasions.

And when they were all seated in their appointed places, the King turned to Merlin who stood beside his chair, and said, 'What of the four places I see about this wondrous table that are yet empty?'

'They shall be filled at the appointed time,' said Merlin. 'The first by King Pellinore, who rests a while from his questing to be with you this very day; see, his name is already upon his seat, there where the sunlight falls. The second waits for Sir Lancelot, son of King Ban of Benwick your old ally; and he shall be with you before next Pentecost morning. He shall be the best and nearest to you of all your knights, and of all your knights he shall bring you the most joy and the bitterest of sorrow. And the third seat is for Percival the son of King Pellinore, and he is not yet born; but when he comes it shall be as though he were a herald, for by his coming you shall know that in less than a year the Mystery of the Holy Grail shall come to its flowering, here in Camelot, and the knights shall leave the Round Table and ride out upon the greatest quest of all time; and it shall be as though all things draw to the golden glory of sunset, beyond which is the dark. But now it is yet morning.'

And for a moment it seemed that a stillness fell upon the Hall.

Then Arthur said, 'Yet one empty seat remains. Who shall sit there?'

'That is the Seat Perilous,' said Merlin. 'It is death for any man to sit there, until he who it was made for comes to claim it. He shall come at the appointed time – and he shall be the last comer of all.'

And even as he spoke, King Pellinore stood in the doorway.

When King Pellinore had been welcomed and brought to his waiting seat, and the feasting that began immediately after was drawing to a close, there broke out a great baying of hounds in the forecourt, so that for a moment all men thought that it was Pellinore's questing beast, but even as the latest comer half rose from the table to follow it as he must whenever it called him, a white hart came running into the Hall, fleet-footed and touched to silver by the light of the high windows; and hard behind it a milky white brachet, a small hunting-dog almost as fair and fleet; and after them thirty couple of great black hounds in full cry.

The hart fled round the huge table, and after it the brachet, and the black hounds, belling as they went. And as they came towards the door again the hart gave a great bound and swerved towards it, oversetting a knight called Sir Abelleus who was not of the Round Table but among those eating at a side-board. And Sir Abelleus seized the brachet, and springing up strode from the hall. They heard his horse's hooves outside as he rode away. And the hart also fled out through the palace gates, with the black hounds baying and belling after it. And almost in the same instant, while the blood-music of the pack still hung upon the air, a maiden rode into the hall upon a white palfrey, and cried to the King, 'Sir, let me not be so wronged, for the brachet is mine that yonder knight carried away!'

But before Arthur could answer her plea, another rider crashed into the hall, a knight, darkly armed and mounted upon a mighty war horse, who seized the palfrey by its bridle and wrenched it round and so dragged horse and maiden away, she crying and making shrill protest all the while.

For three heartbeats after she was gone, Arthur sat unmoving and stared down at the table before him; for she had made a great clamour, and no man wishes to be embroiled in quests and marvels upon his wedding day. But Merlin brought his strange golden gaze back from following the damosel, and said, 'That was not well done, that a maiden should be dragged from this hall crying for succour, and no men moving to her aid. Such an adventure must be followed to its end, for to leave it lying is to bring dishonour upon you and your knights.'

And Arthur knew that Merlin was in the right of it, and he said, 'I will do as you advise me.'

'Then,' said Merlin, 'send Sir Gawain to bring back the white hart, and Sir Lamorack to bring back Sir

Abelleus and the brachet, for it is right that both of them should follow the first quest of their knighthood this day. And let King Pellinore ride after the damosel and bring her back, and bring back also, dead or living, the knight who carried her away.'

So King Pellinore and the two young knights were armed, and their horses brought from the stables, and they rode away.

Sir Gawain took his younger brother Gaheris with him to be his squire; and together they rode through the town and across the bridge and away through the forest, following the distant dwindling music of the hounds, until they came at last to a great castle. The hart fled across the causeway and in through the castle gate, followed by the few hounds that were still on the hunt; and after the hounds rode Sir Gawain, with Gaheris following hard behind. And in the castle courtyard the hounds overtook the hart and brought it to bay and killed it.

Then out from the armoury doorway came the lord of the castle, fully armed all save his helmet, for he had been at practice, his sword naked in his hand; and he began slashing at the hounds, slaying them one after another, and shouting in grief and fury, 'Die, you brutes that have slain my white hart! Alas, my white hart that my lady gave to me and that I have kept so ill!'

'Stop! Leave off from this butchery!' shouted Gawain, suddenly beside himself with fury at sight of the dead hounds. 'Spend your rage upon me, not upon good hounds who do but follow their nature and their training!'

'That will I!' roared the knight of the castle. 'I have killed the rest of the pack, now for the last of the whelps!'

Gawain swung down from his horse, and in the midst of the courtyard the two met, as though they had indeed been two hounds springing at each other's throats. Their blades hacked through the chain-mail again and again, and the red smell of battle came into the back of Gawain's nose and a red mist before his eyes, until at last, he did not know how it happened, the knight of the castle crashed down at his feet and lay crying his mercy.

Gawain knew that it was against all custom to slay a knight who cried his mercy, but the red mist was still before his eyes, and he swung up his sword for a mighty stroke that should sever the fallen knight's head from his shoulders; but in that instant, the lady of the castle, who had been watching from the window of her bower and come running, flung herself upon her lord's body to shield him; and Gawain could not check the down-sweep of the sword in time, and struck through her slender neck instead of his adversary's.

The red haze cleared from Gawain's eyes, and grief and horror came upon him for what he had done. 'Get up,' he said to the knight. 'I give you mercy.'

'I no longer ask for it,' said the lord of the castle, 'for you have slain my lady, my love, who was more to me than all the world, and it is not in me to care whether I live or die.'

'Grief is on me for that,' said Gawain, 'for I meant the blow for you, and had no thought to harm your lady. I cannot kill you now; therefore rise and go to King Arthur at Camelot, and tell him truly all that has happened. Say that the knight who followed the Quest of the White Hart sent you.'

The silent servants brought their master his horse; and silently he mounted and rode away. And looking after him Sir Gawain said hoarsely, 'I am but an ill knight after all, for I have slain a lady, and had I shown proper mercy to her lord, it would not have come to pass.'

'This is no place to stand grieving,' said Gaheris, 'for

I am thinking that we have few friends here!'

And in the same instant four of the household knights came upon them with drawn swords. 'Stand and fight now, you who shame your knighthood!' cried one. And another, 'A knight without mercy is a knight without honour!' And the third, 'You have slain a fair lady! Carry the shame to the world's end!' And the fourth, 'You shall know what it is like to need mercy, before you go from us!'

And all the while they were thrusting in upon Gawain and young Gaheris who stood back to back and fought them off as best they might. But the odds were two to one, and in the end both were wounded sore and taken captive; and the household knights would have slain them on the spot, beside the dead hounds and the dead lady, had not the ladies of the household come and begged mercy for them, so that they were flung living into a narrow chamber in the bowels of the castle, and there left for the night.

And in the morning the oldest of the ladies, whose hair was silver beneath her veil, came and hearing them groan from the pain of their wounds, asked Sir Gawain how it was with him.

'Not good!' said Sir Gawain.

'It is your own doing,' said the ancient lady, 'had you not slain the lady of this place, you had been less sorely hurt this morning. But tell me now, who you are.'

'I am Gawain, son of King Lot of Orkney, a knight of Arthur's court, and this is Gaheris my brother.'

Then the silver lady went and spoke with the household knights, telling them that their captives were near kinsmen of the High King's, and for Arthur's sake they were set free and given leave to return to Camelot. Only the penance was laid upon them that Gawain should carry the body of the slain lady across his saddlebow, and her head hung by its yellow hair about his neck.

And so those two rode sadly back the long way through the forest that they had come the day before.

Sir Lamorack, meanwhile, had ridden after Sir Abelleus and the brachet; and he had not gone far when suddenly a dwarf stood in his path, and struck his horse such a blow on the muzzle with the staff he carried that the poor beast shook his head and squealed, backing a full spear's length before Lamorack could get him under control again.

'Why did you strike my horse?' demanded Lamorack.

'For that you may not pass along this way until you have jousted with the knights in yonder pavilions,' said the dwarf.

And Sir Lamorack noticed for the first time that two pavilions stood back among the trees beside the way, and beside each pavilion a brightly coloured shield and spear, and a horse standing ready saddled.

'I have no time to spare for such a jousting,' said Lamorack, 'for I am on a quest that may not be left lying.'

'Nevertheless, you shall not pass,' said the dwarf, and raising the horn that hung from his shoulder on a silken baldric, he sounded an echoing blast.

Out from the first of the pavilions strode a fully armed knight, who leapt upon his waiting horse, and taking down his shield, set lance in rest and came spurring towards Sir Lamorack. And Sir Lamorack swung his horse to meet the attack and received him with a spear thrust that tipped him over the crupper of his steed. And before he could rise, another knight came from the second pavilion, and Sir Lamorack received him in the same manner. Then Sir Lamorack dismounted, and stood over the two fallen knights as they lay sprawled on the turf.

'Do you cry my mercy?'

'We cry mercy,' said they, with what wind was still left in them.

'Then mercy you shall have. What are your names?'

'I am Sir Felot of Landluck,' said one.

And the other, 'I am Sir Petipace of Winchelsea.'

'So then, Sir Felot and Sir Petipace, get up, and back on your horses, and ride you to the court of King Arthur, and tell him you were sent by the knight who follows the Quest of the White Brachet. Now God speed you and me.'

And when they were gone, swearing to do as he demanded, and Sir Lamorack was about to ride on, the dwarf, who had stood by watching all this while, came to him and said, 'Sir, pray you grant me a gift.'

'Ask it,' said Sir Lamorack.

'I ask only that you will take me into your service, for I would no longer serve such sorry knights as those. If I were your man, I could tell you where rode the knight with the white brachet.'

'Choose yourself a horse, then,' said Sir Lamorack glancing at the spare mounts that stood under the trees, 'and ride with me.'

So they rode together through the early summer forest.

Towards evening they came upon two more pavilions pitched beside the way; and beside the entrance to one pavilion leaned a shield that was as white as milk, and beside the other, one that was as red as a corn-poppy.

Then Sir Lamorack dismounted, and giving his bridle to the dwarf, went to the pavilion of the white shield and looked in. And there lay three maidens sleeping. He went to the pavilion of the red shield; and there lay a lady sleeping with the white brachet at her feet, which barked at sight of him so that the lady awoke, and her maidens also and came running. And

Sir Lamorack caught up the brachet as it sprang towards him, and carried it out and gave it to the waiting dwarf, the lady and her maidens following after.

'Sir Knight,' cried the lady, 'why do you take my brachet from me?'

'Because Arthur the King sent me in quest of it for another lady who claims it for her own,' said Lamorack, 'and so I must bear it back to him.'

'She lies, that other lady! This is an ungentle thing you do, and you shall not go far without suffering for it!'

'Then I will abide what ill befall me as best I may,' said Sir Lamorack. 'But, lady, I must have the brachet,' and he mounted, and he and the dwarf rode on their way back to Camelot.

They had not ridden far when they heard the furious drum of hooves coming hard behind, and Sir Abelleus ranged up beside them. 'Sir Knight, give back to me the brachet which you stole from my lady!'

'Nay, if you want it, you must joust for it!'

So they set their spears in rest, and fought together, first on horseback, and then when both were unhorsed, on foot, until Sir Lamorack had the victory and Sir Abelleus lay at his feet. 'Now yield and cry mercy!' demanded Lamorack.

But the other cried, 'Never while the life is in me!'

And in that moment, again there came the sound of flying hooves, and out from the trees burst a damosel on a grey palfrey, who cried to Sir Lamorack, 'Sweet knight, for King Arthur's love, grant me what I shall ask of you.'

'Ask,' said Sir Lamorack, still with his sword point at Sir Abelleus's throat. 'And if it may be, I will grant it to you.'

'Then give me Sir Abelleus's head, for he is the worst of living men, and a murderer most cruel!'

Then Lamorack was troubled. 'That was a rash

promise, and I repent me of making it,' he said. 'May it not be that he can make amends for whatever wrong he has done you, and win your forgiveness?'

'Never!' cried the lady. 'For he slew my own brother before my eyes, though I kneeled in the mud an hour to plead his mercy; and for no more cause than that my brother had worsted him in a joust!'

Then Abelleus, hearing this where he lay on the ground, yielded him and cried his mercy.

'It is too late for that,' said Sir Lamorack. 'You could have had mercy, but you would not ask for it.' And he stooped to pull off the other's helmet. But Sir Abelleus squirmed over, and leapt to his feet and ran, and Sir Lamorack after him; and among the trees Sir Lamorack caught up with him and smote off his head.

When he came back, cleaning his sword with a handful of grass, to the place where he had left the dwarf and the horse, the lady on the grey palfrey was still there, and she spoke to him gently, 'Sir, my thanks are yours. And now – you must be weary; come therefore to my house, which is nearby, and eat and rest, and tomorrow return to Camelot.'

So Sir Lamorack went with her, and she and the gentle old knight her husband made him and his dwarf and his horses warmly welcome, and gave him many thanks for his avenging of the lady's brother; and bade him remember that a welcome awaited him always in their manor. And in the morning, fed and rested and with his wounds salved, Sir Lamorack set out once more for Camelot, the dwarf following him with the brachet across his saddlebow.

King Pellinore rode into the forest in yet a third direction, and he had not ridden far before, coming down into a gentle valley, he came upon a well bubbling out from beneath an archway of mossy stones, and beside the well a damosel sitting with a wounded knight in her arms. And seeing King Pellinore she cried out to him, 'Help me, Sir Knight! Help me for Christ's sweet sake!'

But King Pellinore was half deaf in his helmet, and too eager upon his quest to stop, and scarcely heard her even when she cried out after him, 'I pray God you may have as much need of help as I have, before your time comes to die!'

He rode on down the valley; and presently he heard the sound of fighting, and coming to an open space among the trees, he saw two knights, one black-harnessed and the other all in elfin green, locked in furious sword-combat, while a little to one side, the maiden he sought sat her white palfrey captive between two squires. He reined in beside her, and said, 'Lady, I have sought you all the forest ways. Now you must come with me, back to King Arthur's court.'

'That will I gladly, if only it may be,' said the lady, 'for it was by no wish of mine that yonder knight of the black armour dragged me from the King's Hall.'

But one of the squires cut in, 'Yonder two knights are fighting for this lady. Go you and part them and ask their leave, and if both give it to you, then may you take her with you back to Arthur's court.'

Then King Pellinore urged his horse between the two battling knights, forcing them to break off, and demanded, 'Why fight you for this lady?'

'I fight to save her from this foul knight who has carried her off by force, for she is the Lady Nimue, and distant kin to me,' returned the knight in green.

'I fight for what is mine!' swore he of the dark armour. 'For I bore her off by my strength this day from Arthur's court!'

'You lie!' said Pellinore. 'For you came in full harness when we were unarmed and at high feast, and carried

59

her off before any man had time to take up arms against you! Therefore on the High King's order I ride in quest of her, and will take her or die in the attempt.'

Then he of the black armour turned his sword upon King Pellinore's horse and drove it through to the heart, and laughed. 'Fight for her then, but on foot as we do!'

Pellinore sprang clear as his horse crashed to the ground, and ripped his own sword from its sheath, and cried out in fury, 'That will I! And for my poor horse as well as for the lady!' And as the black knight made at him, he swung up his sword, and brought it whistling down, through helm and mail coif and bone, splitting the man's head to the chin, so that he fell dead upon the trampled ground.

Then Pellinore turned to the other knight, but he looked up from staunching his own wounds, and shook his head.

'What? Will you not fight for her?' said Pellinore.

'Nay, there is no need. She will come to no harm at your hands. Take her back to Arthur's court, as your quest bids you.'

'That will I do,' Pellinore said, 'and riding this dead knight's charger since he has slain mine.'

'Nay, come back and lodge with me this night, and I will give you a better horse in the morning.'

So King Pellinore and the maiden Nimue returned with the knight her kinsman to his dwelling-place, supped and slept, and in the morning a tall fine warhorse was brought for him, and he mounted, the lady on her white palfrey at his side.

'Tell me your name before you ride away with my kinswoman in your keeping,' said the knight in green.

'I am King Pellinore of Wales, a knight of the Round Table. Now, in fair exchange for my name, do you give me yours.'

'I am Sir Meliot of Logure.'

'If ever you come to Camelot, you shall find fair welcome,' said King Pellinore.

And he rode on his way.

But when he came again to the well where the lady had cried out to him for help, he found the wounded knight lying dead of his hurts, and beside him the lady, lying with her head upon his still breast, and her bright hair showered all about him, and the dagger which she had taken from his belt driven deep into her own heart.

And looking upon them, all the triumph of his accomplished quest drained out of him like wine out of a cracked cup.

'She cried to me for help,' he said, 'and I was in too much haste to stop and aid her.'

'And there is naught that you can do for her now, nor for the knight she loved, but see that they have fitting burial,' said the Lady Nimue. 'There is a hermitage not far from here. Take their bodies to the hermit and pray him see to all that must be done.'

And when King Pellinore had dismounted and carried them both to the hermitage, the dead knight slung across the back of his horse and the lady in his arms, and bidden the hermit see to all things and bury them together, and take the knight's harness for his pains, they rode on towards Camelot again. 'She was very light to carry,' said King Pellinore; and he rode with his chin sunk on his breast.

And on the way, they were joined by Sir Lamorack with the dwarf and the brachet; and then by Sir Gawain riding sadly, with the headless body of the lady he had slain across his saddlebow.

Towards evening of the day after his wedding and the coming of the white hart, Arthur and Merlin walked alone upon the ramparts of Camelot; and looked out over the roofs of the town to the water-meadows and the shining loops of the river, and the forest beyond that rolled away into the blue heat-haze of summer.

'Soon, very soon now, I shall leave you,' Merlin said.

And Arthur turned from the distant forest to look at him with startled eyes. 'Merlin, why?'

'Because it is the appointed time. I have told you often enough that the time would come.'

'But not yet! Oh, Merlin, what will I do without your guidance and counsel? What will I do without *you*?'

'If I have taught you well, and you have learned well, you will do without me.'

'But you are not old,' Arthur said, seeing the man beside him as tall and upright as ever, his eyes as brightly golden, the darkness of his hair only beginning to be streaked with ash colour.

'My kind do not grow old according to the passing years – not as you understand growing old. But I am tired and the life grows thin within me, and I shall be glad to rest. And there are things that I have to do first. For many years I have shared your fate and your father's before you. Now I go to follow my own.'

Arthur said, 'Tell me at least what it is.'

'The lady who rode into your hall yesterday after the white hart, and was herself dragged away by the knight in black armour – did you not know her?'

'Why should I?' Arthur said. 'Never did I see her before.'

'That was Nimue, the Lady of the Lake who gave you your sword.' Merlin saw the astonishment on Arthur's face, and smiled. 'She is of the Lordly People, and has powers of shape-shifting beyond even my own, for I am half mortal. Yet even I have come to you often enough in the guise of an aged beggar or a child gathering blackberries and you have not known that it was I.'

'But what has she to do with you?'

'She has my love,' Merlin said simply, 'all of it that is

not yours. She has had it a long time. Now I go with her
a while, to give her my wisdom and my powers to add to
her own, as a gift of love, and so that she may use them
in your service, when I can do so no more. And when
she has them all, she will lock me with one of my own
spells into a magic sleep . . . A quiet, long sleep, in a
cave beneath roots of a certain hawthorn tree . . .'

'Then she is wicked!' Arthur cried out. 'Wicked,
even though it was she who gave me Excalibur! And
with Excalibur I will kill her before she does this to
you!'

'Nay, she is not wicked,' Merlin said, looking out
over the forest into the dim blue distance. 'She is of the
Lordly Ones, did I not say? The Lordly Ones are
neither wicked nor good, just as the rain is neither
wicked nor good, that can swell the barley or wash away
the field. They simply *are*.'

'But even so – with your powers, surely there is
something that you can do to escape this fate?' Arthur
cried in desperate misery.

'Oh, yes; and so I would remain with you – with my
powers beginning to fail. But to do so would be to turn
aside from the road appointed for me. She is my fate;
and in some sort she is yours also . . . She will be with
Pellinore when he returns, and when she leaves the
court again, I shall go with her.'

'So soon?' said Arthur.

'So soon,' said Merlin.

Arthur was silent a moment, watching the swallows
darting sickle-winged about the battlements. Then he
said, 'This sleep – will it be for ever?'

'Not for ever, no. We shall both come again, you and
I, when the time and the need call for us.'

Arthur went on watching the swallows. He felt the
warmth of the evening sunshine on his face, and Cabal's
muzzle thrust lovingly into the palm of his hand, and

thought of Guenever's face, and the faces of men who were his friends. 'What will they be like, the people we come back to ? What will it all be like?' he whispered suddenly in anguish.

But before Merlin could answer, a little group of figures rode out from the woodshore towards the bridge; and he saw that they were Sir Gawain and Sir Lamorack and King Pellinore; and that Gawain carried something that looked like a woman's body across his saddlebow, and Sir Lamorack was followed by a mounted dwarf with a white brachet on a long leash, and beside King Pellinore rode a damosel on a palfrey as white as hawthorn blossom.

That evening in the Great Hall, before the knights sat down to supper, Arthur bade the three returned knights to give account of their quests. The Queen and her ladies had come in to listen, and when the three stories were told, Guenever said, 'Oh, King Pellinore, it is a sorry tale you tell, for though you succeeded in your quest, through you this wounded knight died of his wounds beside the well, and his lady also, who loved him too well to live without him; for both might have lived had you answered when she cried to you for help.'

'Indeed I was so set upon my quest that thought of all else forsook me,' said Pellinore. 'I shall grieve for that to my own dying day.'

'If that is so, then you will not again ride past any who need your aid,' said the King. 'Come therefore to your place at the Round Table – your son Lamorack also, for he has earned his place among my knights.' And then he turned to Gawain. 'And you? Think you that you also deserve to sit among them? You who come riding back from your quest with the severed head of a lady hanging round your neck, and her slain body across your saddle-bow?'

Gawain, who had finished his story last, and stood by, ash white, flushed fiery red to the roots of his fiery red hair, and then grew white again. 'I do not know. I only know that I will swear to show more mercy in future days; and for the sake of the lady I slew, to fight for all women who seek my aid and be their knight, truly and in all honour.'

Arthur and he looked at each other straightly, for they were good friends and almost of an age. And then Arthur smiled. He was feeling the need of his friends even more than he usually did, after his talk with Merlin on the ramparts. 'Your name is still gold-written on the back of your seat. See? Come you and sit in it. And remember the oath that you have sworn.'

He looked to Merlin, as though to ask, with no word spoken, whether he had dealt rightly with his three knights, for he knew and accepted that this was the last time he would be able to ask Merlin anything.

And Merlin returned him the shadow of a smile.

Thus, then, was accomplished the Quest of the White Hart and of the Brachet, and of the Maiden who was the Lake-Lady Nimue.

And that evening Arthur received the oaths of all his knights of the Round Table, that always they would defend the right, that they would be the true servants and protectors of all women, and deal justly in all things with all men, that they would strive always for the good of the kingdom of Britain and for the glory of the kingdom of Logres which was within Britain as the flame is within the lamp, and that they would keep faith with each other and with God.

And when the oath-taking was over, and before ever the feasting began, Merlin came and set his hand for a moment upon Arthur's shoulder; and when the young King looked up, feeling the farewell in the touch, he said, 'Remember the things that I have taught you.' And he turned away and walked down the Hall, out of the torchlight and into the dark. And the Lady Nimue rose from where she sat among the Queen's maidens, and walked with him. And the places in the Hall were empty where they had been.

5

THE SHIP, THE MANTLE
AND THE HAWTHORN TREE

Then Merlin went on his last wandering, and the Lady Nimue with him, and ever, when he grew weary, she would make him to sleep with his head in her lap, and sing to him the songs of the Lordly People; so in a while when he awoke he would feel himself young again. And ever, as they went, for a gift of love he taught her his own magic arts to add to the magic of her own that she had already.

And so at last they came overseas to the kingdom of King Ban of Benwick; he who Arthur had aided when he was attacked by King Claudas, and who had after-wards fought beside Arthur at the Battle of Bedegraine. Now King Ban had a son, who was seventeen summers old and training for knighthood; and when he was a child and the kingdom sore beset by Claudas, the Lady Nimue had taken him from his mother and fostered him in her own palace of the Lordly Ones in the midst of the Lake, that he might be safe until the danger was past. And this she had done at Merlin's asking; for Merlin knew that the boy was to be the greatest of Arthur's knights, and the best knight in all Christendom.

But now, the boy remembered nothing of this, for mortals who have been inside the Hollow Hills bring back no memory of that time, lest their lives should be spent in hopeless longing and in seeking for the way back.

Therefore Merlin came to the palace of King Ban with Nimue beside him; and he spoke with the King and with Elaine the Queen, and then asked to see their son Lancelot.

'What would you with Lancelot?' said the Queen, who was always afraid of losing him, after that first time. 'He is as yet no more than a squire.'

'But he shall be more,' Merlin said. 'There are things I know of him that make me wish to see and speak with him this one time.'

'And these things?' asked the King.

'I know that he was christened Galahad,' said Merlin, 'before ever he was confirmed in the name of Lancelot. I know that there was a time when you feared him lost to you. But be easy, I have not come to take him from you again – or not in the way you fear.'

So then, still unwillingly, the King sent for his son.

Lancelot was schooling a young goshawk. All his life he was to have more joy from flying a bird he had trained himself than one that had been trained, no matter how well, by a falconer. When they had shared together the ordeal of the terrible three days and nights that man must carry bird where ever he went, allowing no sleep to either, something grew between them that was lacking if the bird had shared it with someone else. Lancelot had reached that stage with Starstrike and had just won through the second night when his father's summons reached him. He knew that if he set Starstrike down now, it would all be to do again, and the hawk might be marred for ever. So he went to his father's Hall still carrying the weary goshawk on his gloved fist, and stood respectfully before the strange dark man and the lady whom he found there.

And as he looked at them, especially as he looked at the lady, it seemed to him for a moment that he had seen them before. And for that moment there was a kind of mist in his head, like the mist that hangs over lake water, and in the mist some kind of vague half-memory that was gone again even before he knew that it was there.

And Merlin looked at Lancelot searchingly, knowing what he knew of future days. Lancelot was a very ugly young man; even when he was not so tired, he was ugly; with a face under his thick arched crest of dark hair that looked as though it had been put together by someone who had not troubled to make sure that the two sides matched. One side of his mouth was straight-set and solemn, while the other curled up with joy. One of his thick black brows was level as a falcon's wing, and the other flew wild as a mongrel's ragged ear. Presently it would be a fighter's face, and presently it would be a lover's face; and the hand that was not hidden in the great leather hawking glove was already a swordsman's hand. And though Merlin's heart bled for the joys and sorrows of his destiny that he would feel more deeply than most men, it warmed with pride because it was a great destiny and the boy was matched to it.

Then Merlin spoke to the Queen his mother, 'Aye, he is as I believed that he would be; and one day he will be the greatest knight in all Christendom.'

'Shall I live to see it?' said his mother.

'Surely, you shall live to see it, and for many summers and winters more. But though his fame shall be known in Benwick as in all other places, he shall not bide here with you.'

And to Lancelot he said, 'When you come to be eighteen, before the next Feast of Eastertide, let you leave this place and go to King Arthur at Camelot, and pray him to make you a knight of the Round Table.'

Lancelot held himself very still, that he might not disturb the goshawk on his fist. 'Often has the King my father told me of Arthur Pendragon and how they fought side by side at Bedegraine; and the harpers sing of him beside our fire on winter nights. There is nothing in the world that I would rather do than go to him and ask my knighthood at his hands and serve him. But why should he think me worthy? I am all untried.'

'Maybe he will do it for the sake of the fighting that he and I saw together,' said King Ban, who had sat quietly looking on.

But Merlin said, 'Tell him that Merlin sent you; and that it was the last thing he did before he went to find his long sleep under the hawthorn tree. He will give you your knighthood. And your place at the Round Table.'

And the joy flashed in Lancelot's ugly face like a bright blade drawn from a battered sheath.

Merlin rose to go, and the Lady Nimue with him. But before she went, she drew close to Lancelot – so close that he thought it strange, remembering afterwards, that the goshawk did not bate from his fist nor strike at her – and she looked deep into his eyes, her own eyes changeful and water-bright, and again for a moment the mist seemed to rise and swirl inside his head.

'You who were first Galahad and are now Lancelot,' she said in a voice that made him see lake water lapping among feathered reeds, 'when you come to Arthur's court and receive your knighthood, let you take your third name as a gift from me, and call yourself thereafter Sir Lancelot of the Lake.'

And when the mist cleared from his head, they were both gone.

Then again Merlin and the Lady Nimue with him wandered through this place and that, across water and among mountains and through valleys and forests, Merlin teaching her the last of his magic as they went. And so they came at last to Cornwall, where King Marc now ruled in place of Duke Gorloise of Tintagel. And at the appointed time they came to the hawthorn tree, all curdled with white blossom and the scent of it coming and going like breath upon the evening air.

And Merlin lay down under the tree with his head in the Lady's lap; and she let down her straight dark hair so that it hung like a curtain about them both; and she made a singing magic. And listening to it, it was to Merlin as though he heard the humming of wild honey bees among the heather of the hills of his boyhood; and he sank into a sleep that was deeper and quieter than any sleep known to mortal man.

And when she saw that he was deep sunk in his enchanted sleep, the Lady of the Lake arose, and made another magic; a dancing magic this time, woven with her footsteps about and about and about the hawthorn tree. Nine times she circled the tree, and as she circled, a cave opened among the roots, and the grass and the stones and the twisted roots rose up and twined together and roofed it in, and closed the last opening, so that Merlin lay within, and nothing remained but the hawthorn tree growing on a stony mound, to show where he lay.

'Bide there until your waking time,' said the Lady Nimue when she had done, and she went her way.

Now at about the same time, King Arthur rode hunting in the forest that stretched west of Camelot into the mountains, and with him for hunting companions were Sir Accalon of Gaul, and King Uriens the husband of Morgan La Fay – for despite Merlin's repeated warnings that she was a witch and would do him any harm she might, Arthur loved to have his half-sister often about his court. They hunted for three days, making further and further west; and on the third day they put up a mighty hart, and hunted it so far and fast that, grievously, they all three killed their horses under them; a thing which can be done too easily in the heat of a long chase, a horse's heart being willing beyond its strength.

The day was drawing on to dusk, and they knew that the forest was no place for unmounted men at night, and so pushed on, hoping to find a hermitage or a charcoal burner's hut. And so they came out from the trees on to the margin of a broad lake; and on the shore of the lake the hart that they had hunted also lay dead, the hounds all about it. They whipped off the hounds, and stood for a moment looking down at the dead beast; and then Arthur set his horn to his lips and sounded the long sad notes of the Morte for the death of the hart, sending the echoes flying through the shadowy forest. And as the echoes died, the hounds turned and went streaming back the way they had come, as though their huntsman was with them.

And in that same moment, out from behind a spit of the alder-grown shore glided a small ship, and came of its own accord to the bank where the three stood, like a well-trained dog when its master whistles.

'Sirs,' said Arthur, 'let us go aboard this ship, for it is a sorry thing to turn away from adventure when it comes so sweetly to the hand.'

So they stepped on board, and found the ship fine and beautiful and richly hung with silks, but seemingly with no one on board save for themselves. And as soon as they had come aboard it drew off from the bank, for all that there was no hand at the steering oar, nor any to man the sails. And as they went, the dusk deepened towards night about them; and suddenly there sprang up the flames of a hundred torches all along the vessel's sides so that it was lit from stem to stern with a golden glow. And up from below came twelve damosels, the fairest that any of them had ever seen; and they greeted Arthur and his companions and made them joyously welcome and brought them such delicious food and such rare and fragrant wines that Arthur thought he had never supped so magnificently before. They were very hungry, and merry also, and when they had eaten their fill the damosels led them below, each to a chamber that had been made ready for them; and they lay down upon beds that were so soft that they seemed to float upon them as upon thick-piled clouds; and faint music whispered all about them mingled with the lap of water along the vessel's sides. And so they fell asleep, and slept unstirring the night long.

And in the morning King Uriens woke to find himself in his own bed in Camelot, and wondered in great amazement how he came to be there. And when he looked at his wife Morgan beside him, she lay still sleeping, but with a little smile on her face as though she knew a secret that she would not tell.

And King Arthur awoke to find himself in a dark and dismal dungeon, and heard about him the groans and complaints of many other men.

'Who are you that make such grievous complaint?'

asked Arthur when he had gathered his wits about him.

'We are twenty knights who have lain here captive, some of us as much as seven years,' one of them answered him.

'For what cause?' said Arthur.

And another answered, 'Sir Damas, the lord of this castle, is a cruel and unjust tyrant who refuses his younger brother Sir Ontzlake his share of the inheritance they had from their father. And often Sir Ontzlake has offered to fight his brother in single combat for the lands that are his; but Sir Damas knows himself no match for him with lance or sword, and so would have the matter fought out by companions instead. But no knight that he has asked will stand champion for him; so he has taken a hatred against all knights, and captured in these past seven years all who have come within his lands, and cast them into this foul dungeon. Many of us have died here, and we who are left are like to go the same way unless help come soon.'

And even as he spoke there came a damosel down the dark stair, carrying a lamp, for little light of day could come into that place. And she said to Arthur. 'Fair sir, how is it with you?'

'I hardly know,' said Arthur, 'nor do I know how I came to be in this place.'

'It matters not how you came here,' said the damosel, 'you shall go free of it if you will but fight as champion for my father against the champion his brother sends to meet him this day, the victor to become the lord of all these lands.'

Arthur was silent. He had never before fought in an unjust cause; but he was young and the blood hot and rising like spring sap within him, and he thought of life shut away in that dark place far from the light of the sun, and the faces of his friends and the feel of a horse under him; and he thought too of the twenty men around him in the gloom.

'I will fight for the lord your father,' he said at last, 'if I have his promise upon oath that whether I win or lose, the twenty knights here with me shall go free.'

'You shall have his promise,' said the damosel.

'Then I am ready – if I had but horse and armour.'

'Horse and armour you shall have, none better in all the land.'

It seemed to Arthur, looking at her face in the upward light of the lamp, that he had seen her somewhere before. 'Were you ever at Arthur's court?' he asked.

'Nay, I am Sir Damas's daughter and nothing more. I was never at court,' said the damosel; and in that she lied, for she was one of the maidens of Morgan La Fay.

But Arthur believed her, for he was a simple and trusting man; and the little warning whisper that had begun at the back of his mind died away.

And he followed her up the stairs towards the clear light of day beyond the stairhead door.

At the same time as King Arthur woke in his dungeon, Sir Accalon of Gaul woke to find himself beside a deep well in the courtyard of an old strong manor house; so close beside the well that if he had so much as turned in his sleep he must have crashed to the bottom and found his death there. When he saw and understood, Sir Accalon thought, Now God help the King, and King Uriens also, for it must be that the damosels in the ship were creatures of some foul enchantment, not mortal maidens, and have betrayed us all; and if I come out from this adventure with my life I shall slay such witches wherever I meet them!

And at that moment came a dwarf, very ugly, with a great mouth and a flat nose that spread all across his face, and saluted him. 'Sir, I come to you from your love, from Queen Morgan La Fay herself.'

Now Sir Accalon did indeed love Morgan La Fay, better than all else in the world, not knowing that she was even as the damosels of the ship, a witch and a worker of dark enchantments. And his heart leapt within him, and he said, 'What would my lady with me, here in this strange place?'

'She begs you to fight for her against a knight whom she has good cause to hate for an ancient wrong he did her; and that you may fight the better, she sends you King Arthur's own sword Excalibur; and she bids you, if you truly love her, to do battle to the uttermost and show no mercy.'

Then Sir Accalon reached out and took from the dwarf the sword which he held across his hands. It seemed to him strange that she should send him Arthur's sword instead of his own; but he thought that maybe she had done so for the power that was in it. And anyway, wherever Arthur was, it would not harm him to use his sword for this one time. And he felt the power in the sword as though it had been a live thing in his hands, and rejoiced in it. 'Go back to Queen Morgan,' he said to the dwarf, 'and tell her I will fight for her as truly as ever a knight fought for his lady.'

Then six squires came and led Sir Accalon into the Hall of the manor house, and set food and drink before him, and then armed him, and set him upon a fine warhorse, and led him to a fair level field that was midway between the manor house of Sir Ontzlake and the fine castle of his brother.

And at the same time, six squires were doing the same thing for King Arthur. But to King Arthur, in the last moment before he mounted his horse, came another maiden, saying, 'Sir, your sister Morgan La Fay has dreamed that you are to do battle this day, and sends you your sword.'

And Arthur saw that she held Excalibur across her hands, and he unbuckled from his side the borrowed sword that he had belted on, and took his own sword to belt in its place. Then he mounted his horse and rode out, the squires and the twenty freed captives following after. He wished that it had been Guenever and not his sister who had dreamed of his danger and sent him his sword. But he never doubted that it was indeed Excalibur that he carried at his side.

So then, the champions came to the field, and found it ringed about with folk who had come to watch. Their vizors were closed, and both carried maiden shields with no device upon them, so neither knew who the other was. They jousted against each other until both were dismounted, and then fell to with their swords. And great and many were the blows they gave each other, and often the sword in Sir Accalon's hand found the weak points in Arthur's harness and drew blood; but however strong and sure the blows that Arthur gave in return, it seemed that they drew scarcely any blood at all. Then the truth began to wake in Arthur's mind; the sword in his hand was not Excalibur. There was no potency, no battle-power in it, and no protection in the scabbard at his side; and seeing the ground growing red with blood, and none of it his adversary's, he began to be sure that the other knight wielded the true Excalibur. But there was nothing he could do save fight his best with the sword he held. So he struggled on, growing weaker from loss of blood. At last, far spent, he drew back a way, to fetch his breath and find fighting ground that was not yet blood-slippery under foot; and Sir Accalon leapt after him, shouting, 'Nay, Sir Knight, this is no time to be taking your rest!'

Then in a sudden fury of near despair, Arthur stumbled to meet him, and by chance rather than skill, for he was past skill, smote him a side-cut on the helmet that almost brought him to the ground; but with the force of the blow Arthur's blade flew into a score of flashing sherds; and for the second time in his life he was left holding only a useless hilt.

Then Sir Accalon pulled off, and said, 'You are unarmed and have lost much blood, and I am loath to kill you. Therefore yield now to my mercy.'

'Nay!' cried Arthur. 'That I may not, for I have vowed to do battle while the life is yet in me, and I had sooner die a hundred deaths with honour than live without it! If you slay me weaponless, to you is the shame!'

'I will accept the shame,' said Accalon, and dealt him another mighty stroke; but Arthur took it on his shield, and stumbling forward dashed the heavy sword-hilt into his opponent's vizor with such desperate force that it sent him lurching three steps back.

Now among the gaily coloured crowd that thronged the edge of the field stood a lady who had not appeared until the fighting was well started, and no one had seen her come. The Lady Nimue, she who had given Arthur his sword, she who had left Merlin sleeping under his hawthorn tree, was late upon the scene, for time means little to the Lordly Ones, but she had known that the young King was in sore danger from his witch-sister that day, and she had come before it was too late.

And as Sir Accalon steadied himself and raised his sword for another blow, she made the smallest of flicking movements with the blade of grass that she was turning between her fingers, and the true Excalibur seemed to twist from the hand that held it, and landed at Arthur's feet.

Arthur flung aside the useless hilt and swooped upon it, and sprang back out of touch, with his own sword in his hand once more. 'You have been away from me too long,' he said, 'and sore damage have you done me!'

And then, seeing the scabbard still hanging at Sir Accalon's side, Arthur flung away his shield, and plunged forward under the other's guard, and grasping it, dragged it free, bursting straps and buckles, and hurled it far behind him.

Then he leapt upon Sir Accalon and dealt him such a blow on the head that he crashed to the ground, the red life-blood bursting from his mouth and nose and ears.

Arthur stood over him with sword upraised. 'Now it is for me to slay you, unless you cry my mercy.'

'Slay me then,' groaned Sir Accalon. 'I never fought with a better knight, and I see that God is with you. But I swore to do battle with you to the uttermost, and therefore I cannot cry your mercy.'

And it seemed to Arthur that he knew the voice, which he had not had time to do before. And he lowered his blade and said, 'You are a valiant knight. Of what name and country are you?'

'I am of King Arthur's court, a knight of the Round Table, and my name is Accalon of Gaul.'

Then grief and dismay rose in Arthur, and he remembered the magic of last night's ship and the morning's awakening, and asked, 'Ah, Sir Accalon, how did you come by Excalibur?'

'I had it from Morgan La Fay, whom I have loved above all else these many years. This morning she sent it to me, bidding me fight to the death for her sake against a knight who should this day come against me.' He groaned again with the pain of his desperate hurts. 'But tell me, who are you whom she would have had me slay?'

'Oh, Accalon,' said Arthur , 'I am your King.'

Then Accalon cried out, for grief at what his lady would have done more than for any other thing. 'Fair, sweet lord, now I cry your mercy, for we are both betrayed, and I did not know you.'

'How should you?' said Arthur. 'Alas, all this is the doing of my sister. Again and again Merlin warned me against her, telling me what she was, and what she would seek to do; but still I trusted her and delighted to have her about my court. But never again,' said Arthur in a weeping voice, 'never again.'

Then all the people gathered about the field came and knelt to the High King, crying his mercy also; and Arthur gave it to them, and summoned together Sir Damas and Sir Ontzlake, and made judgement between them, that Sir Damas should give over to his brother all the manors and estates that were his by inheritance, but that Sir Ontzlake should pay fee for them with the yearly gift of a palfrey. 'For that,' said Arthur in contempt, 'is a more fitting steed than a warhorse for such as you, Sir Damas the Valiant!' And he laid upon Sir Damas also that he should return to the twenty knights their weapons and armour and let them go free, and never again lay hand upon stray knights who came by following their own adventures.

And Sir Ontzlake he bade come to him presently at court.

Then, learning that there was an abbey of nuns near-by, he mounted, and with Sir Accalon drooping in the saddle beside him, he rode that way.

At the abbey they rested, and their wounds were tended. But from that last great blow dealt by Excalibur, Sir Accalon had lost so much blood that on the third day he died. Arthur recovered well and quickly, and in cold rage he had his friend's body laid on a horse-bier, and summoned six knights from Sir Damas's castle, and said, 'Now bear this to my sister, Queen Morgan La Fay, and tell her that I send it to her for a gift. And tell her also that I have my sword Excalibur again.'

*   *   *

Meanwhile, at Camelot, Morgan La Fay, knowing nothing of what had passed, thought that Arthur must by now be dead, and once she was wedded to Sir Accalon of Gaul they could seize the throne of Britain between them as she had always had it in her dark mind to do. And seeing King Uriens asleep on their bed, she decided that the time had come for the next thing that must be done. So she called to her softly one of her maidens, and said, 'Go, fetch me the King's sword.'

And the maiden looked into her face and saw the smile upon it and the darkly glittering eyes, and cried out in horror, 'Madam, no! No! I beg of you! If you slay your lord, you will never escape!'

'That is not a thing you need to trouble for,' said the Queen. 'This is the day and the time I chose long since. Go now and fetch the sword.'

But the damosel fled to Sir Uwaine, the Queen's son, who was newly made a knight of the Round Table, and begged him, 'Come quickly to my lady your mother, for she is set upon slaying the King your father, and has sent me to fetch his sword that she may do it while he sleeps in his bed!'

'Go swiftly and do as she bids you,' said Sir Uwaine. 'I will see to the rest.'

So in a little while the damosel brought the sword and gave it with shaking hands into the steady hands her mistress held out for it. And Morgan La Fay took the sword and unsheathed it, never seeing that Uwaine had come in behind the damosel and remained hidden in the shadows of the hangings by the chamber door. And she stood for three breaths of time looking down at the sleeping man and deciding which would be the best place to strike. But as she swung up the heavy blade for the death blow, Uwaine sprang from his hiding place and seized her sword-hand and wrenched it aside; and as she whirled round to face him, he stood there panting, with a face like one that had taken his own death blow. 'Fiend!' he shouted. 'What would you do? If you were not my mother, and would God that you were not, I would plunge this sword now into your heart.'

'Nay, but the fiends of Hell tempted me!' cried his mother. 'It was their doing, not mine – and see, the madness has passed from me. Oh, sweet son of mine, have mercy, and I promise that never again will I listen to their evil whisperings in my ear.'

'Swear!' said Uwaine.

And shaking and shuddering under his merciless gaze, the Queen swore; and the young knight sheathed his father's sword and turned and walked away.

Towards the end of that day came the six knights with Sir Accalon's body and the High King's message.

Then Morgan La Fay's heart almost broke within her, for she had indeed loved Sir Accalon in her fashion, and it was more than her hopes of usurping the crown of Britain that lay dead upon his bier. But she hid her grief for her own safety; and knowing that if she were still at court when Arthur returned all the gold of the Hollow Hills would not buy her life, she contrived to learn from one of the knights where it was that her brother lay; and before full dawn next day she sent for her horse from the stables, and saying that she wanted none with her save certain of her ladies, she rode away.

She rode all that day and part of the night, and by noon of the next day came to the abbey where Arthur lay not yet fully mended from his wounds.

She asked of the Lady Abbess where the King might be, and was told that he was sleeping. 'Then do not wake him,' she said fondly. 'But I am his sister, and have ridden far to be with him, hearing of his wounds. Therefore I will sit with him a while, and maybe wake him myself later.'

And since she was his sister, neither the holy ladies of

the abbey nor the knight who kept watch before his chamber door thought to deny her. So she went in.

I cannot slay him, she thought, or only at the cost of my own life, with all these about him. But at least I can steal away Excalibur, and later maybe have him at my mercy. But when she crossed to the bed, she saw that though Arthur was indeed asleep, he lay with Excalibur gripped in his right hand. Only one hope of harming him remained to her. The blade in his hand was naked. She looked about and found the scabbard lying on a great carved chest at the foot of the bed. She knew the powers of the scabbard as well as Merlin had done; and she took it up and hid it in the folds of her mantle. It was less than she had hoped for, but it was better than nothing.

Then she sat beside the bed for a while, lest any should look in. And presently she rose and went out, saying to those in the outer chamber that the King slept so sweetly it would be a sorry thing to wake him. And so she mounted her horse and rode away, her ladies following.

Presently Arthur awoke and found his scabbard gone. He demanded in anger to know who had come beside him while he slept. And when they told him Morgan La Fay, he cried out on them, 'Falsely have you kept your watch over me!'

'Sir,' said the Lady Abbess, 'we dared not disobey your own sister's command.'

Then Arthur called for his armour and his horse, and for Sir Ontzlake to arm and come to him. And when Sir Ontzlake came in all haste, they rode out after Morgan La Fay.

Within a while Arthur caught sight of his sister far ahead, with her damosels all about her, and struck spurs to his horse to ride her down. But she, finding him hard behind her, spoke in her horse's ear, and sent it forward, fleet-footed as a Faery steed, and all her damosels streaming after her. But Arthur and Ontzlake were not to be easily shaken off, however fast she fled through the forest ways; and as she came at last skirting the margin of a dark lake among the trees, she cried out within herself, 'Whatever comes to me, at least my brother shall not have his scabbard to protect him again!' and flung the gleaming thing out into the centre-most depths, where it sank at once, borne down by its weight of gold and jewels.

She knew now where she must go for refuge, and in a while, riding her desperate race with the hunt hard behind, she burst out from the trees into an open valley set about with many great stones standing in the grass. And there she made a swift and urgent magic. And when the magic was made, suddenly in the blink of an eye, there were seven more great stones in the valley than there had been before; and of Morgan La Fay and her ladies, no sign.

And the King, following on, saw what had happened and, when he could not even make out which of the stones were his sister and her ladies, thought that it was the vengeance of God, and despite his anger was even a little sorry for their fate. He hunted the valley for his lost scabbard, Sir Ontzlake helping him; but at last gave up the search and went heavily away, with none of the triumph in his heart that he felt he had a right to.

And when he had left the valley, Queen Morgan La Fay turned herself and her maidens back into their own likeness again, and said, 'Now, my damosels, we may go where we will.'

Arthur never found his scabbard again, and so had to have another made to sheathe Excalibur. It was as rich and beautiful as the old one had been, but it had no special virtue; and from that day forward, when he was wounded he bled as other men bleed.

Arthur, with Sir Ontzlake at his side, rode wearily back to Camelot, and there Queen Guenever and all the court were greatly rejoiced to see them.

But on the very first evening of the King's return, as they sat at meat in the Great Hall, there entered a damosel bearing a mantle of cloth of gold soft and heavy with furs and sparked with precious stones; the most splendid mantle that anyone there had ever seen. And she brought it to King Arthur and bowed before him. 'My Lord King, your sister Morgan La Fay sends me to beg your forgiveness for the evil that she has done, and to promise you truly that the evil spirits that tempted her have departed from her; and she will seek to harm you no more, and to show her sorrow for what she sought to do, she sends you this mantle, begging that you will wear it often, and find pleasure in it.'

Arthur looked at the mantle and saw how beautiful it was, and he thought that maybe the evil had indeed gone out of his sister – always he was over-trusting. And he put out his hand to accept the gift. But before he could touch it, there was a swift movement among the ladies in the Hall, and he dropped his hand and looked around. And the Lady Nimue, who nobody had seen enter, was standing at his side. 'Sir,' she said, 'do not put on the mantle, nor touch it, nor let it come near any of your knights, until you have first seen it upon the shoulders of her who brings it to you.'

Arthur looked at her a moment, and saw through her shape-shifting – maybe she let him see – that she was that Lady of the Lake whom Merlin had loved, and who had given him his sword Excalibur. And he re-membered Merlin saying, 'The Lordly Ones are not good or evil, any more than the rain that swells the barley or washes the field away, they simply *are*.' And then he seemed to be not remembering Merlin's voice, but hearing it afresh, speaking in his ear, 'Trust her.

Whatever she is, *you* may always trust her. For a while, she is your fate as well as mine.'

The voice was silent, and Arthur saw that his knights were looking at him strangely, as though wondering why he stood listening while no one spoke.

Then he said, 'Lady, I accept your counsel.' And to his sister's messenger, 'Damosel, I would see this mantle first upon you.'

'Nay, sir,' she said quickly. 'It would ill become me to wear a king's mantle.'

'Nevertheless, you shall wear this one, before ever the King puts it about his shoulders,' said Arthur, and he made a sign to two squires standing nearby; and they seized the damosel and the mantle, and by force wrapped it close about her. And in that same moment, while she screamed and struggled, there was a bright flame of fire that leapt up between the squires' hands almost to lick the roof of the Great Hall, and of the damosel and the mantle nothing was left but a little smoking ash upon the ground.

From that time forward Morgan La Fay never dared to seek to do Arthur harm, but fled to her husband's kingdom of Gore, to a castle of her own that she had there, and fortified it strongly, and there she stayed. And so the kingdom was rid of one more of its enemies.

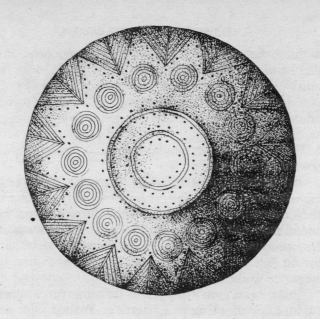

6

SIR LANCELOT OF THE LAKE

Just as the High King and his knights were about to sit down to supper on the eve of Easter, one of Arthur's squires came to him, saying that there was a stranger at the threshold who wished for speech with him but would not give his name. And Arthur looked away down the Hall and saw a young man standing in the doorway, and said, 'Bring him to me. It may be that he will tell *me* his name.'

So the young man came up the Hall and knelt wordlessly at the King's feet. He was a raw-boned and very ugly young man, with two sides to his face that did not match each other, so that one side of his mouth ran straight and sullen and the other lifted towards joy and laughter, and one of his black brows was level as a falcon's wing and one flew wild and ragged like the jaunty ear of a mongrel that has just come well out of a fight. But out from under those brows looked a pair of wide grey eyes that the King thought were the steadiest that he had ever seen.

'Who are you?' Arthur said. 'And for what purpose do you come to me?'

And the young man said, 'I am Lancelot, son of King Ban of Benwick, who fought beside you at Bedegraine. And I come because I have wished to for as long as I can remember, and because Merlin bade me, to ask for knighthood at your hands. He bade me tell you that I was his last bequest to you before he went to find his long sleep under his hawthorn tree.'

'Knighthood you shall have, on tomorrow's morning, the fair morning of Eastertide,' Arthur said; and gave his hand to the ugly young man, who bent his head for a moment to touch his forehead upon it.

'I thank you, sir,' said Lancelot; and then he turned a little, and Arthur saw that a russet-haired young man had come quietly up behind him. 'Sir, here stands my cousin and good friend Lional, who came with me to be my squire; but he is at least as worthy of knighthood as I am myself.'

And the King looked at the russet-haired squire, and said, 'What says Lional as to that? Would you also be made knight upon Easter morning?'

'I would be made knight,' said Lional, 'but not on Easter morning; for then how could I play squire to my cousin Lancelot at the same time? I would not that some strange squire should see to his armour, and attend him through the ceremony.'

'That is well spoken,' said the King. 'You shall serve him as squire for three days, and if you are a good squire, you shall come to your knighthood on the fourth.'

For he liked the seeming of the young man, and beside Lancelot's own seat and the other three that waited, there were already empty places at the Round Table, whose knights had fallen during the past year; and those places must be filled. There would always be empty places, he realised suddenly, as though it were something he had not known before; and always they must be filled . . .

So all that night young Lancelot kept his vigil in the castle chapel, kneeling at the chancel steps with his sword and his armour laid before the altar in front of him. And all night long he prayed, and watched the moonlight through the high window move silvery across his harness, and prayed again, and thought long thoughts that he could not have shared with anyone.

Now Lancelot was as odd and ill-matching in his hidden inmost self as he was in his face for all to see. And maybe because of those strange lost years in his childhood, he always felt as though he was searching for something. He never felt he was quite like other boys; quite like other men. He had a great and terrible hope in him, more fitted to a monk than to a knight, that one day, if he proved himself worthy, God would let him perform a miracle. But for that to happen, he would have to be the best knight in all the world. So kneeling there in the moon-whitened chapel all night long, he prayed that he should become not just the strongest and bravest and most skilled knight, but the best. He prayed that he might never do anything to stain his honour or anybody else's; and he prayed for his miracle.

And the moon sank and the sun rose, and when the proper ceremonies of bath and arming were over, he received his knighthood from King Arthur in the Great Hall on Easter morning.

And after, two of the Queen's ladies buckled on his

knightly spurs. But Queen Guenever herself buckled
on his sword-belt; and this she did partly because he was
a king's son, but mostly in kindness, because she had
heard Sir Kay, the King's foster brother and Seneschal,
sneering to another knight about the newcomer's ill
looks and saying that he would not likely find a maiden's
favour to wear on his crest at the jousts and tourna-
ments.

The buckle was stiff, and though she was well used to
fastening Arthur's sword-belt for him, the Queen found
it hard to make the tang go into the right place. And
Lancelot, seeing this, put his own hand to help her, and
so their fingers touched – and instantly they looked up
from the buckle into each other's eyes. And having
looked, they did not know how to look away again.
They both paled to curd white and the black pupils of
their eyes grew enormous. For a long moment it seemed
that nothing moved or sounded in the Hall, and even
the fire on the hearth stopped crackling. Then they
pulled their eyes away from each other, and Guenever
finished securing the buckle. But her fingers were
shaking.

During the next three days there was a certain
muttering and complaining among some of the knights,
led by Sir Kay, that a man so young and all untried as
yet should have been knighted and given a place at the
Round Table. And afterwards men thought this was the
reason that Lancelot set off so soon on his first quest.
They thought that he went to prove himself, and to
quiet the muttering. And Lancelot let them think it;
but he had another reason. On the first evening after his
cousin Lional had been made a knight also, when
supper was over in the Great Hall and the King and Sir
Gawain were playing chess, he fell, without knowing it ,
to watching the Queen as she sat with the torchlight
meshed in her dark hair, listening with her chin cupped

in her hand to an old song that the King's harper was singing.

'Aye, is she not fair?' said Lional softly beside him. 'Surely she would be the fairest damosel in all this Court, if she were not the Queen.'

And Sir Lancelot said, 'Yes' and began instead to watch his own hands. And in a little, he said, 'I shall ask the King's leave to go on a quest.'

'Let me ride with you,' said his kinsman.

And as soon as the game of chess was over, Lancelot went and knelt before the King and asked leave to ride out next morning in quest of adventure, his cousin Lional with him.

The King looked at him a moment and then said, 'Pay no heed to them. Sir Kay was an unhappy boy and he's an unhappy man, and I fear me he always will be.'

'As to that,' said Lancelot, 'I do not care greatly whether Sir Kay thinks me worthy of my knighthood and my place at the Round Table, but I care whether I think myself worthy of them.'

So King Arthur gave him leave for the quest, and Lional also, and next morning after hearing Mass they rode out in search of whatever adventures awaited them.

And adventures they were like to find in plenty, for although the Sea-wolves and the men from the dark North and the western mountains had been overcome and driven back to their own places, the land was not quiet, for the long years of warfare had left behind them much unrest. There were many lords who had come to think that the strong arm was all that mattered, and right was the same thing as might. And as the months of spring and summer passed, Sir Lancelot and his cousin met and fought with many such, and overcame them. And when they were defeated and cried his mercy, Sir Lancelot would make them swear to be the High King's men thenceforth, and send them to swear fealty to Arthur. But sometimes the battle was to the death, as it was when he met with a certain Sir Carrados. Sir Carrados would not cry quarter, and Sir Lancelot slew him after a mighty battle, and freed the captives he was holding to ransom in his tower. And then he rode on his way, seeking the next thing.

But the time was to come when he would remember Sir Carrados.

Meanwhile, on a day of late summer when the air shimmered like a midge cloud with the heat, the two cousins came to a great old apple tree heavy with half-ripe fruit, that grew close beside a hedge. They were far over on the very borders of the land of Gore, though they did not know it. The shade lay deep and cool under the tree, and Lancelot, who was weary with riding and fighting and the aching heart that he carried within him for Guenever's sake, felt a great desire to lie down in that shade and sleep. So they dismounted, knee-hobbled the horses and turned them free to graze, then lay down themselves in the blissful coolth of the long grass under the apple boughs.

Almost at once Lancelot was asleep, his head on his helm for a pillow. But lying beside him, Lional could not sleep, and in a while he sat up again, and propped his back against the apple trunk, and sat there chewing grass stems and idly watching the horses graze.

Presently he heard the hoof-beats of other horses, hard ridden, and looking out over the open country before him, he saw three knights riding for their lives, and behind them a fourth in hot pursuit, who was the biggest and most powerful looking knight Lional had ever seen, and riding a warhorse that made the horses of the other three look no more than jennets. And even as Lional watched, he reached and overtook the first of the fleeing knights and struck him to the ground, then thundered on to serve the second and the third in the same way. Then he dismounted and, leading his own horse, returned on his tracks and flung each fallen knight across the back of his own mount, bound him there with his own reins, and then remounting, rode on, driving the three shamefully before him.

Sir Lional got up quietly and laced on his helm, taking care not to waken his cousin; for all that summer Lancelot had had most of the fighting, and he thought, Now this is surely my adventure; and if I can overcome this knight and free his captives, I shall win much honour. So he freed his horse's hobbles and, mounting, rode hard after the little group now almost lost in the late summer haze.

Riding hard, he overtook them at last, and shouted to the huge knight to halt.

The other turned without a word, and setting his lance in rest came charging back upon Sir Lional, and got in a blow to the shoulder-piece that hove him backwards clean over his horse's crupper; then he dismounted, bound Sir Lional and slung him over his own saddle, just as he had done with the others, and rode on, driving the four horses ahead of him. And when he reached his own manor, he had them stripped and beaten with thorn branches, and then flung into a stone chamber deep underground, where there were many doleful knights that he had taken captive at other times.

Now a short while before this, Ector of the Marsh, Lancelot's half-brother, had arrived at Camelot, craving knighthood; and finding Lancelot and Lional both away on quest, he asked leave to follow them, and rode out on his search. For a while he searched in vain, until one day he met with a forester, and knowing that wherever there was promise of adventure, there his kinsmen would be most likely found, he enquired,

'Good fellow, is there any place near here where adventure is to be had for the asking?'

'That there is, Sir Knight,' returned the forester. 'Not more than a mile from here there stands the strong fortified manor house of Sir Tarquine; and close by the house the river runs over a ford – a good place for horses to drink – and over the ford there leans a great willow tree, and from the branches of the tree there hang the shields of many knights who Sir Tarquine has overthrown and flung into a dungeon beneath his house. On this tree also hangs a basin of finest copper. Beat upon it with the butt of your spear, and Sir Tarquine himself will come out to fight with you. And may the good God be gentle with your soul.'

Sir Ector thanked the man, and rode on by the way that he had pointed out, until soon he came to the ford, and saw the ancient willow tree leaning over it; and hanging from the branches many shields, some of them rusted and weather-worn, others bright and new; and among them the shield of his cousin Lional. The anger rose in his throat, and seeing the copper basin, he beat upon it with the butt of his spear until all the forest rang and the wood pigeons clattered up from the trees. Then, since no one came, he rode knee-deep into the ford to let his horse drink. And while he was still in the water a great voice cried out to him from the bank, 'Sir Knight! Since you have summoned me, come up from the water and make ready to joust with me!'

Striking spurs to his horse, Sir Ector came plunging up from the ford, setting his spear in rest as he came, and charged the huge knight he saw waiting and ready for him on the bank with such dash and fury that he got in a blow which sent horse and rider plunging round in a full circle.

'That was well struck! A knightly blow!' said Sir Tarquine, and he laughed, and charged Sir Ector in his turn, and got him under the arm and lifted him clean out of the saddle and bore him away at a plunging gallop through his gates and across his courtyard and into his hall and flung him down all asprawl on the rush-strewn floor. 'Now you are at my mercy,' said the huge knight. 'Do you cry quarter?'

'Never!' said Sir Ector through his teeth.

'You shall have it, none the less; prisonment instead of death, for your boldness pleases me,' said Sir Tarquine; and he called his servants and men-at-arms and had Sir Ector stripped and beaten with thorn branches and flung into the dark stone place beneath the house. And there he found many knights before him, the owners of the shields he had seen hanging from the willow tree. And among them Sir Lional.

When they had greeted each other, sorrowfully enough, Sir Ector said, 'But tell me, where is Sir Lancelot my brother, for it was told me that you two rode together.'

'Alas!' said Sir Lional. 'I left him sleeping under an apple tree this very noon, when I rode off to follow the tyrant lord of this place. And for all I know, he sleeps there still.'

And under the apple tree meanwhile, Sir Lancelot lay sleeping until well into the afternoon. And while he slept, there came by four queens riding on white mules, and with four mounted knights in attendance on them, holding up a canopy of green silk upon the points of spears to shield their delicate complexions from the sun. And as they came near, Lancelot's horse caught the scent of the others and whinnied; and looking that way, they beheld a knee-hobbled warhorse, and hard by, a knight sleeping under an apple tree, fully armed save that his helm was off and serving him for a pillow. And one of them – it was Morgan La Fay – knew him by her magic powers. 'It is Sir Lancelot of the Lake,' she said, 'he that shall be the greatest of all my brother's knights.'

Then all four queens looked down at his sleeping face, seeing in its ugliness what most women saw in it all his life, and began to quarrel over which of them should have him for her lover.

'We need not bide here making war over him,' said Morgan La Fay at last. 'I will cast a web of sleep upon him, that he shall not wake for three hours, and we will carry him back to my castle; and when he wakes, he shall choose among us for himself.' For in her own dark heart she was sure that she had more beauty than the other three, and that if her beauty failed her she could win him to her by her spells.

So she dismounted, and kneeling beside him made the spell of sleeping, and laid it upon him with her two forefingers touching his closed eyes. And when she was mounted again, the knights laid Lancelot, sleeping now as deeply as Merlin beneath his hawthorn tree, upon his own shield, and so bore him between them, his own horse following aft, back to the Queen's castle, that was called the Castle Chariot, and laid him sleeping still upon a pallet bed in one of the castle dungeons.

When Lancelot awoke and found himself in his strange prison, he found also a young maiden standing beside him with a platter of bread and meat and a cup of wine.

'How is it with you, Sir Knight?' she asked, kindly enough.

And Sir Lancelot looked about him in bewilderment and said, 'How did I come to be in this place, when I fell asleep under an apple tree?'

'Nay, there is no time now for words,' said the maiden. 'Make what cheer you may; and you shall know more in the morning.' And her voice was soft, for she was sorry for a young knight in the clutches of her mistress and her mistress's fellow queens. And she went away.

Lancelot did not touch his food, but lay hungry and wakeful and afraid and raging through the night.

In the morning the door opened again and the four queens came in, dressed each of them in her fairest silks and sparkling with her brightest jewels. And one of them, still beautiful but as old as his mother at home in Benwick – he did not know that she was Morgan La Fay – said to him, 'Ah, Sir Lancelot of the Lake, we know you, though you do not know us; we know that you are a king's son, and fated to be the greatest of all King Arthur's knights, and we know that there is one woman only in your heart, and she King Arthur's Queen. Yet now, you shall lose her and she shall lose you, for you shall never leave this place alive unless you choose one of us to be your love in her stead.' And she smiled and arched her neck, sleek and purring as a well-fed cat, sure of what his choice would be. 'Choose, then, sweet knight.'

'This is a hard choice that you set before me,' Sir Lancelot said, standing before them, 'to die or to choose one of you for my love. Yet I do not find it hard to make. If it must be so, I will die in this place, rather than take one of you to my heart, for you are all false enchantresses, and with death at least I shall not lose my honour. As for the Queen, my Lady Guenever – give me back my horse and harness and I will prove in combat with any champion you may bring against me, that she is the truest lady to her lord the King that ever lived!'

'So you refuse us?' said Morgan La Fay, and she narrowed her eyes like a cat's before it spits. 'You refuse *me*?'

And they turned and swept out, trailing the scent of musk and rose-oil behind them; and the prison door clanged shut once more.

Presently, when the light through the small high windows showed that the day was drawing towards evening, the young damosel returned with more meat and bread and wine, which she set down on the wooden stool beside the bed, and asked Sir Lancelot again, 'How is it with you?'

'I think that it was never so ill with me as it is now,' said Sir Lancelot, 'for I have gained the anger of the four queens who hold me here, and they will be quick to take some ugly revenge unless I can escape from them.'

The maiden looked at the food that she had just set down, and sighed a little. 'That is true, for I have heard them talking; and for refusing their love indeed they love you not!' And then, as though making up her mind all in a breath, she turned and looked into Lancelot's face. 'Indeed it grieves me to see you in the power of these queens, for they have been the downfall of many good knights. I have no love for them nor duty to them, and I will help you, if you in turn will help me.'

Lancelot returned her look searchingly, wondering if he could trust her, and thought he could. 'Help me to escape,' he said, 'and I will do whatever you ask of me, if it be not against my honour.'

'Then, sir, my father King Bagdemagus has cried a tournament for next Tuesday, between himself and the King of Northgalis, whose queen is one of the four who hold you here. A great tournament of many knights, and at the last such tournament three of those who are to fight on Tuesday overthrew my father. Fight on his side that day, and I will contrive your escape.'

'I have heard of your father as a good knight and a just ruler,' said Sir Lancelot, 'and gladly I will fight in his ranks at this tournament.'

'Then tomorrow morning before light, I will come for you and lead you out of this place, and bring you your horse and armour.'

Next morning the maiden returned with a great bunch of keys in her hand. 'I have given drugged wine to the guards,' she said, 'but they will not sleep long. Therefore come quickly!'

And she led Sir Lancelot out by twelve locked doors; and the last door of all was a narrow postern in the curtain-wall of the castle, so that outside it was the scent of the forest in the early morning, and the scent of freedom. Then she brought him across the open ground to a hidden place among the elder and wayfaring trees of the forest verge where his horse and armour were waiting for him, and helped him to arm and mount.

'Twelve miles north of this place,' she said, 'there is an abbey of Dominican monks. Wait for me there and I will bring my father to you.'

'By the grace of God, I shall not fail you,' said Sir Lancelot, and he urged his horse forward into the forest ways.

Towards evening, he came to the abbey, and the brethren made him welcome and stabled his horse and gave him supper and a place to sleep. And there he remained two days, waiting for the coming of King Bagdemagus. And on the third day came the maiden with the King her father and a brave company of knights. And that was on the Sunday; and on the Tuesday they rode together to the chosen tournament ground where the King of Northgalis and his knights waited for them, in a fair open meadow set about with pavilions striped and chequered in all the colours of a summer garden. And there, Sir Lancelot fought so nobly and so strongly among the knights of King Bagdemagus – none knowing who he has, for he carried the white shield, the Virgescue as men call it, such as knights carry who have as yet no device of their own – that he brought down three knights of the Round Table as well as many others, and King Bagdemagus was accounted the victor in that tournament.

And when Sir Lancelot had spared the lives of those knights he had brought down, he bade them go and swear fealty to King Arthur, saying that the Nameless Knight had sent them. And this he did because he would have no ill feeling between himself and his fellows of the Round Table.

And when the day was over, he returned to their own castle with King Bagdemagus and the maiden his young daughter, who could never of course return to her place as one of Morgan's handmaidens, after aiding Lancelot to escape. And there they made him warmly welcome and offered him many rich gifts. But these he would not accept, saying, 'Nay, the thing was a straight bargain between your daughter and me, and each of us has kept our side of it.'

And in the morning, he took his leave, for he had no thought now but to go in search of Sir Lional his cousin, who had disappeared from him while he slept under the apple tree. But at parting, he said to the King's daughter, 'If ever you should have need of my aid again, pray you let me know of it, and I will not fail you if I be yet living.'

And he rode away, never knowing that the King's daughter stood looking after him with the salt taste of her own tears on her lips.

For many days Sir Lancelot rode about the forest while the blackberries ripened on the bramble domes and the first gold kindled among the green fronds of the bracken, but could never come by any word of his cousin, until one day, following a narrow path among the trees, he came up with the forester whom Sir Ector had met, and asked him much the same question as Sir Ector had asked him, and received much the same reply. And so he came at last to the fortified manor house beside the ford, and the great willow tree leaning over the water, and the shields hanging like strange fruit from its drooping branches; and among them he saw the shields of his cousin Lional and his half-brother Ector.

Sir Lancelot rode in among the branches, and finding the copper basin, beat on it with the butt of his spear until the bottom fell out. But nobody came. He watered his horse at the ford, and then rode to and fro before the gates of the manor, working up a fret that made his horse fidget under him. At last he saw far off along the woodshore a huge knight in full armour and mounted on the tallest warhorse he had ever seen, and driving before him another horse with a knight lying bound across its saddle. And as they came nearer, Sir Lancelot recognised the device on the shield hanging from the saddlebow of the captive knight, and so knew him for Sir Gaheris, the younger brother of Sir Gawain.

So he turned from the manor gateway and rode to meet them. 'Fair sir!' shouted Sir Lancelot, 'set that wounded knight down off his horse and let him rest, while we two try our strength against each other, for you have caused shame and suffering enough to my brothers of the Round Table. Therefore defend yourself!'

'Willingly,' shouted back Sir Tarquine. 'The more so if you be of that fellowship. I defy you and all your brothers!'

'That is enough of words,' said Sir Lancelot, 'now is the time for fighting!'

And Sir Tarquine turned loose the horse with Sir Gaheris across its saddle, and he and Lancelot drew apart the length of the broad meadow before the manor house and, setting their spears in rest, pricked their horses to a gallop, and came thundering together, so that their spears, taking each other in the centre of the shield, brought each other crashing down, horses and riders both.

And when they had rolled clear of their horses' threshing hooves, they drew swords and came together again like a pair of stags in October, and so they battled, with great swinging strokes that cleaved each other's armour and drew blood wherever they found a joint, until the best part of two hours was gone by, and both were spent and weary, and drew off a space, leaning on their swords.

'You are the best and strongest knight that ever I fought with,' said Sir Tarquine, his breath coming and going heavy through the slits of his vizor. 'And ever I have loved a good fighter. I will strike hands with you, and free into your keeping all of the knights that lie captive in my hold – so that ye be any knight but one, in all the world.'

'And what knight is that?' asked Sir Lancelot.

'Sir Lancelot of the Lake; he who slew my brother Sir Carrados whom I have sworn to avenge.'

'Alas!' said Sir Lancelot. 'I am that one knight in all the world! I slew Sir Carrados in fair fight, but if you have sworn vengeance for him, then what must be must be.'

'That is sure,' said Sir Tarquine, 'and never we two shall part from each other or from this place until one of us is dead.'

So they fell again to their fighting, both blind and stumbling-weary as they were; and at last Sir Tarquine's guard wavered and went down; and Sir Lancelot, dropping his own shield, leapt in and seized him by the helmet-crest and got in a swinging blow to the neck that almost hacked his head from his shoulders. And Sir Tarquine fell with a clash and clatter of armour that echoed to the treetops of the forest.

Then Sir Lancelot went to Sir Gaheris and unbound him, and finding him not too sorely wounded, bade him go to the manor house and set free the knights held captive there. 'And I pray you greet them all from Sir Lancelot of the Lake, and bid them in all courtesy to ride to King Arthur's court before next Eastertide; and at Eastertide I will come and join them there.'

And while Sir Gaheris went up to the manor and threw down the doorkeeper who would have barred his way, and set the captives free, Sir Lional and Sir Ector and Sir Kay among many more, Sir Lancelot washed his hurts in the cold clear water of the ford, then whistled up his horse and rode on his way in search of more adventure.

Hither and yon he rode, while the forests flamed with autumn that chilled to the black and white of winter. And he rescued many damosels out of their distress, and overcame many evil knights, and met with adventures many and strange, while the year grew colder and he had no shelter from the winter rain and nowhere to lay his head at night.

One bitter cold evening when the year was drawing on towards Christmas, with the sun setting red behind the trees and frost already making his horse's hooves to ring upon the ground, he came to a fair manor house, and when he asked shelter for the night from the aged gentlewoman who was the mistress of the place, she welcomed him kindly and saw that his horse was fed and bestowed in a warm stable; and when she had given Sir Lancelot a fine filling supper – for she judged that she knew what boys' appetites were like, and he was little more – she took him to a warm dry garret over the gate, where a bed of last summer's hay, smelling still of clover and sweet fescue grass, was spread with sheets of clean rough linen and thick rugs. And when she was gone, Sir Lancelot took off his armour and clad in his shirt and breeches lay between the sheets and was soon asleep.

He had not slept long when he was awakened by the ring of hoof-beats on the iron-hard ground, a horse ridden at desperate speed, and then a beating on the gate. Sir Lancelot tumbled out of bed and peered down from the window. The world was white with moonlight, and the ground and the ledges of the gatehouse walls were all asparkle with frost, and by the light he saw a knight with his horse backed against the gate, desperately defending himself against three more.

'Three against one is no fair match,' said Lancelot to himself, 'no matter what the rights or wrongs of the case!' There would be no time to rouse the household. Everyone he had seen that evening was as old as its mistress, and like enough deaf. He whipped the sheets from the bed and, knotting them together, tied one end to the window transom and flung the rest out through the window; then snatched up his sword Joyeux from where it lay beside the bed. He flung his shield clanging down among the attacking knights, and climbing through the window, plunged after it by means of the makeshift rope. 'If you would fight three to one,' he roared, 'then fight with me!'

They had given back a little at his down-rush, and dismounting from their startled horses, they did indeed turn upon Sir Lancelot, pressing in upon him and their original quarry from all sides. But Lancelot had snatched up his fallen shield, and used it with such skill that it was like another weapon and behind it he was almost as well covered as a man in armour; and he set his back to the stout timbers of the gate, and laughed, and drove them off. The fugitive knight would have shared the fight with him, but Sir Lancelot shouted him back, 'Nay, three to one they wanted, three to one let them have. Do you leave them alone to me!' And the other, seeming all too glad to obey, pulled his horse aside and took no more part in the fight.

And with six more strokes of Joyeux, that sliced through their helmet-crests and juddered the teeth in their heads but did them no more harm, Lancelot had felled all three.

Scrambling slowly and painfully back to their knees, while he stood leaning on his sword and breathing a little quickly, they all cried out, 'Sir, we yield to your mercy, as a man of matchless might!'

But Sir Lancelot had had time to glance at the fugitive's shield, and knew by the device on it that he was Sir Kay. And then he knew why he had fled so fast and stood aside so readily from the fight, for Sir Kay the Seneschal was in truth no great fighting man. And the laughter rose in Lancelot's throat, and he swallowed it, and said, 'Nay, but I do not choose that you should yield to me. Yield therefore to Sir Kay here instead.'

Then the three knights were crestfallen indeed. 'Sir,' said one of them, 'we chased Sir Kay here, and we would have overcome him easily had you not joined the tourney. Therefore why should we yield to him?'

'Because if you do not,' said Sir Lancelot simply, 'I shall take it that you refuse to yield to mercy, and I shall kill you.'

So they yielded to Sir Kay.

'Now,' said Lancelot, 'you shall betake you to Camelot, to the King's court at Eastertide, and you shall swear fealty to Queen Guenever, and put you all at her grace and mercy, saying that Sir Kay sent you. Now get you back to your horses and go!'

And when they were gone, he turned and beat upon the gate with the pommel of his sword, until the whole household with the aged mistress of the place among them came and opened to them.

'I had thought you were in your bed,' said the aged gentle-woman, surprised.

'So I was,' said Sir Lancelot, 'but I went out of the window to aid a friend and fellow of mine that needed it.'

And when they came into the light, Sir Kay knew him, and said stiffly, for thanks did not come easy to him, but warmly all the same, 'It seems I have to thank you for saving my life.'

'You are very welcome,' said Sir Lancelot, who was almost as ill-at-ease in being thanked as Kay was in thanking.

Then when Kay had been unarmed and food brought for him, they went back to the garret over the gate, and lay down in the warm hay and pulled the rugs over them and slept.

But in the morning Lancelot woke early, while Kay was still snoring, and looking down at the King's foster brother in the sinking light of the night lamp, he remembered Arthur saying, 'He was an unhappy boy and he's an unhappy man, and I fear he always will be.' And he knew that many of the knights made fun of him and never missed a chance to take him down in his own esteem. And he laughed kindly within himself, and taking care not to wake him, he put on Kay's armour, which fitted him none so ill, for they were much of a size, though he had to slacken off the straps across the shoulders. He shall ride proud and unmolested for once, anyway, thought Sir Lancelot, and he took up Kay's shield, but his own sword, and went and bade farewell to the ancient gentlewoman; and then took Sir Kay's horse from the stable and rode away, leaving Sir Kay to find his horse and armour when he woke.

He was many miles away in the forest, when suddenly he wondered if Sir Kay would take the jest kindly, as it was meant, or if it was the cruellest and most conceited thing he had ever done in his life. But by then it was too late to turn back and do anything about it.

The very next day he came upon four knights of the Round Table gathered under an oak tree. And one was Sir Ector of the Marsh, his own half-brother, and one was Sir Segramour le Desirous, and one Sir Uwaine the son of Morgan La Fay, and one Sir Gawain, who was captain of all the Round Table brotherhood. And when they saw Sir Kay as they thought, riding towards them, they laughed among themselves, and Sir Segramour rode out to give him a buffet, whereupon Sir Lancelot lifted him on his spear point clean out of the saddle and dropped him all arms and legs to the ground.

'Surely that man is broader across the shoulders than Sir Kay?' said Sir Ector. 'Well, we will see if his buffet can match mine!'

And Sir Lancelot tipped him out of the saddle to join Sir Segramour.

'By my faith,' said Sir Uwaine, 'that is not Sir Kay! Surely he has slain Sir Kay and stolen his armour!'

And he rode hard against Sir Lancelot – and knew nothing more for some while.

Then Sir Gawain fewtered his spear and came against Sir Lancelot full tilt. And Sir Lancelot, kindling his horse in the last instant before the strike-home, as few horsemen but he knew how to do, brought down Sir Gawain and his horse together.

Then Sir Lancelot rode quietly on; and he smiled to himself inside his helmet, and thought, Well, that is four bruising falls that I have saved Sir Kay, anyway. And he thought also, God give him joy who made this spear, for I never had a better in my hand!

And the four knights gathered their wits and aided each other and caught their horses. 'That was assuredly not Sir Kay,' said Sir Segramour.

And Sir Gawain said, 'I am thinking that it was Sir Lancelot. He was but three days at court after his knighting, but I mind me how he did at the jousts on the second day, and I know him by his riding.'

And they continued on their way, for they were heading for Camelot to keep Christmas at Arthur's court.

And Sir Lancelot rode on through the wintry forest, seeking whatever adventure might befall him, while the winter wore on and the snow came and lay thick upon the ground and the straining branches of the trees, and the wind howled like a wolf pack in the long dark nights.

One day when the winter was nearly spent, he came upon the strangest of all the adventures that he met with in that year of lone riding; so strange that ever after when he looked back upon it, it was like looking back upon a dream.

And the beginning of the adventure was this; that as he rode along a forest track, he met with a damosel muffled close against the cold, who looked into his face – for he rode with his vizor open, as did most men except in time of fighting – and cried out, 'Ah, Sir Lancelot! Now Christ in his gentleness be praised that we are met!'

'How comes it that you know my name?' said Lancelot, who was growing accustomed to being mistaken for Sir Kay by the device on his shield.

'Last Easter I was at King Arthur's court, to watch my brother at the jousting on the day after you were made knight.' And in her desperate eagerness she twisted her hands in his bridle as though to draw him after her, so that his horse was startled and began to dance.

'Softly,' said Sir Lancelot, 'what is it that you would with me?'

'Ah, Sir Knight, I sorely need your help – and for that same brother. For this very day he fought with an evil knight, Sir Gilbert the Bastard. And Sir Gilbert he slew, but my brother was sore wounded, and the wound will not cease from bleeding so that now he lies upon death's threshold. And there dwells in the forest not far from here a sorceress called Allewes, and when in despair I went to her for help, she laughed at me, and said the blood-flow would not cease until I could find a knight valiant enough to go into the Chapel Perilous, where Sir Gilbert's body now lies, and bring out the sword that lies there and a piece of the cloth that covers the body. Then if the sword be touched to the wound, and the cloth bound about it after, the bleeding shall cease, and my brother be made whole again.'

'That is a marvellous thing,' said Sir Lancelot, 'but who is your brother?'

'Sir, he is Sir Meliot de Logure.'

At that, Lancelot was silent a moment, remembering the young knight who had been at Camelot only a short while when he himself came from Benwick, and who, it was whispered, was kin of some kind of Nimue the Lady of the Lake. And the hairs stirred a little on the nape of his neck, and the sense of being in a dream thickened about him.

But he said at last, 'Then he is my brother in the fellowship of the Round Table, and assuredly I will do all that is in my power to aid him.'

'Then, sir,' said the maiden, 'let you follow this track, for it will bring you to the Chapel Perilous. And I will wait here until you come again. And pray God that you *do* come again; for if you do not, then there is no knight living who may achieve this adventure.'

Then Sir Lancelot rode on, following the track where the ice was melting in the ruts, and the half-thawed snow falling from the branches of the trees. And in a while he came to a clearing in the forest beside the way; and in the midst of the clearing a grey and mournful chapel set among night-dark yew trees. Sir Lancelot dismounted and tied his horse to the narrow gate, and went into the churchyard. And then he saw, hanging from the twisted branches of the greatest and oldest tree that grew beside the chapel door, many shields, upside down in token of death. And he saw also, standing among the yew trees, more than thirty knights in black armour and with drawn swords in their hands; taller by a head than any mortal man; and their vizors were open and their faces bare, the faces of the long dead, and he saw that they grinned and gnashed their teeth at his coming, but no smoke of breath came from them upon the cold air. And fear rose like a cold fog in Lancelot, and again, and more strongly, the hair crawled on the back of his neck. But he drew his sword and readied his shield before him, and advanced steadily upon them like a man advancing into battle.

And at his coming, they gave back and scattered, their feet leaving no track upon the puddled snow; and Sir Lancelot passed through them and entered the chapel.

Within, the place was dimly lit by one lamp that hung from the vaulted roof; and beneath the lamp, a dead man lay upon his bier, covered by a pall of crimson silk. And it seemed to him that the cold of that place was ten times deeper than the raw winter's cold outside, for it ate into the very soul.

He drew his sword and, stooping beside the bier, cut a long strip from the crimson silk that covered the stark shape. And as he did so, the pavement tilted under him as though the earth had quaked beneath the chapel, and the lamp swung on its chain, casting weird shadows about the place so that for the moment it seemed full of dark wings, and almost it was as though Sir Gilbert's body stirred beneath the crimson pall. And Sir Lancelot's heart sprang racing into his throat.

But the earth steadied and the lamp hung quiet once more; the dark wings were gone, and the dead man lay still beneath his pall. And Sir Lancelot sheathed his blade, and as he did so, saw a splendid sword lying beside the bier. He took it up, and with the strip of crimson silk crumpled in his shield hand in the hollow of his shield, he stepped out into the grey light of the snowy churchyard.

The black knights still stood there, waiting among the yew trees; and they spoke to him in one voice, and that a terrible one. 'Knight, Sir Lancelot, lay down that sword, or you shall die!'

'Whether I live or die,' said Lancelot, 'words shall not win this sword from me. Fight me for it, if you will.'

And as they had done at his first coming, they fell back before him, leaving no tracks in the snow; and so he came again to the gate where his horse was tied. But beside his horse, a strange damosel waited for him, nothing of her face showing in the shadow of her hood but the darkness of her two great eyes. And she said in a voice as soft and cold as the snow, 'Sir Lancelot, pray you leave that sword behind you; you will die for it else.'

'I leave it not, even for your pleading,' said Sir Lancelot.

And the damosel gave a little laugh with music in it like the chiming of icicles. 'How wise you are! For if you had left that sword at my pleading, you would never have come to Arthur's court nor seen Queen Guenever again. Now, in token that there is no ill-will between us, do you kiss me but once, and go your way.'

'Nay!' said Sir Lancelot, already reaching for his horse's bridle. 'God forbid!'

Then the damosel let forth a high wailing cry, and seemed to grow thin and shaken as though the wind blew through her very bones. 'Alas! I have had all my labours in vain. For many times I have seen you in my dreams, in running water by day and in the fire at night, and grown to love you; and it was I who raised the Chapel Perilous to entrap you and web you round with my spells as the spider webs the blundering crane-fly with her silk; and had you kissed me, you would have

111

lain this moment dead in my arms, and been mine for all time, you who are the flower of all King Arthur's knights. But there is that in you which is too strong for me, and you have torn through all my spells. Have pity on me, now that I am torn and broken . . .'

Then Lancelot guessed that she must be the sorceress Allewes, of whom Sir Meliot's sister had told him; and he crossed himself strongly. 'Now God preserve me from your subtle crafts,' he said, and rounding from her to his horse, mounted and rode away.

He followed the track by which he had come, until at last he found Sir Meliot's sister standing where he had left her. And when she saw him she clasped her hands and wept for joy. Then she set her hand, lightly this time, on his horse's bridle, and led him to her brother's castle nearby, where Sir Meliot lay upon his bed with the physician and his squires standing helplessly about him, and the red life-tide still ebbing from the wound in his flank.

Sir Lancelot crossed to the bedside, and drawing the sword that he had brought from the Chapel Perilous, laid the blade against the streaming wound, then wiped and cleaned it with the strip of crimson silk, and at once the blood-flow ceased and the edges drew together, and Sir Meliot sighed, and sat up on the bed as well and whole as ever he had been.

And for one shaken heartbeat of time, Sir Lancelot wondered whether this was his miracle; the miracle that he had prayed so long and hard that one day God would allow him to perform. But then he knew that this was something of quite a different sort. This was magic and enchantment. And it came to him also, that if ever he were allowed to work his miracle he would know it by something in himself, some knowledge that the power of God had passed through him like flame and a high wind.

He had broken a spell, no more than that.

But still, he was glad that he had saved Sir Meliot, his fellow of the Round Table. And the three of them were joyful together, and he remained with them several days. But when the snow melted, he said to Sir Meliot, 'I must be on my way; for it ill befits one on a quest to sleep seven nights in a goose-feathered bed; and there are matters yet to be adventured before I return to Arthur's court at Eastertide. Come you back to court also at that time, that we may meet again.'

Far and wide through the forest country rode Sir Lancelot, and by marshways where the land was half water and flamed at sunset under the crying and calling of the geese as they began their northward flight, and up into the high moors and the mountains of the West, and back to the forest ways again, while the world woke from winter into spring around him, and the celandines starred the wayside banks and the wild cherry foamed into blossom, and the larks tore his heart with the sweetness of their singing high above the cultivated land. And he met with so many adventures that if a weaver of tales were to tell them all, the telling would never be done. And he made for himself a name on men's lips, though he was still but nineteen, a name like a banner, such as men weave into a harp-song for warriors and women to tell their children by the fire.

And in the last days before Easter, he rode back to Camelot.

When he came into the Great Hall, bareheaded but still in Sir Kay's armour, Sir Gawain and Sir Ector of the Marsh, Sir Uwaine and Sir Segramour saw indeed who it was who had felled them all with one spear, and there was a gale of laughter among them. And then Sir Kay, with his colour making two red spots on his cheek-bones, told how Sir Lancelot had rescued him, and of the exchanging of their armour and how he had ridden home in peace, none daring to interfere with him in Sir Lancelot's harness. He could not find laughter, as the others could, in the story against himself, but he told it none the less; and Sir Lancelot felt as though he had been forgiven for something, and laid his arm for a moment across the Seneschal's shoulders.

And then came in King Bagdemagus, and Sir Meliot de Logure, and behind them the knights whom Lancelot had rescued from Sir Tarquine, and the knights whom he had overcome and bidden yield themselves to King Arthur or to the Queen, until there was scarce room for all of them in the Great Hall.

It should have been the proudest and most triumphant moment of Sir Lancelot's life, as he came forward and knelt to the High King. But the Queen had also come into the Hall to welcome him back and to receive the freed captives and vanquished knights who he had sent to her; and she sat beside the King in a gown of golden damask, her eyes brighter in the torchlight than the jewels about her neck.

'We have heard of your deeds these many months past,' said the King. 'You have indeed proved yourself, and no man now will question your right to receive knighthood so young.'

And the Queen leaned forward a little, and said, 'The time has seemed long while you were away, and we are glad that you are come home.'

And Lancelot moved to kneel before her with a suddenly pounding heart. It was for her that he had ridden away on his year-long quest, and now the year was over, and he had come back; and Guenever was still here, and nothing was changed.

7

SIR GAWAIN
AND THE GREEN KNIGHT

Of all the knights who had their places at King Arthur's Round Table, Sir Gawain seemed always to be the one who had something strange about him. Gawain of the flaming red hair, and the temper that flamed to match it, as swift as fire to spring up and as dangerous, but as swift to sink again. He was of the Old People, the Dark People, but then so was Gaheris, and Agravane their younger brother who by now had also joined the court. So was his cousin Uwaine, and so was Arthur himself on his mother's side. It was more than that. Strange stories were told about Gawain; the country folk said that his strength waxed and waned with the sun. So it was fitting that one of the strangest adventures ever to befall the knights of the Round Table should come to him.

On the Christmas that Sir Lancelot was still away upon his own quest, Arthur held his court at Camelot, for the time had not yet come when he kept his Christmases at Carlisle. Yuletide went by with many festivities, and it came to New Year's Eve. Now Christmas was chiefly a matter for the Church, but New

Year's Eve was for banqueting and merrymaking, and so when dusk came, the whole court gathered to their feasting in the Great Hall; the knights of the Round Table each in their places; the lesser knights and the squires at the side boards. Even the Queen and her ladies had come to join the feast and look on from under their silken canopy at the upper end of the Hall, for there would be dancing after the banquet was done. Already the serving squires were bringing in the great chargers of goose and venison, and swans and ships and towering castles made of almonds and honey. The wine glowed red in crystal goblets and the Hall leapt with torchlight and lilted with the music of the harper who sat at the Queen's feet.

The boar's head was brought in, wreathed in scented bay leaves and heralded by trumpets and carried high on the shoulders of four pages. But just as it was set on the table, the great doors of the Hall flew open, and a gust of wind burst in, making the torches stream sideways and the flames of the huge log fires crouch down upon the hearths. And a little snow eddied in on the dark wings of the wind.

The harper fell silent between note and note. The voices of the revelling company fell away, as every face turned towards the door and the night beyond. And a great silence took the Hall, where the cheerful sounds of merrymaking had been.

And into the silence came the clang and bell-clash of horse's hooves upon the frostbound courtyard stones, and out of the darkness into the torchlight and firelight that steadied and leapt as though in greeting, rode a great man, almost a giant, upon a warhorse that was of a fitting size to carry him.

At sight of him a long gasp ran through the Hall, for he was the strangest sight that any man there had ever seen, mighty of limb and goodly of face and holding himself in the saddle like a king, wearing no armour but clad from head to heel in the fierce fine green that is the colour of the Lordly Ones and not of mortal men. His jerkin and hose under his thick-furred cloak were all of green, and green was the jewelled belt that circled his waist. His saddle was of fine green leather enriched with gold, so were his horse's trappings which chimed like little bells as the great beast moved. Spurs of greenish gold sparked the heels of his boots that were the colour of moss under ancient oak trees. Even his thick crest of hair and his curling beard were of the same hue, and the great horse beneath him green from proud crest to sweeping tail, its mane fantastically braided and knotted up with golden threads. In one hand he carried a huge axe of green steel inlaid with the same strange greeny-gold; and high in the other a young holly tree thick with berries that sparked like crimson jewels in the torchlight. But save for the holly berries of Christmas, all else, even the sparks that his horse's hooves struck from the stone pavement as he rode up the Hall, was green; blazing and fiery green; the living green of springtime itself.

When he came halfway up the Hall, he reined in, and flung down the holly tree upon the floor, and sat looking about him on all sides. And it seemed to everyone there, from the King himself to the youngest page, that the golden-green eyes, like the eyes of some proud and mighty forest beast, had looked for a moment directly and deeply into his own.

Then he cried out in a voice that boomed from wall to wall and hung under the roof and brought a startled spider down out of the rafters, 'Where is the lord of this Hall, for I would speak with him and with no other!'

After the thunder of his voice, for three heartbeats of time all men sat as though stunned, and there was no sound save the whispering of the flames upon the hearths. Then Arthur said, 'I am the lord of this Hall, and I bid you right welcome to it. Now pray you dismount, and while my stable squires tend to your horse, come and feast among us, this last night of the Old Year.'

'Nay, that I will not,' said the stranger. 'I have not come to feast with you; nor have I come in war. That, you may see by my lack of armour, and by the green branch that I bear. But word of the valour of your knights has reached me in my own place; and for a while and a while I have been minded to put it to the test.'

'Why, then,' said Arthur, 'I doubt not that you will find enough and to spare among my knights willing and eager to joust with you if that is your desire.'

'That is as may be,' said the Green Knight, 'but for the most part I see here only beardless bairns who I could fell with one flick of a bramble spray! Nay, it is a valour-test of another kind that I bring here for a Yuletide sport. Let any man here stand forth as champion against me, and he may take from my hand this axe which has no equal in the world for weight and keenness, and with it strike me one blow. Only he must strike the blow in the place of my choosing. And he must swear to yield me the right to strike the return blow in the same place, if I am yet able, a year and a day from now.'

And again there was silence in the Hall; and the knights looked at each other and away again, and here one drew a quick breath, and there one licked his lower lip. But none dared to take up the challenge of the beautiful and terrible stranger.

Then the Green Knight laughed, long and loud and mocking. 'Not one of you? Is this indeed King Arthur's Hall? And you who feast here but dare not take up a simple challenge, are you indeed the knights of his Round Table? The flower of chivalry? Nay, let you go hang your heads in shame, I see I have had a bootless journey!'

Arthur sprang to his feet, though well he knew that it was not for the High King to take up such a challenge, and flung his shout of defiance in the stranger's face. 'Yes! One! Off your horse now, give me your axe and make ready for the blow!'

But almost in the same instant, Sir Gawain also was on his feet. 'My lord the King, noble uncle, I claim this adventure, for still I carry with me the shame of the lady's death whose head I cut off, and I have yet to prove my worthiness to sit at the Round Table!'

He seldom called Arthur 'uncle', for they were almost the same age, and so when he did, it was as a jest between them. And now the familiar jest cut through the King's rage and reached him, and he knew that what Sir Gawain said was true. And so he drew a deep breath and unclenched his hands, and said, 'Dear my nephew, the adventure is yours.'

Then as Sir Gawain left his place and strode into the centre of the Hall, the Green Knight swung down from his horse, and so they came together. 'It is good that I have found a champion to meet me in Arthur's Hall,' said the Green Knight. 'By what name are you called?'

'I am Gawain, son of Lot King of Orkney, and nephew to my liege lord King Arthur. By what name do men call you?'

'Men call me the Knight of the Green Chapel, in my own North Country,' said the stranger. 'Swear now to the bargain between us; that you will strike the one blow in the place of my choosing, the one blow only. And that in a year and a day you will submit yourself to my blow, the one blow only, in return.'

'I swear by my knighthood,' said Gawain.

'Take the axe, and be ready to strike as I bid you.'

Gawain took the mighty and terrible axe in his hand,

and stood swinging it a little, feeling its weight and balance; and the Green Knight knelt down on the floor, and stooping, drew his long flame-green hair forward over the top of his head to lay bare his neck.

For a moment all things in the Hall seemed to cease, and Gawain stood as though turned to stone.

'In the place of my choice,' said the Green Knight. 'Strike now.'

And life moved on again, and Gawain in a kind of fury swung up the great axe with a battle yell, and putting every last ounce of strength that he possessed into the blow, brought it crashing down.

The blade sheared through flesh and bone and set the sparks spurting from the pavement as though from an anvil; and the Green Knight's head sprang from his shoulders and went rolling along the floor almost to the Queen's feet.

There rose a horrified gasp, and while all men looked to see the huge body topple forward, the Green Knight shook his shoulders a little, and got to his feet, and walked after his head. He caught it up and, holding it by the hair, remounted his horse that stood quietly waiting for him. Holding his head high, he turned the face to Sir Gawain, and said, 'See that you keep your oath, and come to me a year and a day from now.'

'How shall I find you?' asked Gawain, white to the lips.

'Seek me through Wales and into the Forest of Wirrel; and if you bring your courage with you, you shall surely find me before noon of the appointed day.'

And he wheeled his horse and touched his spurred heel to its flank, and was away out into the darkness and the eddying snow, his head still swinging by its long hair from his hand. And they heard the beat of his horse's hooves drumming away into the winter's night.

Behind him he left great silence in the Hall, and it was

a while before the harper drew his hand across the bright strings again, and men returned to their laughter and feasting.

The snow melted and the buds began to swell along the wood shores. And at Eastertide Sir Lancelot returned from his questing, as has been told. The cuckoo came, the foxgloves stood proudly along the woodland ways and then were gone; and in farms and manors up and down the land the harvest was gathered in; and it was the time of blackberries and turning bracken once again. And at Michaelmas it was time for Sir Gawain to set forth upon his terrible quest.

King Arthur held his court at Caerleon that Michaelmas; and there gathered Sir Gaheris and Sir Agravane, and Lancelot and Lional and his brother Bors who was new-come from Less Britain to join him, Sir Uwaine and Sir Bedivere, King Bagdemagus and Sir Lamorack and Sir Gryflet le Fise de Dieu and many more. And their hearts were sore within them so that there was no joy nor savour to the feasting, for the sake of Sir Gawain, who was riding away from them and would surely never come riding back.

And Sir Gawain with his squire's help armed himself and belted on his sword, and mounted Gringolet his great roan horse, and set out.

For many days he rode through the ancient border country of Wales until he came to the wild dark mountain lands of North Wales; and he rode by steep valleys and roaring waters and mountain-clinging forests. And many times he was attacked by wild animals and wilder men and must fight for his life, knowing all the while that death must be waiting for him at the end of his quest. Autumn had turned to winter when he reached the end of the mountain country, and came down by Clwyd to the Holy Head near to Saint Winifred's Well on the shore of the broad and grey-shining Dee. He forded the river mouth at low tide, and barely winning clear of the sands and saltings before the tide came racing in again, he came to the black and ancient forest-fleece of the Wirrel.

And as he rode, whenever he came up with a forester or a wandering friar or an old woman gathering sticks, and whenever he found shelter at night in a swineherd's bothie or a charcoal-burner's hut (those were the nights he counted himself lucky; on other nights he slept huddled in his cloak under a pile of dead bracken or in the root-hollow of a tree brought down by the storms of some past winter), he asked for tidings of the Green Knight of the Green Chapel, but no one could tell him what he needed to know.

And the time was growing short . . .

On Christmas Eve, weary man on weary horse mired to the belly from the forest ways, he came out from among ancient trees that seemed to reach their twisted lichen-hung branches across his way as though to seize him and draw him into themselves, and saw before him open meadowland set about with fine tamed trees, a willow-fringed stream winding through; and beyond the stream, the land rising gently, crowned by a castle that was both strong and beautiful in the last light of the winter's day.

Now God be thanked, thought Sir Gawain, and he gently pulled Gringolet's twitching ear. There will be food and shelter to spare in this place and they will not refuse us welcome upon this night of all the year. And he forded the stream and rode up to the castle gate and beat upon the timbers with the pommel of his sword.

The gate opened almost at once, and the porter appeared in the entrance.

'Good fellow,' said Sir Gawain, 'pray you tell your master that a knight of King Arthur's court rides this way upon a quest; and begs shelter for himself and his horse.'

'My master, the lord of this castle, has a welcome for all comers, especially any who come on this night of all the year,' said the porter, standing aside, and Gawain rode through into the outer court of the castle. Squires came hurrying to take Gringolet to the stables, while others led Gawain himself through the inner court and then into the castle Hall, where the lord of the castle himself stood before a roaring fire with three great wolfhounds lying all about his feet, their bellies to the warmth.

He was a big man, broad across the shoulders and running just a trace of fat; his face weather-beaten, kindly and open, his mane of hair as red as Gawain's own; and as his guest entered the room, he thrust the wolfhounds aside and came striding to meet him with hands outstretched.

'Welcome, knight-at-arms, my home is your home, and all that I have is yours for as long as it pleases you to bide here.'

'My thanks, noble sir,' Gawain said, his heart warming to the man in instant friendship. 'God be good to you, for the goodness of your hospitality.'

And they clapped each other upon the shoulders as though they were old friends indeed.

The squires led Gawain to the guest chamber high in the keep, where they helped him to unarm, and brought him a robe of thick russet wool lined with the softest dappled lynx fur; then they escorted him back to the Hall, where another chair had been set for him opposite the lord of the castle; and one of the hounds came with proudly swinging tail and laid its chin on his knee.

Meanwhile the squires and pages were setting up the table boards and spreading them with fine white linen; and bringing in the food and setting ready the wine jugs.

And the soft warm hunger-water ran into Sir Gawain's mouth at the sight and smell of the dishes; and the warmth of the fire and the heavy furred robe seeped through his chilled and weary body, and he was very well content.

When supper was over, the lord of the castle said, 'Come, Sir Gawain, for you have not yet seen my lady, and she will be eager to greet you.'

And they went together, by the stairway behind the Hall, to the Private Chamber; a fair chamber whose walls were painted green and scattered with small golden stars; and the lady of the castle sat beside the fire with a little silky lapdog on her knee, and her maidens all about her. And Gawain thought when she smiled at him that she was the fairest lady he had ever seen; fairer even than Queen Guenever. She made him sweetly welcome, while her maidens brought a chessboard with men of silver and crystal, for her lord and his guest to play; and the evening passed as happily as any that Gawain had ever known, so that for a little while he was almost able to forget the dark quest on which he rode.

And when the time came for sleep, the squires took him back, making a candle-lit procession of it, to the guest chamber, and left him with a goblet of spiced wine beside the bed.

Four days passed, with all the singing and feasting and rejoicing that goes with Christmas time; and always the lady of the castle stayed close to Gawain and talked to him and smiled upon him and attended to him in all things.

But on the evening of the fourth day Gawain knew that he must stay no longer from his quest. When he told the knight and the lady of this, they grieved, and would have had him stay longer. But Gawain held to his purpose. 'I have stayed too long already, happy in your company, and my quest calls me. I must meet the

Knight of the Green Chapel by noon of New Year's Day; and as yet I do not even know where this Green Chapel may be.'

Then the lord of the castle laughed, and slapped his great hand upon his broad knee. 'That makes good hearing indeed; for the Green Chapel I know well; it is not two hours' easy ride from here! Bide with us then until the morning of New Year's Day, and then one of my squires shall guide you to the place, and have you there before the sun stands at noon.'

'Then gladly will I bide here,' Sir Gawain said, 'and warm me with your kindness, and do in all things as you will.' (For he thought, if these be the last three days of my life, it were sweet that I should spend them among friends.)

'So then, we have three good days to spend,' said the lord of the castle, 'and I shall spend them as always I spend the three last days of the Old Year, hunting in the forest. But you, who have ridden so far and hard, and have, I doubt not, some great ordeal to face at the Green Chapel, shall abide here and take your ease, and keep the company of my lady who ever complains of her loneliness when I leave her to follow the boar or the red deer. And in the evenings we will make merry together.'

'That will I do most willingly,' said Gawain.

The lord's eyes flickered with laughter in his weather-beaten face. 'And since this is the time for games and jests, and I have a fantastic mood on me, let us make a covenant together – that each evening I will give you whatever I have gained in my day's hunting; and you shall give me in exchange whatever you have gained here in my castle. This exchange let us swear to, for better or worse, however it may turn out.'

'That is a fine covenant, and gladly will I swear to it,' said Gawain; and they struck hands like men sealing a bargain.

Next day the lord of the castle summoned his companions and his hounds and rode away to hunt the red deer through the forests of Wirrel and Delamare. But Gawain lay abed, with a most unusual drowsiness upon him, for he was not used to late lying. And presently the lady of the castle came, stepping lightly, and sat down on the edge of the bed, as blithe as a linnet on a hawthorn spray, and began to tease him. And by little and little, from teasing she slipped into love-talk, and spoke sweet words as though half in jest. And Gawain took them as though they were all in jest, and turned them aside lightly and courteously as though they played some kind of game. And at last the lady rose to go. 'God save you for a pleasant hour,' she said. 'But I find it hard to believe that you are Sir Gawain, as you claim to be.'

'Why so?' asked Sir Gawain, startled.

And she laughed. 'Would Sir Gawain ever have tarried so long with a damosel and never once asked for a kiss?'

'Faith, lady, I feared to displease you,' said Sir Gawain, 'but since it seems that you give me leave, I do indeed beg you most humbly for a kiss.'

So the lady took his face between her hands, and kissed him most sweetly, and went her way. And Gawain called for the chamber squires, for he would get up.

At evening, the lord of the castle came home with the carcass of a fine red deer slung across the back of a hunting pony. And he bade his huntsmen lay it before Gawain, who had come to meet him in the courtyard. 'See, now, here is the fruit of my hunting, which I give to you according to our bargain.'

'I accept the gift with all thanks,' said Gawain, 'and bid you to sup with me, though in your own Hall, tomorrow, when it is cooked. And now in return I give to you the thing that I won here in the castle this day.' And he set his hands on his host's shoulders and kissed him, once.

'So; that was a fine gift, and much do I thank you for it,' said the lord of the castle. 'Yet gladly would I know who gave you that kiss.'

'Nay,' said Sir Gawain, 'that was no part of the bargain.'

And presently they sat down to supper in great good fellowship.

Next morning the lord of the castle sent for his boar hounds and rode hunting again. And again Gawain lay in his bed with the sweet unaccountable drowsiness upon him, until again the lady of the castle came and sat down on the edge of the bed, with the little dog pattering after, to cuddle in the floor-folds of her gown. And again she fell to teasing him softly, playing with words and trying to coax words of love from him in return. But Sir Gawain continued to turn them all aside, lightly and with courtesy that held no unkindness nor rebuff; and at last she left him, though this time with two kisses instead of yesterday's one.

That evening, the lord of the castle returned home at dusk, and his huntsmen laid at Gawain's feet the grizzly carcass of a boar. 'Here, guest of mine, I bring you the spoils of my day's hunting.'

'I accept the spoils of your hunting,' Gawain said, 'and bid you to sup with me again tomorrow night.'

'And what have you to give me in return?'

'These, that I have come by since you rode out this morning,' said Gawain; and putting his hands on the other's shoulders, he gave him two kisses. 'This, and no more, I have gained, and now I give them to you.'

And together, with the rest of the castle knights, they supped royally on the red deer that had been Gawain's gift of the night before. And the lady, coming in with her maidens, smiled at Gawain and sent him sweet dark glances that he pretended not to see.

That night, Sir Gawain thought that for other reasons beside his quest it would be better if he rode on his way next morning. But when he said so to his host, the big man said, 'Nay, but why?'

'Tomorrow will be the last day of the year; and by noon of the next day, I must be at my meeting-place with the Green Knight.'

'Have I not sworn on my knightly honour that the place is but two hours' ride from here, and you shall come there long before noon on the appointed day? And there is yet one day of our bargain still to run.'

So the next morning, the morning of New Year's Eve, the lord of the castle called for his huntsmen and his hounds and rode away into the dark forest, while Sir Gawain still lay sleeping, tangled in troubled dreams of his meeting with the Green Knight that was now so cruelly near.

He woke to find thin winter sunshine streaming into the chamber, and the lady of the castle bending over him. When she saw that he was awake, she gave him one kiss, lingering a little, then stood back, looking down at him, laughing still, but a little sadly under the laughter. 'But one little kiss,' she said, 'does your heart freeze in the winter? Or have you a damosel waiting for you at court?'

'No damosel,' Sir Gawain said gently, 'and my heart is still mine to give; but lady, fairest and sweetest lady, I may not give it to you, for your lord and the lord of this castle is my host. If I were to love the wife, that would be to shame my knightly vows.'

'But my lord rides hunting and will not be home till dusk, no one will ever know, not even he, and so he will feel no hurt. Can we not love in this one day, that all my life may be sweeter remembering that Gawain of

Orkney once held me in his arms?'

Gawain shook his head. 'The wrong would be none the less because no one knew of it. No, lady, it cannot be.'

For a long while she besought him, but he turned her pleas aside; and at last she sighed as one admitting defeat, and kissed him again, and said, 'Sir Gawain, you must be the truest to your vows of all knights living. So – I will plague you no more. But give me something of yours to remember you by; that I may cherish it, and it may comfort me a little in my sorrow.'

'Alas,' said Sir Gawain, 'I have nothing to give, for I travel light upon this quest.'

'Then will I give you something of mine. Take this green girdle and wear it for my sake.'

'Lady, I cannot be your knight and wear your favour.'

'Such a little thing,' said the lady, 'and you need not wear it openly as my favour, but hidden where no man shall see, and only I shall know of it. Pray you take it, for you ride into sore danger, that I know; and there is magic woven into it, that while you wear it you shall bear a charmed life. Only keep it hid, and tell not my lord of it.'

And with his meeting with the terrible Green Knight so close, the temptation was too great, and Gawain took the girdle of gold-worked green ribbons and knotted it round his neck under his shirt.

And the lady kissed him for the third time, and went her way.

That evening at dusk, the lord of the castle returned from his hunting bearing with him nothing but one fox-skin swinging from his hand.

'Alas! I have had scurvy hunting,' he said when Gawain met him in the courtyard, 'and this is all that I have to give you on the last of your three days.'

129

'Then it seems that my winnings have been better than yours. For I have this to give you,' said Gawain, and setting his hands on his host's shoulders he gave him three kisses.

Then with great jest and merriment, their arms across each other's shoulders, they went back into the Great Hall where supper was made ready, and feasted on the boar which the knight of the castle had brought home from his hunting the day before.

But Gawain spoke no word of the green ribbons lying round his neck under his shirt and his borrowed robe.

On New Year's Morning, Sir Gawain arose early, having slept but little, and called for the squires to arm him – keeping the green ribbons well hidden beneath the neck-band of his shirt the while. They brought him food; dark crusty bread and cold pig-meat, a cup of wine, and a platter of last summer's little withered yellow apples; but there was small wish for food in him; he drank some wine and ate one of the apples, and that was all. Then he went down into the courtyard, where the stable squires had brought out Gringolet looking sleek and well-fed.

Gringolet whinnied with pleasure at sight of his master, and Gawain fondled him a moment, then sprang into the saddle. 'Fare you well; the sun and the moon on your threshold,' he said to the lord of the castle, who had come down to take leave of him. Of the lady, there was no sign. 'If I might, I would do aught in my power to reward you for your kindness. But I think that I shall not see the rising of another sun.'

And he rode out through the gates that had been flung wide, with the squire who was to guide him riding hard behind; out over the causeway and away through the grey light of a low sullen dawn, with sleet spitting down the wind. By forest and mire and dreary waste-land they went, until they came to the lip of a broad valley between steep rocky slopes, and reining in, sat looking down, and saw the whole valley full of swirling mist.

'Sir,' said the squire, 'I have brought you as far as I may. Down yonder under the mist is the Green Chapel you seek; and down there the Green Knight will be waiting, as always he waits to fight with and slay all who would pass him by. None who come into combat with him may escape living. Oh, sir, do not go down there! None shall ever know; I will not betray you, that I swear as I hope for knighthood myself one day.'

'My thanks,' said Gawain; 'but my honour's lost and my knighthood shamed if I turn away now from my tryst. God knows how to save his servants if he wills it so.'

'Then your death is on your own hands,' said the squire. 'Follow the cliff path yonder and it will bring you down into the deep-most heart of the valley; a stream runs down the valley, and the Green Chapel stands upon the opposite bank. I bid you farewell, Sir Gawain, for I dare come with you no further.'

So Sir Gawain gentled his horse into the cliff path, and held on down, the rocks rising sheer on his right hand and dropping sheer into the mist on the other; and out of the mist came the sound of rushing water, rising to meet him. At last he came as it were down through the mist into the clear air below it, and reached the valley floor, and saw a deep narrow stream swirling its way in a tumble of white water among rocks and the roots of lichen-hung alder trees. But he could make out no sign of any chapel, until after a while of looking about him he saw a short way upstream and on the far side a low green mound covered with alder and hazel scrub; and as he rode doubtfully towards it, he heard above the rush and tumble of water, a sound as of a scythe on a whetstone coming up from somewhere deep within the heart of it.

This must be the Green Chapel, he thought, and green it is indeed; and no Christian chapel but some secret place of the Hollow Hills. And within it the Green Knight is making keen his weapon that must surely be the death of me this day.

But he set his horse to ford the stream at a place where it broadened and ran for a few yards shallow over a gravel bed, and came out close below the green mound; and there he dismounted and hitched Gringolet's bridle to an alder branch. And standing in the strange grey light scarfed with mist, he called, 'Sir Knight of the Green Chapel, I am here as I vowed, to keep our New Year tryst.'

'Wait until I have done sharpening my axe,' came the great booming voice he remembered, echoing from the cavernous heart of the mound. 'I shall not be long. And then you shall have the greeting that I promised you.'

And Gringolet pricked his ears and tossed his head and showed the whites of his eyes; but Gawain stood unmoving, and waited on.

And in a while the sound of scythe on whetstone ceased, and out from a patch of darkness beneath the hazel branches came the Green Knight, just as he had been when he rode into Arthur's Hall a year and a day gone by, beautiful and terrible, and swinging lightly in his hand a long axe with a blade of green steel that looked sharp enough to draw blood from the wind.

'Now welcome, Sir Gawain!' he cried. 'Three times welcome to so brave a knight! Now off with your helmet and make ready for the stroke I owe you for the one you dealt me in Arthur's Hall a year ago last night.'

Gawain unloosed and pulled off his helmet, and thrust back the chain-mail coif from his neck. And taking a last look at the wintry world about him, he knelt and bent his head forward for the blow. 'Strike, then,' he said.

The Green Knight swung up his great axe, and as he brought it sweeping down, Gawain heard the whistle of it, as the crouching bird must hear the wing-rush of the swooping hawk. And despite himself, he flinched back and ducked out from under the blow.

The Green Knight stood leaning on the long handle of his axe, and grinned at him, the grin of some wild thing out of the forest. 'Can this indeed be Gawain of the bold heart? When it was you that swung the axe, I never flinched from *your* blow.'

'Your pardon. My courage lacks the knowledge that I can set my head back on my shoulders when you have done with it,' said Gawain with a flare of grim laughter. 'But I will not shrink again. Come now, and strike quickly.'

'That I will,' said the Green Knight, and again he swung up the fearsome blade and again he brought it whistling down. But this time Gawain remained as still as though he had been one of the rocks of the stream-side. And the axe-blade missed his neck by the width of a grass-blade, and dug deep into the mossy turf beside him.

'Strike!' shouted Gawain. 'It was no part of our bargain that you should play with me thus!'

'Why, nor it was,' agreed the Green Knight, 'and now your head out a little further . . .'

And for the third time he swung up his axe, and swung it singing around his head, and brought it down. And this time Gawain felt a sting like a gad-fly on the side of his neck, and a small trickle of blood running down inside his coif, and the axe stood quivering in the turf beside him.

Then Gawain sprang from his knees and leapt clear, drawing his sword as he did so. 'Now I have borne the blow and you have drawn the red blood, and if you strike again, I am free of my vow and may defend myself!'

The Green Knight stood leaning on his axe and laughing a little; and suddenly Gawain saw that though his garments were still green, they were but the garments in which a man rides hunting, and he was not the Green Knight at all, but his kindly host of the past week. And then he saw that he was both.

'Gawain, Gawain,' said the knight, 'you have indeed borne the blow, and I am in no mind to strike again. Indeed, had I been so minded, your head would have lain at my feet the first time I raised my axe.'

'Why, then, this game of three blows?' Gawain asked, breathing quickly.

'The first two blows that touched you not, these were for your promise truly kept, for the one kiss and the two kisses my wife gave to you while I rode hunting, and that you rendered up to me when I rode home at evening. The third blow that drew blood was for your promise broken, when you gave me her three kisses but not the green ribbons from her waist.' He saw the look on the young knight's face, and his great smile broadened. 'Oh, I know all that passed between you. It was at my will that she tempted you, and had you yielded to her tempting, and dishonoured your knighthood and my house, then indeed you would now be lying headless at my feet. As for the green girdle, you took and hid it but for love of your life. You are young, and he must be a sad man indeed who does not a little love the life God gave him. So now that I have drawn blood for it, I forgive you the girdle.'

Gawain pulled the green ribbon girdle from its hiding-place and held it out to him. 'I am ashamed, none the less. I am unworthy of my place at the Round Table.'

'Nay,' said his host the Green Knight, with booming

kindness. 'You are only young with the life running hot in you. And did I not say that you are forgiven? There will be few knights at the Round Table with a better right to sit there than you. Keep the green girdle in remembrance of this adventure; and come back with me to my castle, that we may end the Twelve Days of Christmas in joy.'

But Gawain, though he put the green ribbons round his neck again, would not stay. 'I must away back to my liege lord,' he said. 'But before I go, pray you tell me, noble sir, who you are, and how you came to be both lord of the castle where I have been made welcome and happy this week past, and the terrible Green Knight, who dies not when his head is struck from his shoulders?'

'My name is Sir Birtilack,' said the other. 'I was minded to test for myself the courage of Arthur's champions of the Round Table, having heard much of the High King's court, even here in my northern wilderness. For the rest – question not the ways of magic.'

So they parted as dear friends who have known each other a lifetime. And Gawain rode back through the Forest of Wirrel and the wild border country of Wales, until he came again to Arthur's court, and his own place that he had fully earned among the foremost of the brotherhood of the Round Table.

8

BEAUMAINS,
THE KITCHEN KNIGHT

It became King Arthur's custom that at Pentecost, when all of the Round Table knights who were free to come gathered each year to his court at Camelot, that he would not sit down to dine until some strange thing had happened or some marvellous sight been seen or a quest begun.

And on one Pentecost, a while before noon, Sir Gawain, looking from a window of the Great Hall, saw three men enter the inner courtyard on horseback, and with them a dwarf on foot. The three men dismounted, and left their horses in the dwarf's care; and as they turned towards the keep, one of the men leaned upon the shoulders of the other two; and he was taller than either of them by a head or more.

'Here comes your strange happening, if I mistake not, my Lord King,' said Gawain, turning from the window, back to where the King and his knights were waiting; and in a few moments more, the three men came into the Hall, the young giant in the centre still leaning on the shoulders of the other two, as though he was maybe too weak from his own height to stand without them. All three were shabbily dressed and journey-stained, but the tall one, for all his seeming weakness, was the goodliest young man to look upon that anyone present had ever seen, brown-skinned and barley-haired, with eyes as clearly blue as the sky on a March morning; long limbed and broad of shoulder, and with hands that, for all their huge size, Sir Lancelot, looking at him, recognized at once for a swordsman's hands and a horseman's hands. And Sir Lancelot was a judge of such matters.

When the three of them had come the length of the Hall, and checked before the dais where King Arthur sat, the tall young man dropped his arms from the others' shoulders, and stood up straight as a tilting lance. And without waiting for the King to speak first, he said, 'Now God save you, my Lord King, and all your fair fellowship. I am come to ask of you three gifts.' The corners of his wide mouth tilted upward. 'Not unreasonable gifts, but such as you may grant with honour. And the first I will ask of you now, and the other two I will ask of you this day a twelve-months.'

'Ask,' said Arthur, who liked the look of the young man on sight, 'and you shall have what you ask for.'

'I ask that you give me food and shelter until the twelve months be up,' said the young man.

'Nay, lad, ask for something better than that.'

'There is nothing that I want – until this day a twelve-months.'

'So be it, then, food and shelter you shall have. For I never denied that to any man,' said Arthur. 'And now, tell me your name.'

'That I had rather not, until the proper time,' said the strange young man.

'It must be as you choose,' said Arthur. 'Yet I would be glad to know who you are, for you are one of the goodliest young men that ever I have seen.'And he gave the young man over into Sir Kay's keeping, bidding him to give the boy food and lodging as though he were a lord's son.

'Assuredly he is not that,' said Kay with a sniff, 'nor even a gentleman's son, or he would have asked for horse and armour. I will give him warm lodging in the kitchen, and all the food he wants. And I make no doubt he will be as fat as a yearling porkhog by the time the year is out. And since he will not tell his name, I shall give him one; I shall call him Beaumains, Fairhands, for indeed I never saw bigger and finer hands – nor ones that looked less used to work.'

At this, Sir Gawain frowned deep between his red brows, for he too liked the look of the young man, and did not much care for Sir Kay and his thin barbed wit; and Sir Lancelot said quietly, 'I'd have a care there, Lord Seneschal, for the boy looks to me to have had other uses for his hands than chopping wood and turning a spit; and I'd not be surprised if one day he used them to make you regret that mockery.'

But Arthur said nothing, for he thought, The boy has the look of endurance about him. If he must come to his knighthood by the hard way, it is of his own choosing, and I dare say he will take no harm by it.

And Beaumains said nothing at all.

So for a full year he served in the kitchens, and the

other scullions jeered at him because he did not know how to do the things that were easy and familiar to them – until he learned their skills himself, and then they learned the unwisdom of such jeering. And Sir Kay made his life a misery with petty punishments and waspish jests. Both Sir Gawain and Sir Lancelot offered to take him as their squire, even without knowing who he was; but he thanked them with a courtesy that was like the gentle courtesy of a great hound, and remained in the kitchens. He had his fill of food, and a warm place by the fire at night, but the only kindness he received was from the dogs, and from Sir Gawain who clapped him on the shoulder once or twice in passing, and from Sir Lancelot, who gave him three silver pieces at Christmas to buy a warm cloak. And in all the while, he never returned evil words to Sir Kay, or complained, or seemed the least out of temper with his fellows, even when he tried, as he sometimes did, to teach them better manners by ducking one or other of them in the horse trough.

So the time drew again to the Feast of Pentecost.

And on Pentecost morning, as the knights were gathered in the Great Hall, a damosel came running, and knelt before the King and begged him for aid.

'For whom?' said Arthur. 'For yourself? What is this adventure?'

'For my sister, the Lady Lioness,' said the damosel, 'who is held captive in her own castle, besieged there by a cruel tyrant, the Red Knight of the Red Lands, who has laid waste her estates, and now demands that she gives herself to him.'

Almost before she had done speaking, Beaumains, who had been standing by the inner archway that led from the kitchen stair, came forward eagerly to stand before the King. 'My Lord Arthur, I thank you for the food and drink and lodging that I have had in your kitchens this twelve-months past. Now I ask for the remaining two of the three gifts you promised me.'

'Ask, then,' said Arthur.

'Sir, firstly I ask that you will give me the adventure of this damosel, for it is in my mind that I have earned it!'

'In mine also,' said the King, 'and the third gift?'

'That Sir Lancelot of the Lake shall ride with me until he judges that I have earned knighthood; for I would be made knight by him and by no one else.'

The King glanced questioningly at his friend, the foremost among his knights, and Lancelot nodded. 'It shall be as you wish,' said the King.

But the damosel had risen from her knees. 'So I am to have none but your kitchen page to aid me, when here in your Hall sit the best knights in Christendom?' And the colour burned in two fiery spots on her cheekbones, and her eyes were bright with angry tears. 'Then keep your aid, for I want none of it!' And she swept from the Hall, shrilly calling up the page who was walking her palfrey to and fro in the courtyard, and mounted and rode furiously away.

And while they still heard the beat of the palfrey's hooves, a page brought word to the King that the dwarf who had come with Beaumains last year stood in the forecourt, with a warhorse and a fine sword, and said that he waited for his master.

So, followed by most of the company in the Hall, Beaumains strode out, and greeting the dwarf as an old henchman, took and buckled on the sword, and mounting the great warhorse, rode away, the dwarf following on his sturdy cob.

And Sir Lancelot, sending for his own horse and his war gear, armed and mounted and in a while rode after him.

But he did not ride alone, for Sir Kay also had sent for

his horse and armour, saying, 'I also will ride after my kitchen knave, though not to give him knighthood, but a good drubbing for thrusting himself forward in this way!'

'Better you bide at home, man, and eat your dinner,' said Sir Gawain. But Sir Kay was too angry to listen; and Sir Lancelot only smiled a little, his twisted half-sad smile inside his helmet.

Riding hard and alone – Lancelot had fallen behind a little to keep clear and watch what happened – Sir Kay caught up with Beaumains just as Beaumains caught up with the damosel. 'Beaumains!' he shouted. 'Hi! You kitchen knight, if you want to leave your cooking-pots and play at chivalry, here I come to teach you the game!'

And Beaumains pulled his horse round, and said in a voice quite different from the voice that anyone had heard him use before, 'First learn that game yourself! Sir Kay, I know you for an ungentle knight. Therefore, *beware of me!*'

Then Sir Kay set his spear in rest and spurred straight in upon him. But Beaumains, having no spear, drew his sword and at the last instant, wrenched his horse aside and struck up the other's spear with the flat of the blade, then thrust the sword point under the fluted rim of the other's shoulder-piece, and tipped him from the saddle, with a wound trickling red into the summer dust. Then Beaumains dismounted, and taking up Sir Kay's spear and shield, swung back into the saddle and rode on his way.

Many small cruelties and injustices had been repaid with that blow.

And Sir Lancelot also dismounted, made sure that the wound was not serious, and heaving Sir Kay on to his horse again, patted the beast's neck, saying, 'Take him home. You have more sense than he has.'

Then he too remounted and rode on.

Meanwhile Beaumains had again overtaken the damosel; but he got no kind greeting, for indeed though she was fair enough to look upon, her name, which was Linnet, was the gentlest thing about her. 'How dare you come following after me?' she cried. 'Get back to your kitchen, Beaumains. Aye, I know your name, given to you by the knight you have felled by a foul blow. Given because your hands are so big and coarse – hands for plucking geese and turning a spit!' And then, growing shriller yet, 'At least ride further off from me, for you stink of greasy cooking.'

'Say what you will,' said Beaumains steadily, 'I shall not turn back, your adventure is mine to achieve, given to me by the High King, and I shall not swerve aside from it while the life is in me!'

'Achieve my adventure, you kitchen knight?' she jibed. 'Nay, but before long you shall meet with such a foe that you would give all the rich broth you ever supped in Arthur's kitchens rather than stand your ground against him!'

'I shall do the best I may, and we will see how it turns out,' said Beaumains gently; and rode on, a little behind the damosel.

Before long they came to a dead thorn tree, from whose branches hung a black spear and a black shield. And under the tree sat a huge knight all in black armour, his raven warhorse grazing nearby.

'Now flee away down the valley before that knight can mount his horse,' said Linnet, 'for that is the Black Knight of the Black Lands, and none may stand against him.'

'My thanks for your warning,' said Beaumains, and held straight on as though she had not spoken it.

And when they drew near, the Black Knight got to his feet, and said, 'Damosel, is this your champion, brought from King Arthur's court?'

'Nay, Sir Knight, this is but a greasy scullion, who follows me whether I will or no. Therefore I beg of you, teach him to turn back from me; for I am sick of the kitchen smell of him.'

'Why then,' said the knight, whistling up his black charger, 'I will knock him out of that fine saddle, for a kitchen knave has no right but to go on foot – and his horse is a fine one and will be of use to me.'

'You make mightily free with my horse,' said Beaumains, 'and indeed he is yours if you can take him! Come then and try, or stand aside and let us pass, this damosel and I.'

'Nay,' said the Black Knight, 'that is not a fitting thing – that a kitchen knave should ride against her will with a fine lady.'

'That would depend on the kitchen knight and on the lady,' said Beaumains, stung out of his usual steady quietness. 'But indeed I am no scullion, but a gentleman born, and of nobler blood than you!'

Then the Black Knight mounted his horse and took down his shield and spear from the dead thorn tree, and the two rode apart the proper distance and turned and thundered towards each other; and the black spear shattered on Beaumains's shield; but Beaumains's spear took his foe in a joint of his armour, piercing through mail and flesh, and the Black Knight pitched from the saddle all tumbled like an arrow-shot bird. When she saw the Black Knight lying dead, the damosel wrenched her palfrey round, and striking her heel fiercely into its flank, rode off without a word.

But Beaumains dismounted, and stripped off the dead knight's armour – beautiful plain black armour with a blue-purple sheen where the sun caught it – and put it on. Only he kept his own sword and Sir Kay's spear. And while he was securing the last buckle with the help of his dwarf, Sir Lancelot, who had sat his horse quietly at a little distance, looking on, came up. 'And do you judge that you have earned your knighthood now?'

His vizor was up, and Beaumains looked him straight in his odd twisted face and smiled. 'Yes, sir,' he said, and knew that he had been right; there was nobody else from whom he would choose to receive his knighthood.

'I also, with all my heart,' said Sir Lancelot. 'But first tell me your name – I will keep it under my helmet for so long as you wish.'

'Sir,' said Beaumains, 'I am Gareth, youngest son of King Lot of Orkney – youngest son but one of Queen Margawse.'

There was a little silence in the forest clearing, and somewhere afar off sounded the alarm call of a jay.

'How comes it, then, that Sir Gawain, and Sir Gaheris and Sir Agravane, all your brothers, none of them knew you when first you came to court?'

'It was eight years since any of them had seen me; and even a brother changes between nine and seventeen,' said Beaumains, who was now Gareth, simply. 'But truly, I think Gawain felt something for me from the first, for he has shown me kindness in this past year, even as you.'

'Kneel then, Gareth of Orkney,' said Lancelot.

And when the young man knelt before him with his bright sandy head bent, Lancelot gave him the light buffet between neck and shoulder which, when vigil and ceremony were stripped away, was all that was really needed for the making of a knight.

'Rise, Sir Gareth, and go on your way; when you return you will surely find a place at the Round Table, for already you begin to be a worthy knight.'

Then Sir Gareth got up, and put on his helmet and mounted the black horse, leaving his dwarf to lead his own. And he and Sir Lancelot parted, one to ride back to Camelot, the other to ride on after the Lady Linnet.

When Gareth caught up with the damosel, she cried out on him, shrill as a hawk, 'You need not think to be my accepted knight because you have killed a better knight with a coward's blow! Faugh! Ride down wind of me, for your smell sickens me! But at least I shall not have to suffer that long, for in a while we shall meet with a champion who will treat you even as you have treated him whose armour you wear. Therefore flee while you may!'

'I do not flee from any man,' said Gareth, 'nor, while the life is in me, do I leave off from following you until the adventure is accomplished.'

Before long as they rode, the damosel angrily in front, Sir Gareth a little behind and his dwarf bringing up the rear, they heard the beat of horses' hooves and a crashing in the undergrowth, and out on to the track ahead of them rode a knight all in green; green surcoat over his armour, green shield and spear, green housings on his horse, and the crest of cut silk that topped his helmet fluttering green like young beechleaves in springtime.

'God's greeting to you, damosel,' he said, reining across the way. 'Is that my brother the Black Knight who rides with you?'

'Nay,' said Linnet, 'it is a mere kitchen knave who has slain him most foully and stolen his armour.'

'Then you slew a good knight,' said the man in green, 'and I shall slay you, in payment for the foul blow!'

'No foul blow,' Gareth said, 'I slew him in fair fight – indeed the advantage was to him, for I had no armour but my jerkin. So did I take his armour which was mine by right, as the spoils of conquest.'

Then the two set their spears in rest, and fell to most furious jousting, there upon the woodland track, until their spears were all in splinters and they betook them to their swords. And when Gareth unhorsed the Green Knight they fought on foot. And all the while the damosel Linnet mocked the Green Knight and cried out upon him for being so slow to finish off a mere scullion in stolen armour, until in his rage he struck such a blow at Gareth that his shield was hacked in half.

Then Gareth shook the broken halves from his arm and, taking both hands to his sword, leapt in upon his foe, swinging the bright blade high, and brought it down in such a buffet upon the green crested helm that he dropped like a stoned hare, and lay half stunned, with his wits away. And lying so, he cried quarter.

'Whether you have quarter of me is for the damosel to decide,' said Gareth, standing over him. 'For unless she plead for you, you shall surely die.'

'Then he must die,' said Linnet, 'for never will I plead with a scullion!'

'Fair Sir Knight,' said the fallen man, 'spare my life, and I will forgive you the death of my brother; I will be your man, and my thirty knights who follow me.'

'Willingly will I spare it, if the damosel begs me.' And slowly Gareth raised his sword as though for the death stroke, the eyes of the Green Knight straining up after the blade.

'Stop!' cried Linnet. 'Do not slay him! I beg it of you, you – kitchen knave!'

Gareth lowered his sword, and bowed his head to her in all courtesy. 'It could have been asked more kindly, but you have asked it, damosel, and it is my pleasure to do your will.' Then to the fallen man, he said, 'Sir Knight of the green harness, I give you your life. Go free and get you to Camelot, your thirty knights with you. Swear allegiance of King Arthur and tell him that the Knight of the Kitchen sent you to him.'

'Truly I thank you for your mercy,' said the Green Knight. 'But the day draws on to evening. Come back with me to my manor and rest for the night; and in the morning we will go our ways, I and my knights to Camelot, and you and the damosel on the road of your adventure.'

So that night they lodged with the Green Knight; and the damosel cast scorn upon Sir Gareth and would not suffer him to eat with her at the same table. 'Shame it is, to see you treat this scullion as an honoured guest,' said she.

But the Green Knight said, 'Worse shame would it be to treat him with dishonour, for he has proved himself a better fighting man at least than I am.' And he set Sir Gareth to eat at a side table, but himself ate there with him.

Next morning they set out upon their separate ways. And as before, Linnet jibed at Sir Gareth for his kitchen smell and big hands, and bade him ride downwind of her. And as before, Sir Gareth bore it all quietly, giving her no angry retort, but saying only, 'Damosel, you are uncourteous to mock me so; for I have served you well till now, and it may be that I shall serve you better in time to come.'

'That,' said the damosel, 'we shall see!' But for the first time she looked at him as though he were human, and she herself a little puzzled; and she bit at her lower lip.

Presently the track they followed led out from the trees, and in the distance rose the walls and towers and crowding roofs of a fine city; and between the wood-shore and the city was a fair meadow, newly scythed, and all about the meadow stood pavilions of dark blue silk, and all among the pavilions wandered knights and ladies in trailing silks and damasks of the same deeply glowing blue, and pages walking slender gaze-hounds whose collars were of fine blue leather, and squires exercising horses in rich trappings of the like colour.

And in the midst of the meadow was a pavilion bigger and finer than all the rest, a blue spear standing upright beside the entrance, and a blue shield propped against it.

'Now indeed it is time for you to flee,' said the damosel, 'for there is the pavilion of Sir Persant of Inde, who men call the Blue Knight, one of the greatest champions in all the world, and his five hundred knights camped about him; and even Sir Lancelot and Sir Gawain would be hard put to face him under arms; therefore I bid you again to flee while there is yet time for fleeing.'

But she spoke a little less harshly than before.

'Almost it seems as though you do indeed fear for my skin,' said Sir Gareth; and there was a flicker of easy laughter in his voice, as he snapped his vizor shut.

'Nay, your skin is no concern of mine; but the castle where my sister is besieged is not seven miles from here, and the dread grows on me that you may be overcome, now that we are so near.' And then it was as though she heard what she had said, accepting him for her champion after all. And she looked at him quickly, but could see nothing of his face behind his closed vizor; and she said with her breath, still half angry, caught in her throat, 'Now what manner of man are you? A gentleman indeed? Or a mere spiritless creature of dumpling-broth after all? For never did woman treat knight so shamefully as I have treated you, and yet always you have answered me courteously and never departed from my service.'

'Damosel,' said Sir Gareth, 'your harsh words have served a useful purpose; for they angered me, and anger strengthened my arm against those whom I must fight. As to whether I am gently born – I have served you as a gentleman should, and whether or not I am one, you shall know when the time comes.'

Then out from the tall pavilion appeared a squire, and he came to Sir Gareth, saying that his master bade him ask the Black Knight whether he came in war or peace.

'Go back to your master and tell him that is for him to choose,' said Sir Gareth.

And the squire went away. And in a short while another squire came from behind the pavilion leading a tall iron-grey warhorse, who trampled the ground beneath his hooves and fretted at his bit; and out from the pavilion came Sir Persant himself, in armour that took the sunlight with the blue flash of a beetle's wing, and mounted the horse, and taking shield and spear, turned to where Sir Gareth waited.

'So, he chooses war,' said Sir Gareth, and he struck spur to the black stallion's flank and broke forward to meet the Blue Knight.

And with the shock of their meeting, each had his spear shattered into three pieces, and both horses were brought down. Both knights sprang clear of the lashing hooves, and drawing their swords fell upon each other, hacking and hewing till the sparks flew; and at last Sir Gareth got in a blow to the Blue Knight's crest that burst the lacings of his helmet and tore it off and flung him to the ground.

Then, without waiting for the demand, the damosel begged for mercy on the fallen knight, and Sir Gareth instantly lowered his upswung blade, and said, 'Mercy you shall have, because this damosel asks it; and because you are such a knight as my heart warms to, and sad pity it would be to slay such a one. Therefore do you take your knights and ride to Camelot, and there do homage to King Arthur, saying that the Knight of the Kitchen sent you.'

'That will I surely,' said the Blue Knight, 'but first, since the shadows are already lengthening, do you and the maiden you ride with sup and sleep here as my guests.'

So that night they were the guests of the Blue Knight; and the damosel Linnet no longer railed at Sir Gareth; but when the meal was over, she told Sir Persant how they rode to save her sister besieged in her castle by the Red Knight of the Red Lands, and of her companion's fights along the way. And 'Sir Persant,' she said, 'pray you make this gentleman a knight before we ride on, that he may be able to challenge the Red Knight as one of equal rank challenges another.'

'Most gladly will I do that,' said Sir Persant, 'if he will receive his knighthood at my hands.' -

'And right gladly would I receive it of you,' said Sir Gareth, 'but that I received it yesterday at the hands of Sir Lancelot of the Lake.'

'So, and by what name, then, were you knighted?' asked Sir Persant.

'By my own, I am Gareth of Orkney, son to King Lot and Queen Margawse.'

And the damosel looked at Sir Gareth, and opened her mouth as though to speak, and shut it again, saying no word.

And the Blue Knight looked at both of them, and smiled a little.

Next morning they parted and rode their ways, Sir Persant towards Camelot with his knights, Sir Gareth and Linnet on towards the castle of the Lady Lioness; and well before noon the seven miles were behind them, and they came to the edge of a great level plain, and Gareth saw a little way off a fair castle, whose turrets rose up tall and proud in the morning sun. And between them and the castle was a spreading camp of tents and pavilions all of scarlet red, and knights coming and going among them whose armour, like their weapons and the trappings of their horses, were all the colour of cornfield poppies. A fair sight it would have been, save for a dark thicket of trees in the midst of the camp, from the branches of which, Sir Gareth saw as he rode closer, the bodies of some forty knights hanging as though from a gibbet. Still fully armed, their shields round their necks, their gilt spurs on their heels; and all dead, long and shamefully dead.

'Yonder is an ugly sight,' said Sir Gareth.

'Alas! There hang the bodies of those who came here before you, to save my sister,' said Linnet. 'Have you enough courage to succeed where they failed?'

'I can but try,' said Sir Gareth between his teeth, 'and that without delay.' And seeing a great ivory horn hanging from the branch of a sycamore that was the tallest tree in the thicket, he made towards it.

'Nay!' cried the damosel, behind him. 'Do not touch that horn! Not yet!'

And when Sir Gareth turned to look at her questioningly, she told him, 'When that horn sounds, the Red Knight comes out to do battle with him that sounds it.'

'So I had supposed.'

'But all morning long, the Knight waxes in strength until at noon he is stronger than seven men, but when noon is past his strength wanes until by sunset he is a strong and terrible champion indeed, but no more. Let the horn sleep until noon be past, or by sunset you will hang among those others.'

'I should deserve no better,' said Gareth, 'if I were to lie in wait to come upon him at his weakest time.'

And he took down the horn, the greatest he had ever seen or handled for it was carved most wonderfully from a whole elephant's tusk, and set it to his lips and sounded a note that rang back from the castle walls and brought all those within running to the windows, and the followers of the Red Knight from their pavilions to see who sounded such a blast. And the Red Knight himself came striding from his pavilion, armed and armoured all as red as blood; and two squires brought him his roan warhorse, and he sprang into the saddle.

But Sir Gareth was looking up at one of the windows of the castle, from which looked back at him a girl's face, as pale as a windflower and lit with a sudden wild hope. A pair of white hands fluttered to him beseechingly. And it was as though something in his breast took wing and flew up to the girl in the window that he knew would never return to him again.

'That is my sister, the Lady Lioness,' said Linnet, seeing where he looked.

'I knew that it must be she,' said Gareth, still looking. 'And truly I ask for nothing better than to fight for her and call her my lady.'

'And there,' said Linnet, 'comes the Red Knight!'

And Gareth pulled his gaze back from the face at the window, and looked round to see the Red Knight spurring towards him, all ablaze in the morning sun.

'Aye, leave your looking at yonder maiden, and look at me!' shouted the Red Knight. 'For I am the last thing that you shall see before you join the carrion hanging from those branches!'

Sir Gareth urged his horse forward, clear of the dark trees with their sad and dreadful burdens; and in the clear space between the camp and the castle, they parted their horses the proper distance; then turned with spears in rest, and hurtled towards each other so that they came together with a clash like noontide thunder. Each spear struck true to the heart of the other's shield, and splintered into kindling wood, and their horse-harness burst as though it had been but strands of silk, and horses and knights fell in one great tangle to the ground. Both horses were dead, and both knights stunned and lay so long unmoving that all the watchers thought that they had broken their necks, and marvelled at the stranger knight in the black armour, who even in the moment of his own death, could so overcome the Red Knight while the sun was yet an hour short of noon.

But in a while, both knights stirred, and got them to their feet, staggering, and drew their swords, and so crashed together that it was like the last struggle of wounded lions. For an hour they fought, and the walls of the castle rang with their bladestrokes as with the ding of hammer on anvil, and the sparks flew red in the sunlight. And at the hour of noon the Red Knight struck Sir Gareth's sword from his hand and hurled himself upon him and by sheer weight brought him crashing down.

For Sir Gareth the world began to spin and grow dark; but then through the confusion in his head, he heard Linnet's voice crying to him, 'Oh, Sir Beaumains, what of your courage now? My sister weeps at her window to see you down and all her fair hopes with you!'

And the last of his strength rose in him, and he heaved himself up from under the Red Knight, and got him in a mighty grip, and wrested the sword from his hand, and tore off his helmet to end the fight.

'Mercy!' groaned the Red Knight. 'I cry your mercy! If you are a true knight, spare my life!'

'Did you spare the lives of those who hang yonder from your death trees?' roared Sir Gareth, and raised his sword.

But the other choked out, 'Not yet! Hold your hand and I will tell you all the reason for that!'

'The reason had best be a very good one!' said Sir Gareth.

'You shall judge. Once I loved a maiden. Never loved man more than I! But she told me that her brother

Carrados had been slain by Sir Lancelot of the Lake, and she would have none of me until I had avenged him by slaying a hundred of King Arthur's knights and hanging them up like carrion. Then and only then would she be my love.'

Then the maiden Linnet added her plea to his. 'All this has been wrought by Queen Morgan La Fay, hoping to bring grief and shame upon Arthur and the flower of his knights; but through your strength and courage she has failed. And indeed this man fallen at your feet did all that he did under her spell, though this I might not tell you until now. His death will not bring back to life the men he has slain; therefore, pray you let him live.'

So Sir Gareth lowered his sword, and stood leaning on it, breathing hard. 'I spare your life,' he said. 'Get you to King Arthur and swear fealty to him, saying that the Knight of the Kitchen sent you.'

And the Red Knight stumbled to his feet. 'As you command, so I obey, for you have vanquished me in fair fight.'

Then they went to the red pavilion, where the afternoon sun shining through the silken walls made all to glow like the heart of a ruby. And the maiden Linnet salved and bound the hurts of both of them. And while she did so, a chaplain came out from the castle, and the poor broken bodies were taken down from the dark thicket and given Christian burial.

The horses were brought, and the Red Knight mounted, his head hanging low on his breast; and with his knights behind him, he rode off towards Camelot.

And the damosel said to Gareth, 'Come you.'

And together they went up to the castle and across the echoing drawbridge that had been lowered for their coming, and into the outer court. The people of the castle thronged about them, loud in their rejoicing, but to Sir Gareth they all seemed like the people of a dream, as he followed Linnet into the inner courtyard. And there on the threshold of her hall, in a gown of green worked all over with little flowers like a summer meadow, stood the Lady Lionese.

'Sister, here is the champion I brought to save you,' said Linnet.

And the Lady Lionese held out her hands in greeting, and said, 'Ah, Sir Champion, by what name shall I thank you?'

'I am Gareth of Orkney, son to King Lot and to Arthur's sister, brother to Sir Gawain,' said Gareth, and he knelt, and took the hands she held out to him, and felt how little and soft they were; but the world was swimming under him, and he heard the Lady Lionese weeping, as though from a long way off. 'Oh, his wounds! He is fainting – he is dying! What shall we do?'

And Linnet's voice saying, 'Call the squires and have him carried to a guest chamber, and send to the kitchen for hot water and clean linen. And broth afterwards. I will tend him.'

For several days he lay sick of his wounds, while Linnet dressed them with evil-smelling salves until the heat went out of them and they began to heal. And the Lady Lionese came and sat beside him with sprays of honeysuckle and dove-winged columbine in her hands, while her minstrels played beneath the window for his pleasure.

But in truth he needed no more pleasure than to lie and look at her.

One day when his wounds were on the mend, he said to her, 'Maiden, these have been the sweetest days of my life; and when I am well enough to ride from here, I shall leave all joy behind me unless you promise me what I ask.'

'And what is that?' said she, looking low under her

eyelashes.

'That you come back with me to Arthur's court and marry with me there.'

Then Lionese put her arms round his neck and kissed him gravely, and spoke no word; but none was needed.

That night as the sisters sat together braiding their hair, she said, 'Dear sister, I wish you could be as happy as I. It should be you he loves, not me, after all the dangers that you have shared together for my sake.'

'After all my foul words to him?' said Linnet; and she laughed. 'Nay, for all that he is so big and strong and valiant and faithful, he is too gentle for me. I should be weary of him in a twelve-month!'

'But you will come with us to Arthur's court?'

'That will I,' said Linnet. 'It may be that I shall find there a knight with a temper to match my own.'

And so, when Gareth's wounds were far enough healed, they rode together for Camelot, with Sir Gareth's dwarf riding behind.

And at Camelot they found the Green Knight and the Blue Knight and the Red Knight, each with their followings, already there. And all had sworn fealty to the High King, saying that the Knight of the Kitchen had sent them. And the King and Queen and all the fellowship of the Round Table greeted them warmly; and Sir Lancelot said, 'Would you think that the time is come now, for telling all men who you are?'

So, standing before them all, Sir Beaumains the Kitchen Knight said simply, 'I am Gareth of Orkney.'

Gawain let out a shout. 'What of your Knight of the Kitchen now, Sir Kay? I knew it! Did I not feel kinship with him from the first? Did I not always say the lad had good blood in him?' And he came to fling his arms round his young brother and beat him joyfully on the shoulders, and Gaheris and Agravane with him.

And when the cheerful tumult had somewhat died

156

down, and by one and another the story of Gareth's adventures had been told, he took Lionese by the hand, and asked the King's leave to marry her.

'My dear nephew and my youngest knight,' said the King, 'if the maiden pleases, your wedding shall be in three days' time.'

And so three days later Sir Gareth and the Lady Lionese were wed. And after the ceremony in Saint Stephen's Church, came the wedding feast in the Great Hall; and when the feasting was done, the squires cleared back the tables in the lower part of the Hall for minstrelsy and dancing. And as the evening wore on, finding themselves together in a corner with a cup of wine between them, Lancelot and Gawain fell to watching the dancers led by Gareth and Lionese. And Gawain said, 'If it had been me, I would sooner have taken the younger sister.'

'The golden shrew?' said Sir Lancelot. 'Aye, well, the heart makes its own choices, though sometimes they be unlikely ones.' And he sounded as though he were forty instead of twenty-four. And he took good care not to let his eyes go to the Queen where she sat beneath her silken canopy looking on.

Instead, he watched where Gaheris and Linnet danced behind the bride and groom, and saw how their eyes flicked and flashed upon each other, every time the circling pattern of the dance brought them together. A fine fierce wooing they would make of it, those two, he thought; but he said only, 'I think Linnet will come to another of your kin before the leaves turn brown.'

And so indeed she did.

9

LANCELOT AND ELAINE

Before the wedding of Gaheris and Linnet, Sir Lancelot
was off and away, riding errant on another adventure.
Of all the knights of the Round Table, he was the one
who most often rode away; and people thought that it
was to gain honour that he went, sometimes up to the
castle of Joyeux Gard in North Wales, which he held
from the High King, but more often simply disappear-
ing into the wilderness in search of danger and
adventure. But in truth it was to save his honour and the
Queen's that he went. For his love for Guenever and

hers for him grew stronger as the springs and summers and winters went by; and when he could no longer bear to be at court, seeing her every day, talking with her, hawking with her, touching her hand in the dance, and knowing all the while that she was Arthur's Queen, then he would send for his horse and his armour, and ride away, lonely, leaving his heart as though pulled out by its root-strings behind him.

So in the autumn of Gaheris's wedding, he was far away, and riding through a strangely barren land, where the fields about the few settlements had a threadbare look, and the trees that in other parts of the forest would have been glowing with autumn fire of gold and copper, raised only a few withered brown leaves against the buttermilk sky. And so he came by chance over the bridge of Corbenic, and saw before him a tall tower, and huddled about the tower, the roofs of Corbenic town. And as he crossed the bridge, people came flocking from their houses and their work; and they gathered about his horse clinging to the bridle and stirrups and crying out to him as someone who they knew and respected. 'Welcome, Sir Lancelot, flower of knighthood! Now our lady will be saved from her dreadful fate!'

'What fate is that?' said Sir Lancelot, hard put to it among so many voices to make out what they said.

'Here within this tower she lies imprisoned in a bath of scalding water,' the townsfolk told him, 'and has been so for five long years, bound by the spells of Queen Morgan La Fay and the Queen of Northgalis, from jealousy because she is fairer than they – so fair that men call her Elaine the Lily – and there she must remain until the best knight in the world shall come to set her free!'

And all the while they told him this, they were urging his horse on up the street towards the tower.

'I see not why I should succeed, if other good knights before me have failed,' said Sir Lancelot. 'But I will do what I may.' And he dismounted before the arched entrance of the tower, and went on up the winding stair within, the townspeople still flowing at his heels. And so he came to an iron door at the head of the stair. It was bolted and barred from within, but the bolts and bars flew back as he set his hand to it; and he thrust the door open, and went in. The chamber was full of steam which lapped about him; but there in the midst of it he could make out a great butt of seething water, and in the butt, the Lady Elaine, holding out her hands to him imploringly. He strode forward through the eddying steam that was thinning in the draught from the open door; and he took her by the hand, and she rose up and stepped out of the scalding water. Then the women who had come up behind him gathered round her, and one took off her own smock and slipped it over her head, and another wrapped her in her cloak, for she was as naked as a needle.

And when she was clad, she put her hand back into Sir Lancelot's, and said, 'Sir, I thank you for my deliverance. And now, if it please you, let us go to the chapel that is near here, and give thanks to God.'

So they went down the stair and along the narrow way to the chapel, the people still crowding after, filled with silent joy. Then Sir Lancelot and Elaine the Lily knelt together before the altar to give their thanks. And for a little Sir Lancelot wondered again whether this was his miracle that God had given to him; and again he knew that it was not, but only the undoing of a magic spell.

And when they came out into the sunlight again, he looked at the maiden now that the flush of the boiling water was gone from her and her hair was drying to pale gold; and he saw why men called her Elaine the Lily, for it seemed to him that she was the fairest lady that ever he had seen – saving only Queen Guenever.

She turned her head and smiled at him, very gravely and sweetly, and said, 'Sir, now that we have given thanks to God, will you take me home?'

'Most gladly,' said Sir Lancelot, 'if you will tell me where that may be.'

'It is but at the other end of the town,' said the maiden. 'For it is the Castle of Corbenic, and my father is the king of this land.'

Then Sir Lancelot understood the withered trees and the air of desolation, for he had heard, as all men had heard, of King Pelles of Corbenic who was also called the Maimed King because of a wound that he had from long and long ago, that never healed; and how, at the same time as he got his wound, his land itself had been wounded, so that there had been droughts and lean harvests and a shadow as of grief lying over it ever since. Strange stories he had heard, also of Corbenic Castle itself . . . But it was no time to be standing and thinking of such things, with the maiden standing looking at him, with her hand in his, and waiting to be taken home.

So he mounted his horse and took her up before him, and rode with her through the town, the people following quietly after, and some beginning to drift away, until he came to the tall grey castle crouched at the highest point, where the rocky hillside fell away to the half-dried bed of the great looping river far below.

In the broad outer courtyard, the castle people were waiting to greet them, and Elaine's women came with soft cries of joy and concern to carry her away to her own apartments, while squires came to take Lancelot's horse to the stable, and others to lead Lancelot himself to the guest chamber to help him unarm, and then later to the Great Hall of the castle, where the tables were already set up and spread with white linen for the evening meal, and King Pelles, looking like the gaunt shadow of a man, lay on a gilded couch with the knights and ladies of his court about him, and Elaine sitting close at his side holding one of his wasted hands in hers.

'Ah, Sir Lancelot of the Lake,' said King Pelles – for like his people, he knew who the strange ugly knight was – 'God's blessing upon you, and my everlasting thanks for that you have saved my daughter when so many others have failed, and brought her back to me.'

Then all the gathered company followed him in thanks and greeting to Sir Lancelot, and he was given an honoured place at the High Table, and so they all sat down to supper.

And then, while the tables before them were still bare, a strange thing happened – or seemed to happen. Lancelot was never sure afterwards whether it was all a dream; one of those strange waking dreams he had had as a boy, and which he sometimes thought had to do with those lost years of his childhood that made him feel not quite like other people.

He thought that he looked up at the great window in the far gable-wall, and saw there against the sunset light a dove hovering on outspread wings, and hanging from her bill a little censer all of gold; and the faint smoke that wafted from the censer about the Hall was fragrant with all the sweetest spices of the world. And suddenly the great doors that were below the window opened wide, and in came a maiden all robed and veiled in white, and bearing in her hands a cup veiled also in white samite. And from the cup, even through its veiling, there shone a light so dazzling that none might look upon it fully. And the maiden, seeming to float rather than touch her feet to the ground, came up the Hall, holding the cup high before her, and passed about the tables, and so out of the door again. And the doors closed of themselves behind her.

And in the quiet that followed the cup's passing, it seemed to Lancelot that he had eaten and drunk better than ever mortal man. Indeed he could never afterwards remember that any other food came to table that night, nor that anyone there felt the need of it.

He lifted his face, which he had bowed into his hands as the cup passed, and asked, 'My Lord King of the Waste Land, what is this marvel?'

'A marvel indeed,' said King Pelles, 'for this that has passed before you is the Holy Grail, the cup from which Our Lord drank at the Last Supper, before His crucifixion, and in which, afterwards, was caught His holy blood. You know, as all men do, that this cup was brought to Britain by Joseph of Arimathea; and first it was lodged in Avalon of the Apple Trees in the holy place that he founded in this land. And after, it was lodged here at Corbenic, and I, who am kin to Joseph of Arimathea, and who men call the Maimed King, am also called the Grail Keeper. In time to come, the Grail shall pass about Arthur's table at Camelot, as tonight you have seen it pass around mine, summoning all the knights of the Round Table to the greatest and the last quest of all. And then shall be the flowering time for Arthur's Britain, and the flame of Logres shall shine at its brightest, before the darkness closes over it once more.'

For several days Lancelot remained at Corbenic, though he never saw the passing of the Grail again. He had ridden out from Camelot to escape his love for the Queen, but he had only brought it with him. And since by riding he could not outride it, it seemed to him, for a little, that there was no reason to be riding anywhere else. And the maiden Elaine was often in his company, as they rode together and played chess together, and talked much in the unkempt castle garden in the last warmth of the autumn sunshine. And with his heart full of Guenever, Sir Lancelot never knew that she was falling in love with him, nor guessed how many nights she wept herself to sleep.

But Brissen, her old nurse, knew.

And Brissen spoke with King Pelles, and heard what he had to tell; and she was of the Old People, the Dark People, and had skill with herbs and the spells that women use, and like many of her kind she had, too, something of the second sight. And from the King's chamber she went to Elaine, and said, 'Little bird, never weep so sorely, for though he loves only Queen Guenever, you shall have him for your loving lord for a little while; and you shall bear him a son and call him Galahad which is his father's first name, and he shall be the best knight in the world and heal your father's wound and bring the Waste Land out from the shadows.'

And she set herself to bring the first of these things about.

Next evening Elaine and her old nurse went secretly from the castle. And a while later a man, who Lancelot did not know was the husband of Dame Brissen, came to him privately and put something into the hollow of his hand; and when he looked, it seemed to him that it was a ring Queen Guenever often wore. And his heart began a slow drubbing beat that shook his rib cage, and he asked without looking up, 'Where is my Lady the Queen?'

'In the Castle of Case, not five miles through the forest. She is alone, and she bids you come to her.'

Then Sir Lancelot called for his horse, and rode wildly through the night and the autumn gale, with one of the grooms to guide him. And the bare trees lashed and moaned overhead, and always it seemed that Guenever's face with its soft hair streaming glimmered in the dark ahead of him.

In the courtyard of the Castle of Case he dropped to the ground, and asked the first person he saw, 'Where is the Queen?'

'She was weary, and has gone to her bed,' said Dame Brissen. But he was deaf and confused with the gale and the beating of his own heart, and he had scarcely seen her at Corbenic, and so he did not know her for Elaine's nurse, nor think it strange that she should be there.

'Come you first into the Hall, and drink a cup of wine by the fire,' said the old woman, 'for you are wet and must be weary with hard riding on such a night as this.'

He followed her; and there was warmth and quiet in the Hall, and no light but the flame-flicker of burning apple logs on the hearth. And then there was a crystal cup of warm spiced wine in his hands, and he drank it; and as soon as he had done so, a warm glow spread through him and it was as though he saw everything through a golden haze, and a great joy swelled in his breast because Guenever was so near . . .

'Come now,' said Brissen, and led him up a winding stair.

The great chamber above the Hall was in black darkness, so that he could not even see the window slits. He said, 'Guenever?' and walked forward into the dark.

In the morning when he woke, the cobweb grey of dawn was seeping in through the chinks in the shutters; and he turned to find the Queen his love in the bed beside him. And saw instead that Elaine lay there still asleep. Then a great bewilderment rose within him; and as he remembered all that had happened the bewilderment changed to grief and rage.

He shouted, 'Traitress!' and sprang from the bed and caught up his sword from the chest where it lay, and drew it from its sheath. 'You have betrayed me! I will kill you for this!'

And Elaine woke, and lay looking up at him with frightened eyes, never seeking to move as he stood over her with the naked sword.

'I have lived too long, and now I am shamed!' he said. And then, as still she did not answer, he cried out again like one in mortal pain, 'Elaine, why did you do this thing to me?'

'Because of the prophecy,' she said then, 'because we have to make Galahad, who shall heal my father and lift the shadow from this land and achieve the Quest of the Grail. And because – oh, Lancelot, I did it all for love of you; because I might not live without you, and save in courtesy you never looked my way!'

And she knelt up in the great bed, weeping.

Then Lancelot flung his sword into the corner, and said, but as though the words strangled in his throat, 'I will not kill you. It was not your fault, and I forgive you. See – I will kiss you to show that I forgive you.' And he took her in his arms and kissed her awkwardly between the brows.

But when she tried to kiss him in return, the grief and horror rose again in him, and with a great cry he sprang for the window, and flinging back the shutters leapt out. He landed in a bed of late sad roses, and sprang up, bleeding where the thorns had lashed his face and body – for he was clad only in his shirt – and still making his strange heartbroken outcry, ran for the half-fallen wall at the foot of the castle garden; and scrambled over, and fled on, down the rocky hillside and across the dried-out river, and was lost in the dun shadows of the autumn woods.

Christmas passed, and Easter, and the woods were shouting with cuckoos. But no word of Lancelot came back to Camelot; and then when a year was gone by, Sir

Bors his cousin determined to wait no longer, but to go seeking him. And in his search, it happened by chance that he came to the Castle of Corbenic, and there he was made welcome by King Pelles, and by his daughter, the Lady Elaine.

And the Lady Elaine carried a very young baby in her arms.

And when, bowing before her in all courtesy, Sir Bors came to a closer view of the babe, it stirred from sleep and opened its eyes at him; and he recognised the wide grey eyes in its small sleep-crumpled face; and he looked at Elaine, startled, and knew that the babe at her breast never had those eyes from his mother.

And the Lady Elaine smiled a little, both proudly and sadly, and said, 'Yes, Sir Knight, this is Lancelot's son as well as mine; and his name is Galahad, and he shall be a better knight even that his father, for he shall be the perfect knight of all Christendom.'

'Sir Lancelot?' said Bors. 'Is he here?'

'He *was* here,' said the Lady Elaine. 'Alas, no more.' And she told Sir Bors how Sir Lancelot had come to Corbenic, and how he had run mad and fled into the forest, and no one had been able to find him or gain any word of him since.

Then Sir Bors was sorely grieved; and next morning after hearing Mass he rode sadly away, turning his horse's head back towards Camelot.

And back at Court, when the Queen asked him if he had gained any news of Lancelot, he told her no, not wishing to cause her the grief that his news must bring. Yet the thing was too heavy and too sore in his breast for him to carry it alone, and so in a while he told Sir Ector of the Marsh and Sir Owain the Bastard and certain others; and a secret once told to two or three is a safe secret no more; and so, none knowing quite how it came about, it began to be known through the court that Sir

Lancelot had a son by King Pelles's daughter, and that he had run mad. And so it came to the Queen after all.

For a while, Guenever herself was half mad with grief and anger, which tore at her all the worse because she must keep it hidden, while King Arthur, forced to stand by and pretend even to himself – above all to himself – that she was but grieving for the loss of a friend, came near to breaking his own heart without anybody noticing.

And so another year, and part of a third year went by; and though Sir Ector and Sir Gawain and many others of the Round Table rode out in search of him, none brought back any word.

Then one day – it was Candlemas, and the first chill snowdrops were in flower in the tangled garden of Corbenic Castle – the Lady Elaine and her maidens came out into the garden to pass an idle hour. They had a ball of gilded leather to play with, for it was too cold to sit in the overgrown arbour or stroll to and fro along the half-lost paths. And in a while, as they played, tossing the ball from one to another, it fell into the midst of a clump of bushes by the old half-empty well at the garden's foot. One of the maidens ran to fetch it, and came back without it, and with her eyes wide in her startled face.

'Madam!' she shouted. 'There is a wild man asleep by the well! – oh, madam, it must be the Man of the Woods, let us run away!'

'Nay,' said Elaine, 'first I will look upon him for myself.' And a great quietness came upon her. It was as though she knew, even before she parted the bushes and stood beside the well . . .

She knew him at once; Sir Lancelot lying there with his head pillowed on his arm, asleep with the deep-spent exhaustion of a creature that has been run far and fast by the hounds. He was gaunt as a wolf after a famine winter, clad only in the rags of the shirt that he had been wearing when he disappeared into the forest, and the skin of some animal bound about him; and his hair was grey.

And Elaine sank to the ground beside him, weeping as though her heart must surely break.

Then came Brissen her nurse, and bent over her, saying, 'Do not wake him, for it may be that the dregs of the madness are still there, and if you rouse him now, he may run mad again.'

'What shall we do?' whispered Elaine. 'Oh, my love, my love, what shall we do?'

'I will cast a sleeping spell upon him, so that he shall not wake for an hour,' said the old nurse. 'And while he sleeps, we will bear him within doors, out of this cold, and lay him in the tower chamber, where he may be warmed and cared for.'

So she wove her magic, a small magic made with the fingertips and a singing-charm. And the maidens brought a fine deer-skin rug, and they muffled Lancelot in it, and bore him by a private stair into the tower chamber, and laid him on the bed there. And while some kindled scented apple logs in the brazier to warm him, Elaine and her old nurse stripped him of his rags, and bathed and salved his hurts. He was scarred and gashed like an old hunting dog, with the thin silver scars of ancient spear wounds from his knightly days, and the bruises and briar scratches he had got only that morning, and one great scar, scarce healed over and still darkly purple, on his flank.

'That was a boar's tusk,' said Dame Brissen, 'and must have come near to letting out the life.'

And Elaine wept again as she looked upon him; the gaunt man lying on his deer-skin, the famine hollows under his ribs and the scars he carried, and the marks of grief on his sleeping face.

Then they laid him under warm covers, and left him with Dame Brissen to watch beside him, while Elaine went to tell her father that Lancelot was with them once more.

And save for Elaine herself, the King her father, her old nurse and her maidens, no one in Corbenic knew who lay in the tower chamber.

The magic sleep that Brissen had laid upon him passed back into true sleep, and it was not until far on into the next day that Sir Lancelot awoke. He lay looking straight above him at the canopy of the bed, where a white hart with a golden crucifix glimmering between its antlers ran endlessly through a green silk-worked forest, pursued by white hounds. There was a deep frown between his eyes, and they were shadowed with bewilderment, but the madness that had held him two years and more was all gone from them, and they were clear again. In a while, he began to look about him, and as Elaine came swiftly from where she had been sitting in the window embrasure, to bend over him, he strained up on to his elbow and cried out to her, 'How did I come here? For God's sweet sake, lady, tell me how did I come here?'

'Sir,' said Elaine, 'I scarcely know. There have been stories in these last months, of a man of the woods . . . If you were he, as you look to be, you have been wandering through the Waste Land like a madman, your wits all gone. But yesterday your wanderings brought you back to Corbenic, and we found you sleeping by the well in the garden. But now the madness is passed, lie still, and eat and sleep, and soon you shall be well again.' And almost before she had done speaking, he was asleep once more.

For two weeks Sir Lancelot lay in the great bed, tended by the Lady Elaine and her old nurse. For two weeks he lay gazing up at the white hart for ever fleeing from the white hunting dogs; then as he grew stronger, sitting in the carved and cushioned chair in the window and gazing out on the wintry countryside. He was courteous and grateful in all things to the Lady Elaine; but she had hoped that he would come to show her more than courtesy and gratitude; and he never did. Nor did he ever ask to see his son.

And when he was strong enough to ride, he asked for clothes and a horse, and took his leave of King Pelles, and of Elaine the Lily.

'My father would give us a castle,' said Elaine, 'and I will love you always. I will live for you if that pleases you even a little. I will die for you if by that I can serve you better.'

'Neither live nor die for me,' said Sir Lancelot. 'One day there will come another knight who will love you as I cannot.'

And the Maimed King on his gilded couch said nothing, for Galahad was born, and to him that was the only thing that truly mattered.

And Elaine watched from the ramparts as Sir Lancelot rode away. And she wept no more, for it was as though all her tears were dried up, like the living rain that never fell on the Waste Land.

Sir Lancelot rode straight back to Camelot, and all the court rejoiced and marvelled to see him return to them out of his long, lost darkness. Only the Queen, though she stood beside her lord the King to welcome him back, showed no joy in his coming.

For three days she nursed her coldness towards him. But after that she could bear it no longer, and sent one of her maidens with word that the Queen would speak with him in her own apartments. There was nothing strange in such a summons, for often Guenever would invite those she liked best among the Round Table knights to come and talk with her in her chambers or in the castle garden, or ride hawking with her or hear the music of her harper. But Sir Lancelot knew that no pleasantly idle hour was before him, and his heart beat hard in his throat as he climbed the stair to the Queen's apartments.

The Queen's maidens were gathered about the fire, playing with a gaze-hound puppy and listening to the music of a little Welsh harp played by an old grey harper in their midst. But the Queen had drawn aside into the tall west window of the chamber to catch the last light of the evening on her embroidery. She glanced up as Sir Lancelot entered, and moved her hand towards the wall-seat opposite her. Then she went on with her stitching. She was working a fiery crimson dragon upon golden damask; a new shield-cover for the King.

The window embrasure was almost like a little room in the thickness of the wall, full of the pale clear winter sunshine, while the rest of the chamber was already shadowy. Even the struck notes of the harp sounded shadowy. Sir Lancelot knelt at the Queen's feet, holding himself still, until at last she looked up from her stitching, and said in a small clear voice as though she were speaking to a stranger, 'And so you have come back to us, Sir Lancelot.'

'I have come back,' Lancelot said. 'It has been a long time.'

She saw his grey hair and the marks of grief on his strange crooked face, and her heart whimpered over him. But she only agreed, 'It has been a long time,' and pulled a new strand of scarlet thread from the tangle beside her. 'Truly, I wonder that you have come at all.'

'I had to,' said Sir Lancelot.

'I do not see why. Surely once your senses returned to you, you had all that you could wish for at Corbenic.

They say King Pelles's daughter is very fair, and indeed it must be so, that they call her Elaine the Lily.'

'She is very fair,' said Sir Lancelot, 'but it is you that I love.'

And that was the first time that ever the words had been spoken between them. And while the sudden silence lasted, the harper struck three lingering chords on his harp.

Then Guenever said, 'It is Elaine that you gave your son to.'

And Sir Lancelot said, 'Guenever, it was not as you think. They brought me a ring like the one you wear, and told me that you bade me come. They gave me something to drink; and the room was wolf-dark. And I thought that it was you.'

The thread of scarlet silk snapped in Guenever's hand, and she looked up from her embroidery and met his gaze; and so they remained looking at each other. And not another word was spoken between them at that time.

But from that day forward, the love between Lancelot and Guenever was changed from what it had been before. It was stronger than ever, but it was no longer as simple as it had been, for doubt and jealousy and regret had been added to it; and before long, guilt, for it was from that time that they gave up trying to keep apart from each other. And from their coming together, there came sorrow and loss and darkness, upon themselves and upon Arthur and upon Arthur's kingdom, even as Merlin had foretold before he went to his own darkness under his magic hawthorn tree.

And Elaine? After Sir Lancelot was gone she drooped and dwindled away like a lily starved of the sun and rain. And the spring went by, and summer ripened and fell. And the snowdrops came again in the castle gardens; and when the second summer came, she knew, and all those about her, that her life was almost sped. Then she sent Galahad to a certain abbey, bidding the nuns of the place to care for him and bring him up in the ways of God; and when he grew older, to see that he was schooled by men who could train him in all things fitting to a knight.

And she spoke to her father and her old nurse and all those about her, telling them what she would have them do when the life was gone from her. Weeping, they promised that all things should be as she wished. Then she called for parchment and ink and quill, and she wrote a letter. And when the letter was written, there was nothing more that she must do, and so, like a bird taking wing, her spirit flew from her body and was gone.

Then her attendants did all that she had bidden them. They dressed her in her finest silken gown, and laid her in a litter, with the rolled parchment in her hands, and bore her from the Waste Land and away through the late summer forest, until they came to the looping narrow waterway that joined itself at last to the broad river that flowed past Camelot on its way to the sea. And there they made ready a barge hung all over with black, and laid her in it, scattering the flowers of late summer over all; and with one old dumb man-servant to steer the barge, they left her to the river.

And the river carried her on until it joined the other that flowed by Camelot, and still on, through dark stretches overarched by alder trees and out into open meadow stretches between banks thick with meadow-sweet and tall purple loosestrife, until the barge came to rest at last, against the bank below Camelot town.

Arthur and the Queen were speaking together at a window that looked far down upon the river – the same window where she and Lancelot had spoken together after his long absence – and they saw the black-draped barge come down on the quiet silver flood, and settle into the bank above the bridge. And Arthur called to Sir Kay, 'See you that black barge? It is in my mind that there is a strangeness about it. Take Sir Bedivere and Sir Agravane, and go and look more closely, and bring me back word.'

So Sir Kay went, and the other two with him; and in a while he returned and said, 'Sir, in that barge there lies the body of a fair damosel, and there is no one else in the barge but an ancient man at the steerboard, who will speak no word; and indeed I think that he is dumb.'

'Here is a strange thing indeed,' said the King. 'We will come now and look upon the body of this lady.' And he held out his hand to the Queen, and together, with many knights following, they went down through the narrow streets of Camelot town where the swallows still darted among the eaves, and across the water meadow to the river bank. And there lay the black barge at rest, and in it the body of the lady, clothed in cloth-of-silver, and with her fair hair parted and combed upon her breast, and she lying as though she smiled in her sleep.

'This is a sorry sight,' said the King. And he asked the old man who she was, but could get no answer.

And the Queen said softly, 'How fair she is. Like a lily cut down by an early frost.'

And then they saw the letter in the lady's hands that lay folded on her breast; and the King climbed aboard the barge and gently took the parchment and broke the seal and read what was written within.

'Most noble knight, Sir Lancelot, my most dear lord, now has death taken me as you would not. I loved you truly, I that men called Elaine the Lily; and therefore to all ladies I make my moan, and beg them pray for me.

Give me honourable burial and pray for my soul, Sir Lancelot, as you are a true knight above all knights.'

And that was all.

Now Sir Lancelot was among those who had come down with the King and Queen; and he had taken one look at the lady's face and then stood as though turned to stone and deep-rooted there in the riverside grass. And when Arthur had done reading the letter and while all the company were murmuring for sorrow, he covered his face with his hands and groaned. And when he took his hands away, he said, 'My Lord Arthur, I am sorry at heart for the death of this lady. God knows I never desired her death, but I could not love her as she loved me.'

'Love comes as it chooses, or does not come; nor can it be fettered,' said the King, half as though he answered Sir Lancelot, and half as though he spoke to his own heart. And he gave orders for the bestowing of the lady's body until the time of her burial, and turned away.

And as the Queen turned also, she said to Sir Lancelot, 'You might have shown her something of gentleness, to save her life.'

And Sir Lancelot felt the world reel under him, for he was in many ways a simple man, and he never understood women, least of all the Queen.

Next day the Lady Elaine was buried worshipfully in the Church of Saint Stephen, and Sir Lancelot offered the Mass Penny for her soul, and strewed the last of the summer's roses and strands of honeysuckle on her grave.

And when all was done, the old dumb servant turned again to the river where the barge waited for him, and pushed off from the bank, and poled back upstream.

And Sir Lancelot was left with a new grief and a new

guilt to carry. He thrust it deep down into himself and grew a scar over it; but he carried it all his days.

10

TRISTAN AND ISEULT

The years went by and the years went by, and the names
on the high backs of each seat at the Round Table
changed as knights died in battle or upon some
hazardous quest and new young knights took their
places. And among the lost names were those of King
Pellinore and his son Lamorack, slain in a family feud
by Gaheris and Agravane in vengeance for the death of
their father King Lot of Orkney. And after that, four
seats beside the Seat Perilous were empty for a while;
for though King Arthur knew that he must bow to the
old laws of the blood feud, he sent both slayers away on
a long and difficult quest by way of penance. And his

heart was sore within him, and he wished that he still had the good counsel of Merlin beside him.

That year, on the Eve of All Hallows, the knights gathered about the Round Table were deeply aware of the empty places in their midst. For on that night of the year, the time of Ingathering, when the cattle were brought in to their winter quarters, many people set a place at their table and left it empty for the ghosts of their dead if they should come wandering home in search of shelter for the dark months ahead.

On this particular Hallowe'en, winter was coming in with a gale of wind and rain that beat like dark wings about the walls of Camelot; and at the height of the storm, just as they were ending supper, a squire entered with word that a stranger stood outside, asking shelter for himself and his horse.

'Bring him in,' said the King, 'on this night of the year all men are welcome at all firesides.'

And so the stranger came in. A tall man, and dark, dark as the storm outside as he came into the torchlight; wet and windblown, he might have been some creature of the storm. Yet about him there was a great stillness.

He came up the Hall, and as he thrust back the heavy folds of his cloak, all men saw that he carried under its shelter a harp in its bag of finely broidered mare's skin.

'God's greeting to you,' said the King as the man knelt at his feet. 'Both for your own sake and for the sake of the harp you carry, for a harper with a new song to sing, a new tale to tell is most welcome on such a night as this. Eat and drink, and warm yourself, and then maybe of your courtesy you will wake the magic of the harpstrings for us.'

'That will I, most willingly,' said the stranger.

He was given a place beside the hearth, and food freshly brought from the kitchen, and a cup of wine. And when he had eaten and drunk and his cloak had ceased to steam in the warmth of the fire, he took his harp from its bag; a beautiful harp of black bog-oak with strings of findruim, the white Irish bronze, and began to tune it, and when every string sang true, he asked, 'Now, what would you have, my Lord King? A song of war? Or hunting? Or love?'

'Any song, so that it be a new one,' said the King.

'Love,' said Queen Guenever, who had come in with her ladies to listen.

The harper was silent a little, his face in the firelight looking as though he listened to something very far off, or deep within himself, as his enquiring fingers woke random note after random note from the shining strings. Then he said, 'I will give you the tale of Tristan and his lady Iseult.'

Then there was a murmuring and a stirring of interest up and down the Hall, for Sir Tristan's name and his reputation as a knight-at-arms were known to many there. They settled themselves to listen, and sometimes telling it as a story, sometimes letting it drift into song in time to the haunting harp-music, and then back to story again, the harper wove for them this tale.

When King Marc of Cornwall was young and new to his kingship, there was war between Cornwall and Ireland. And word of it came to another King, Rivalin of Lothian. And for no other reason than that it was the sea-faring season and he thought it time his young men were blooding their spears, he called out his ships and his warbands and they coasted round Britain to King Marc's aid. Then together they won a great victory over the Irish; and when all was over, King Marc gave his sister in marriage to Rivalin for a bond between their two peoples.

For a year Rivalin lived happily with his Cornish princess, but at the end of that time, bearing their son, she died. And for Rivalin it was as though the sun went out. For a long while he could not bear even to look at the child. He called him Tristan which means Sorrow, and gave him to the Queen's old nurse to rear. And when the boy was seven, he took him from the nurse and gave him to a young knight called Gorvenal to train as a prince should be trained. And from the first, Gorvenal loved him as a much younger brother, and taught him to ride and handle sword and spear and hawk and hound, to sleep hard and bear pain unflinching, to think for himself and to keep his word, and many other lessons beside. And from somewhere deep within himself he learned to play the harp so that it was as though he played upon the very heartstrings of those who heard him.

One day when Tristan was sixteen years old, he and Gorvenal were sitting beside the fire; and Gorvenal looked across at the boy who was leaning elbows on knees and gazing into the heart of the flames. 'What do you see in the fire?' asked Gorvenal.

'I see far countries,' said Tristan.

And Gorvenal knew that this was the time he had long expected. 'Tristan,' he said, 'I too have been thinking of far countries. Here in Lothian there is no man now who can outmatch you in the princely skills – but for a prince to be foremost among his father's subjects might be a somewhat easy glory, after all.'

'I do not care for easy glory,' said Tristan.

And next day he went to his father and asked him for a ship, that he might go seeking adventure.

The King his father agreed, and the ship was made ready, and when the sailing weather came after the winter storms, Tristan and Gorvenal and a handful of young companions set sail.

Now it had long been in Tristan's heart to visit his mother's country, for his old nurse had often told him stories of the land and its magic; and so they made the long coastwise voyage and came at last to the southern coast of Cornwall; and there they landed and bought horses and rode north towards Tintagel.

So they came at torch-lighting time to Tintagel Castle on its rocks high above the sea, and stood at last before King Marc in his Great Hall. And he and Tristan looked at each other and their hearts warmed together in that first moment. Then the King greeted his guests and asked them from what land they came.

'From Lothian,' said Tristan.

And the King looked at him more closely, as though suddenly he were seeing another face within his, and said, 'Did ever you see my sister, the Queen of Lothian?' and then he sighed. 'Fool that I am, you would not have been born when she died.'

'I was born on the day she died,' said Tristan. 'I am her son.'

And the King put his arms round him, and would have wept, had he been a man for tears.

For two years Tristan and his companions were of King Marc's court; and as it had been in Lothian, so it was in Cornwall, there was no one who could ride swifter on the hunting trail than Tristan or master him at sword play; the King's harper could not make music so sweet, and he could throw any wrestler in the kingdom.

And then a sore trouble fell upon the land; and this was the way of it.

The war with Ireland, that had first brought Rivalin from Lothian, had flared again a few years later, and the patched-up peace had left Cornwall pledged to pay a yearly tribute to Ireland in corn and cattle and slaves. Cornwall had paid the tribute for a year or two, and then both sides had let the matter drop. But now the Queen of Ireland's own brother, the Morholt, mightiest of champions, sent word that the time had come for paying the old debt, and that because it had been owing fifteen years, it must be paid all in slaves; one child in every three born in Cornwall in all those years. If they would not pay, then let them make ready to defend themselves in battle, for he was coming with a fleet of ships – or else let them find a champion to fight him, the Morholt, in single combat.

Then Marc's fighting men began to make ready for war, though with little hope of victory, for Ireland had grown strong under the Morholt's leadership; and the women, weeping, began to seek out places to hide their children.

Then Tristan sought out the King his uncle, and said, 'Better than all this ready-making for war, if we were to send the Morholt his champion for single combat.'

'Much better, if we had such a champion. But the Morholt has the strength of four men,' said King Marc.

'I have skills that you have not seen me use as yet,' said Tristan. 'I will go out as Cornwall's champion, if you will have me.'

'You are only a boy! To let you go would be to throw your life away!'

'It is my life,' said Tristan, 'and I am your nephew, your nearest kinsman, I have the right to go!'

And King Marc knew that this was true. So he sent word to the Morholt that a champion of the royal house of Cornwall would meet him in single combat. The place was set – a small island just off the Cornish coast – and on the appointed day Tristan and the Morholt came together upon the island. They landed there alone, Tristan from the shore, the Morholt from the Irish ships that lay waiting out to sea. The Morholt moored his boat where the dark rocks gay with tufted sea-pinks came down to the water's edge. But when Tristan had landed he pushed his boat off and let the tide take her.

The Morholt stood watching, dark and menacing as thunder in his black armour. And 'That was surely a strange thing to do,' said he, when Tristan drew near, 'to push your boat off again when you landed.'

'Two of us came to this island,' Tristan said, 'but only one will need a boat to carry him away.'

Then the Morholt laughed sharp in the back of his throat, and drew his sword; and together they went up to the level space in the midst of the island. And there they fought, all the long day. Tristan was the swifter swordsman, but the Morholt had the strength of four men, and his blows fell so thick and fast that at times there was nothing Tristan could do but cover himself as best he might behind his shield. At last, in trying to guard his head, he raised his shield too high, and the Morholt lunged beneath his guard and got in a great blow to the thigh that laid it bare to the bone.

But the fire of his wound and the blood-flow that should have weakened Tristan, seemed to wake a desperate valour in him that he had not found before. And, yelling, he leapt forward with blade upswung, and brought it down in a whistling stroke that bit so deep through the mail and into the bone beneath, that when he jerked it free a fragment of the blade was left in the Irish champion's skull.

With a great cry the Morholt turned and fled, leaving a crimson trail, towards where his boat was tied and other boats from the Irish ships were already putting in for him.

And Tristan walked down the landward shore of the island, trailing crimson also; and he could hear the Cornish warriors rejoicing, but it all seemed far off, and his blood soaked and soaked into the grey shingle.

As soon as the ship that carried the Morholt reached

Ireland, messengers were sent for the King's daughter, the Princess Iseult; for in all the land there was none that had her skill in the healing craft. But not even she could bring a dead man back to life, and by the time she reached him the Morholt was dead of his wound. But she drew out the jagged piece of sword blade from his skull, and laid it carefully by, in case she should ever meet a man whose sword lacked a splinter that shape . . .

Meanwhile Tristan lay for a long while sick of his wound in Tintagel Castle. And when at last it was healed the King, rejoicing, gave him knighthood and determined to make him his heir. But his lords urged him to marry and have sons of his own. And when he would not listen to them, some, who were jealous of Tristan, began to whisper among themselves that it was his doing. And Tristan, knowing this, also urged his uncle to marry. 'Give me three days to think the matter over,' the King said at last, 'and on the fourth morning you shall have your answer.'

And on the fourth morning as he sat, his mind still not made up, waiting for his lords and nobles, in the sunshine before the entrance to his Great Hall, two swallows fell to quarrelling about something high over his head, darting and circling, snatching it from one to the other, until even as the King looked up, they dropped it. A thread like gossamer, but red as flame; it drifted to his outstretched hand, and he saw that it was a long hair from a woman's head; and such a colour as the King had never seen before, so dark as to be almost purple in the shade, bright as fire where the sun caught it. Surely only one woman in the world could have hair that colour; and one woman in the world would be hard to find!

So when the lords came for their answer, Marc showed them the hair, and told them, 'I will marry, as you wish, but only the woman to whom this hair belongs.'

Then Tristan stood forward from the rest, and said, 'My uncle, give me the hair and a ship, and I will go and seek this woman, and if she lives, bring her back to you.'

So a ship was made ready for a long voyage, and Tristan gathered his closest companions, Gorvenal among them, and set sail, to search all the countries of the world, save Ireland, where since the Morholt's death, the King had ordered death for any Cornishman who landed on his shores.

Yet a man's fate is a man's fate. The ship was caught in a great storm and driven hither and yon, and when the storm blew itself out at last, they found their vessel driven hard aground on the shore of a great river-mouth. Far off were other boats, and beyond, hearth smoke and the glint of pale sunshine on roofs and church spires. Then Gorvenal, who had travelled far in his own youth before Tristan came to him, said, 'Now God help us, for yonder is Wexford, and we are held fast upon Ireland's shore!'

And with the folk of the nearby fisher village already coming down in curiosity they took hurried counsel and determined to claim that they were storm-driven merchants from Less Britain. This story they told, and the people believed them, and as they were helping them to get their horses overboard and up through the shallows, the bells of Wexford began to toll; and one said to his neighbour, 'Another good man dead for the Princess's sake.'

And when Tristan asked his meaning, they all told him, taking up the story one from another, how a terrible fire dragon was laying waste the land, and how in despair, for with the Morholt dead they had no champion who could stand against it, the King had offered his daughter the Princess Iseult to any man who could slay the monster. 'Many good knights have tried and failed,' said the last man, sadly. 'It is for the latest of them that the bells of Wexford are tolling now.'

Then Tristan thought, It is I who led my comrades into this sore danger, and if I can slay the dragon, then the King can scarcely have us killed, even if he discovers that we are from Cornwall.

So in the dark hour before the next day's dawn, he got into his mail shirt and bade farewell to his companions and, taking his own horse from among those grazing under guard close by, he rode away.

He knew that he was travelling in the right direction, as the light grew round him, by the scorched desolation of the countryside; and presently he heard a terrible roaring far ahead of him, and across his path came galloping a knot of horsemen who shouted to him to turn back and fly for his life.

But Tristan turned his horse into the way they had come, and rode on. All the country looked as though a heath fire had swept through it, and all around were the blackened snags of tree stumps and the scorched and half-eaten bodies of cattle. And then, rounding a rocky outcrop, he saw before him a cave mouth dark in the side of the hill, and before the cave mouth, coiling itself to and fro in anger, long as a troop of horse and wicked as sin, was the dragon he had come to seek.

He crouched low in his saddle and, levelling his spear, struck spurs to his horse and charged in to meet it. His spear point took it in the throat as it reared up to meet him, wounding the creature sore; but horse and rider plunged on into the heat and poison fumes that made a cloud about it; and crashing against the spiked and glowing breast-scales, the horse dropped dead. But Tristan sprang clear, as the dragon, still with his spear in its throat, roaring in agony and coughing out great gouts of steaming blood, made for the rocks that choked the hillside. And Tristan sprang after it with his sword upraised.

There among the rocks and the scorched hillside scrub they came together. Tristan's shield was charred to cinders in the first onslaught and his ring-mail seared his flesh; but the dragon was weakening as the spear dragged at its throat and breast; and its fire was sinking. And at last, seizing his chance, Tristan sprang in and drove his sword between the breast scales and found the monster's heart.

The dragon reared up with a death-roar that echoed like thunder among the hills, flailing the air with its tail and savage claws, then crashed to the ground, its fire dying out.

With his last strength, Tristan wrenched open its jaws and hacked off the venomous black tongue. But his own hurts were very sore, and he had scarce dragged himself a spear's throw from the great carcass when the ground seemed to rise beneath his feet and a roaring blackness engulfed him.

Now one of the men whom Tristan had seen fleeing from the dragon's lair was the King's steward, who had long desired to marry the Princess Iseult though she had no liking for him at all. And when he saw that Tristan rode straight on despite their warning, he slipped away and turned back also, to see what should befall and whether there might be any gain for him in it. And so he was near at hand when he heard the monster's death-cry; and made bold by that and the silence that came after, he pressed on. And among the rocks he found the dead horse and then the dead dragon, and of the dragon slayer no sign at all. And he thought, The dragon must have eaten him before it died, and there lies my chance. And drawing his sword he fell to hacking at the monster's carcass until his blade was reddened to the hilt. Then he galloped back to Wexford and gathering his henchmen and a cart, returned again with them to hack off the dragon's head and fetch it into the town. And when they had brought it in, he made for the King's Hall to show him the battered head and his blood-stained sword, and claim the Princess in marriage.

The King was torn between joy that Ireland was delivered from the terror that had laid it waste, and grief that his daughter must marry a man she loathed. But he had given his word, and he sent to the women's quarters to bid her come down for her betrothal to his steward.

When she received this word, the Princess thought more quickly and desperately than ever she had thought in her life before. And she sent back word to the King that she was unwell and could not come down to her betrothal that evening or the evening after, but that on the third evening she would come. For she was sure that the steward had not himself slain the dragon but was stealing some other man's glory; and she must play for time.

Then she sent for Brangian, chief among her maidens, and bade her have horses ready at the postern gate before dawn, that they might ride out and look at the place where the dragon had been slain. 'There is some mystery here, and it may be that by seeking we shall find the answer to it,' she said. 'We *must* find the answer to it, for sooner than wed with that man I will die!'

So in the dark of next morning, the Princess and her maiden slipped out and rode away towards the hills. They found the torn remains of the horse, and then the headless carcass of the dragon; and searching further, they found Tristan lying among the rocks and the blackened thorn-scrub. And at first they thought him dead. But when they had stripped off his mail, they found him clawed and scorched from head to foot, but with seemingly no death-wound upon him. And stowed in the breast of his mail shirt the Princess found what she and Brangian both knew for the forked tip of the dragon's tongue.

'Dear mistress,' said Brangian, 'you will not go to your betrothal to the steward tomorrow.'

'Nor any day,' said the Princess; and she put back the hair from Tristan's forehead and looked long into his shut face. Then they set to work to get him across Brangian's horse, and Brangian mounted behind him; and so they returned in the dawn to the King's palace.

When Tristan came back to himself he was lying in a strange chamber with two women bending over him, and one had hair as black as midnight and the other had hair the colour of hot coals. And he knew that whoever she might be, this was the maiden he was seeking, for no other in all the world could have hair quite that colour, the colour of the single hair in the silken packet he wore round his neck. And then as he raised himself on his elbow and looked about him, he saw a silver bowl beside the bed, and lying within it the forked tip of the dragon's tongue.

In a voice that seemed not to be his own, he croaked, 'Well for me that you found and kept that wicked thing, for it is my only proof that it was I who slew the dragon.'

'Well for me also,' said the red-haired maiden. 'For my father the King promised me to whoever could rid Ireland of the monster, and his steward claims that it was he.' And then they both heard what she had said, and there was a startled silence between them.

Then the Princess, when she had done salving Tristan's wounds, gave him a healing broth, and when he had drunk it and was asleep, she and Brangian took his mail shirt and his sword into the next room that they might clean them without disturbing him.

And when the Princess drew his sword, she saw that a small piece was broken out of the blade halfway down.

She laid the sword on the table without a word, and going to a carved chest, brought from it a small packet wrapped in crimson silk; and from the packet she took the fragment of sword-iron which she had taken from the Morholt's skull, and held it to the gap in Tristan's blade. It fitted perfectly.

Across the table she and Brangian looked at each other. 'This is the slayer of my kinsman,' she said in a small cold voice. 'And he lies in my hands for killing or curing.'

Brangian cried out, 'No! Oh no, my mistress! You cannot kill a man lying helpless at your mercy!'

'I can,' said Iseult, 'but I have no need to. I have only to show this to my father.'

'And destroy the dragon's tongue! If this man who slew the Morholt can prove that he also slew the dragon, the King must forgive him. And oh, my lady, remember he is all that stands between you and marriage to your father's steward!'

The Princess stood a long while looking down at the sword blade. Then she said, 'Yes, that is worth remembering.' And began to laugh. And later that night she went to her father and told him of the knight she and Brangian had found, and of her certainty that the steward's claim was false.

'As to that,' said the King when he had heard her out, 'here are two men, both claiming the same thing. Their claims must be heard before the Assembly.'

'Then let the Assembly be called for three days' time,' said the Princess. 'In three days I can heal his dragon wounds and he will be ready to prove his right to the kill.'

Meanwhile, word of how the King's steward had slain the dragon reached Tristan's men waiting beside their ship, but of Tristan himself no word at all; and even when Gorvenal went in secret to the dragon's lair, he found no clue that he could bring back to them, and they could only think that his venture against the monster had cost him his life. But even as they were debating what they should do next, word spread from the palace that another warrior had claimed the dragon-kill, and that his claim and the steward's were to be tried on the next day but one. And before they had drawn breath from that, came a letter from Tristan to Gorvenal written with much difficulty, but telling him what had happened, and bidding them all to be present at the trial, clad in their best, and bearing themselves as befitted bold and honest merchants of Less Britain.

The day came, and the great timbered council hall was made ready for the Assembly, and when the lords and nobles were gathered, and the supposed merchants of Less Britain also, the eyes of all were drawn to the monstrous head that had been dragged in on its cart and set up in the midst of the place. Then the King entered and took his place in the High Seat; and after him came the Princess Iseult walking proud under the royal goldwork that bound her hair.

Then the Horns of Summoning were sounded; and from the door on the right of the hall the steward strutted in, and from the door on the left, Tristan, still weak from his wounds but carrying himself less like a merchant than a king's son, none the less.

Then the King raised the silver rod in his hand for silence, and when all the gathering was hushed, he spoke to them of the dragon that had ravaged their land, and his promise of the Princess's hand to any man who could rid them of this horror, and how many of their best and bravest knights had died in the attempt. 'Now the evil is ended, and the dragon's head lies here before you, and two men claim the kill. Therefore, before you all, I call upon both to prove their claims. And since my steward was the first to make it, let him now be the first to speak.'

The steward stood forward boldly enough, and said, 'My Lord King, I slew the dragon in long and bitter struggle for the love of the Princess: and here lies the monster's head to prove my claim as clearly as though it could speak!'

'And yet a man might come upon such a carcass, slain by another, and cut off the head to claim the kill for himself,' said the King.

'And what man would slay this dragon and walk away?' demanded the steward.

'Let the second claimant answer that,' said the King.

And Tristan stood forward also. 'My Lord King, merchant as I am, I have some skill with weapons. And hearing of the evil fallen upon this land, I thought that if I could slay your dragon for you, it might be good for trade! By God's grace I slew the creature; but being myself sorely hurt, a great blackness came upon me; and it must be that while I lay in the blackness, this fellow came and found the dead dragon and thought to gain the reward that another man had done the bleeding for.'

'Lies! All lies!' shouted the steward.

'One of us lies indeed, but it is not I! My Lord King, has this head been closely guarded so that none might come near it unseen?'

'Night and day,' said the King.

'Then let some of your men force open its jaws. Maybe it could indeed have spoken to prove your steward's claim, *if it were not lacking the tip of its tongue!*'

And when four strong warriors had forced the jaws open, there for all to see, was the black stump of the dragon's tongue! Then Tristan sprang up on to the cart and held aloft the forked tip of the tongue which he had brought with him in a napkin. 'My Lord King, nobles of Ireland, is the proof enough?'

'The proof is enough,' said the King, and the great gathering echoed him.

And when they looked round for the steward, he had slipped away.

But there was yet one more matter to be set right. And going to the King, Tristan knelt at his feet, and said, 'My lord, there is one more thing to be told, and better I should tell it now, than that you should hear it in another way.'

'Tell on,' said the King.

'It is this: four days since, it was I who slew the dragon; two years since, it was I who slew your kinsman, the Morholt.'

A great gasp ran through the Hall, and the King's brows drew almost to meeting. 'You killed Ireland's champion? Do you know what you say?'

'It was done in fair fight,' said Tristan.

'That is true,' said the King, 'and true it is also that the Morholt was slain by no merchant but by Tristan of Cornwall.'

'I am Tristan of Cornwall.'

'Then what brings you of all men to our shores?'

And Tristan told him the whole story of the quest for the Princess of the swallow's hair.

'Then,' said the King, when all was told, 'if I give you my daughter, you will take her not as your own bride, but to be Queen of Cornwall.'

'That is so,' said Tristan, and looked at the Princess; but though she had been watching him ever since he entered the Hall, she never looked back at him now.

The King thought a long while with his chin in his hand. At last he said, 'Maybe it is time that old scars were healed, and there was friendship once more between Ireland and Cornwall . . .'

And so the thing was settled; and beside Tristan's ship, another was made ready, and furnished with all rich things, to take the new Queen of Cornwall to her kingdom. And after three days of feasting and merry-making, they set sail.

At first they had fair weather, but within a day they ran into rough seas, and the Princess and Brangian and all her maidens were direly ill; so at last Tristan bade the shipmaster to put in to the nearest shelter he could find along the Welsh coast, while Gorvenal in the Cornish ship held on to carry word of their coming to King Marc.

At noon, the Irish ship came under the shelter of a long headland, and dropped anchor in a little cove where a stream came down from the steep woods inland; and Tristan and the other men sprang over-board to carry the women ashore. And Tristan held up his arms to the Princess as she came over the side, and carried her up through the shallows and set her down on the white wave-rippled sand. Now this was the first time that ever they had touched each other since she had tended his wounds, and that was a different kind of touching; and as he set her down, their hands came together, and their eyes also, and in that moment it was as though something of Iseult entered into Tristan and something of Tristan into Iseult that could never be called back again as long as they lived.

Before evening Tristan and his companions built a little cabin of green branches up the streamside for the Princess and Brangian, and another for her maidens. And when morning came, the storm was over and the sun shone in a clear sky; but the seas were still running high. They would have to wait another night for the seas to gentle. And Tristan, though he was careful not to be with the Princess again, was glad. He wandered off by himself, and sat among the sand dunes of the headland.

And there the Princess found him after all, and she carrying a little packet of crimson silk in her hand. 'I have something to show you,' she said, and undid the packet and held out the splinter of metal in her palm. 'Draw your sword that I burnished for you while you lay sick.'

And when he did as she bade him, she fitted the sharp fragment into the gap in the blade; and they looked at each other with the sword lying between them. 'So you knew,' said Tristan. 'Even before I told your father, you knew.'

'I knew,' she said.

'Why did you not kill me, Iseult?'

'And marry my father's steward?' But they both knew that was not all the truth. And she tossed the fragment away into the sand as something that no longer mattered, and walked away.

That evening at moonrise, with taper-light glimmering softly from the little branch-woven cabins up the streamside, the shipmaster came to Tristan where he was walking to and fro on the edge of the men's camp, and said, 'The wind has gone round and already the seas are gentling; it will be fine sailing weather tomorrow.'

'Then make ready to sail on the morning tide,' said Tristan.

And he went to tell the Princess.

She was alone in the bothie, and combing her hair by the light of a honey-wax candle. 'I hoped that you would come,' she said.

'I came only to tell you that the seas are gentling, and tomorrow we sail with the morning tide.'

Iseult stopped combing her hair. 'I would that the seas might never gentle,' she said, and made room for him on the cushions beside her; and he sat down.

'Lady,' he said, 'that thought is best forgotten. You will be happy in Cornwall, and King Marc will be a kind and loving lord to you.'

'Kind and loving he may be,' said Iseult, 'but this is the last day that ever I shall be happy, and already the moon is up.'

'You will forget today.'

'Never,' said the Princess. 'Whoever takes me to wife, you are my lord as long as I live; and you know it.'

And Tristan bent his head into his hands and groaned.

'Do you love me?' said the Princess.

'Iseult, I am the King's man.'

'But do you love me?'

And Tristan said, 'Though it is like to be the death of both of us, I love you, Iseult.' And he put his arms round her and they clung together as the honeysuckle clings to the hazel tree.

But they sailed for Cornwall with the morning tide.

And so they came at last to the landing-place below Tintagel; and the King himself with all his court came down to greet the Princess of the Swallow's Hair.

'Until now,' said King Marc, with Iseult's hands in his, 'I thought that this marriage would be for the binding together of the rift between Cornwall and Ireland. But now I know that it is for making music in my heart . . . Your hair is as red as fire, but your hands are so cold; yet mine are big enough to warm them.'

And Tristan, turning aside to greet old friends and old enemies, thought, Dear God! He loves her too!

The wedding day came and went, and Iseult of Ireland was now Queen of Cornwall; and for a long time – or it seemed a long time to them – Tristan never looked her way nor she his.

Autumn and winter went by, and the year turned to spring; and one day Tristan came upon the Queen in the little garden that clung to the rocks below the castle; and she was looking towards Ireland and weeping; and all his love for her that he had pushed down into his dark and inmost places came rushing up to the light again, and he put his arms round her and held her close and kissed her. And after that, there was no going back for either of them to where they had been before.

And as ill luck would have it, they were seen by another nephew of King Marc's, Andret by name, who was jealous of Tristan. And from that day forward he spied upon them, waiting his time.

Again the summer turned to autumn, and the winter passed and the golden gorse flamed along the headlands. And the love between Tristan and Iseult would not let them be, dragging at them as the moon draws the tides to follow after it, until at last, whether they would or no, they came together again.

And all the while, Andret watched.

One night in early summer, the Queen went early to her apartments, saying that her head ached, for there was thunder in the air, and she would be alone. And soon after, Andret saw that Tristan's place in the King's Hall was empty. Then he too slipped out. Soon after, a palace servant with a gold coin hidden in his closed hand came to the King with word that the Queen begged him to go to her instantly in her bower.

And when Marc came striding into the bower, brushing aside Brangian who tried to hold him back, he found Tristan and Iseult held close in each other's arms.

Then the King's wrath was terrible; all the more terrible because of his love for his Queen and his kinsman. And waiting for no excuses, he shouted up the guard. And Tristan, for all that he fought like a wildcat, was taken and dragged away, while the Queen was held captive in her own chamber – until next day they were brought before a council of the chiefs and churchmen and lawmakers of the kingdom.

And Iseult was condemned to die by fire, which

according to the law of the land was the proper fate for a queen who had betrayed her lord, and Tristan was condemned to be broken on a great wheel.

By dawn on the appointed day all the preparations had been made; and great was the grief and loud the wailing throughout the land, for Tristan was the champion and the hope of Cornwall, and the Queen had made herself beloved in her husband's kingdom as she had done in her father's.

Tristan was to die in the morning, Iseult after noon, and so he was led out first by men of the King's bodyguard. Now the chosen place for his execution was some distance from the castle; and on the way to it, they passed a little chapel set high on the edge of the cliff. And when they came to it, Tristan asked leave to go in and pray, saying that he had had no time to make his peace with God before they fetched him out that morning.

And after a little counsel-taking among themselves, the men agreed, and let him go in alone and unbound, seeing that there was no way in or out but the one door, and a high window that no man could get through, above the sheer drop to the rocks beneath.

But Tristan was a slight man and a desperate one, and he got through that window all the same, and dropped into a furze bush below the clifftop that caught and held him from the long fall; and by little and little, using every finger- and toe-hold among the black rocks, he worked his way along below the edge, until he came to a place where he could regain the cliff-top out of sight of the chapel and the bodyguard watching its door. Then he set off back towards Tintagel.

He had not gone far, when round a tump of wind-shaped thorn scrub he came face to face with Gorvenal. They wasted no time in exclaiming nor in greetings. 'Is the hunt behind you?' Gorvenal said.

'Not yet, I will tell you all later.'

'Meanwhile, the sooner we are many miles from here the better. See – here are your sword and your harp. I could not bide in Tintagel, and I could not be leaving them behind me.'

Tristan took his sword and hurriedly belted it on. 'Let you keep my harp for me until maybe I come for it,' he said, and set his hand an instant on Gorvenal's shoulder, and then walked straight on.

Gorvenal swung round after him. 'Are you mad? This is the way back to Tintagel!'

'I cannot leave Iseult to die in the flames,' Tristan said. 'I must save her or die with her.'

Gorvenal drew a deep breath. 'Two swords are better than one. If you are for Tintagel, then so am I.' And they went on together.

Soon they came in sight of the castle; in sight also of the Queen's execution place outside the gates, with the pyre already built and the people crowding round. And they settled down behind some hawthorn bushes to wait. It was no good to make any plan; they could only trust that when the moment came, God would show them what to do. Presently the castle gates opened, and King Marc with the rest of his bodyguard came out. And at the same moment, down the woodland track behind Tristan and Gorvenal, came a small terrible company wearing the long hooded cloaks and carrying the wooden clappers that marked them for lepers.

Gorvenal drew aside, as all men did from such company, but Tristan knew that God was showing him the way, and stepped out into their path and spoke to the leader of the band. 'Where are you away to, friends?'

'To Tintagel, though with heavy hearts, to see them burn the Queen,' the man croaked.

'Would you save the Queen, if you could?'

'That would we – and doubly, if it were made worth our while.'

'Lend me your cloak and clapper, and there will be no burning in Tintagel today,' said Tristan; and to Gorvenal, 'Have you any money?' And he took the gold piece his friend brought from the breast of his tunic, and dropped it into the bandaged hand the leper held out for it.

The man took off his stinking rags, and Tristan flung them on, pulling the hood forward over his face. 'Bide here in hiding, while I go on with your companions.'

'I also,' Gorvenal said.

'No. If aught goes wrong, you must be still free, to get the Queen away.'

And he went on with the lepers, swinging his clapper and crying, 'Unclean! Unclean!'

When they reached the execution place, the Queen had been brought out, and was being bound to the stake, the King standing by with a frozen face to see it done.

'Come,' said Tristan, to the sad creatures behind him, and they went towards the King, all men falling back to let them pass. And kneeling before him, Tristan cried out, making his voice dry and cracked, 'Lord King, a boon!'

'This is a strange time to come asking a boon,' said the King in a voice of stone.

'Not so strange, for we ask that you give us the Queen to be of our company.'

A gasp ran through the crowd. 'If she is to die a shameful death, we can offer her one more shameful than the fire. Slower, but maybe uglier.'

And the lepers clamoured, 'Give her to us! Give! Give!'

And the King's stone face broke up in a sudden agony and he shouted to the executioners, 'Cut her loose and give her to these creatures!'

Iseult began to scream and scream, and when Tristan sprang on to the pyre to seize her, she fought him like a wild thing, while all the crowd shouted in angry protest; and then she heard his urgent whisper in her ear, 'Iseult, it is I. Do not betray me!'

She went on screaming, but she ceased to fight, as though accepting despair, and allowed herself to be dragged down from the pyre into the midst of the lepers, and away up the track towards the woods, while again the people parted to let them through.

When word of Tristan's escape was brought to the King, his wrath was terrible, and he sent out the hunt for him in all directions. They found the lepers, but the Queen was no longer with them and they told how a terrible warrior had torn her from their midst and made off with her across his saddlebow. And of Tristan and Iseult they found no sign. They and Gorvenal had vanished as completely as rags of morning mist when the sun rises.

They held eastward and eastward away from Tintagel towards the sunrise, and so came at last to a little lost valley through which a stream threaded down from the high moors, shaded over by hawthorn and elder, and the small thick-set oak trees of the ancient forest reached up towards it from below. And between the moors and the forest the stream broadened into a little pool where the wild things came to drink at dawn and sunset.

'Surely here we shall be safe,' said Tristan. 'We are full three days from Tintagel, and it is many years since the King hunted these hills.'

'The hunting will be good here,' said Gorvenal, 'and we must hunt if we are to live.'

And Iseult said, 'This is such a place as our valley in Wales. We shall be happy here – for a while.'

So they built a hut beside the stream, and Tristan and Gorvenal made themselves bows from forest yew, with strings braided from the red hairs Iseult plucked for them from her head, and went hunting when they needed food; while Iseult with her knowledge of herbs gathered plants and leaves and berries that were good to eat.

And they were happy – for a while.

It was young summer when they came to the hidden valley, and three times the bracken turned to russet, and three times winter came and they huddled about the fire, while Tristan woke the music of his harp and sang to them the haunting story-songs of Lothian and Ireland. Three times the hazel catkins danced in the March winds, and the hawthorn was curdled with white blossom, and the blossom fell.

And then one evening on the edge of another autumn, Tristan and Iseult sat before their hut at twilight. They were alone, for Gorvenal had gone off on one of his long solitary hunting trips. And suddenly Iseult drew close against Tristan, and said, 'Do you feel anything?'

'A little stirring of the wind,' said Tristan.

'No, not that.'

'A night moth brushed my cheek.'

'No, not that.'

'What, then, Iseult?'

'A shadow,' she said, 'there is a shadow fallen over us. Hold me close.'

Now that very day, far off in Tintagel, King Marc called for his horses and hounds to ride hunting next dawn. And he said to his Chief Huntsman, 'I am weary of the old hunting runs. Are there no hills in Cornwall where we have not hunted before?'

'There are the moors eastward beyond the Tamar River,' said the Chief Huntsman. 'It is many years since we hunted that way, so far afield.'

So the next day King Marc and his companions rode eastward – and three days later they set up their hunting camp below the high moors. They had good hunting, and killed three times, but when the hound pack was counted at evening, one of them was missing. It was a good hound, and the King's favourite, and the Chief Huntsman called out some of his men and set off at once to find it.

All night long they searched until, a while before dawn, he came to a stream threading down from the high moors; and among the stream-side hazels and elders he caught the glimmer of a fire. He hitched his horse's bridle over a low-hanging branch and turned upstream towards the light, meaning to ask whoever was up there if they had seen or heard a strayed hound.

He came to the last red embers of a fire and saw that it glowed before the doorway of a hut, and peering in, he saw a man and a woman asleep on the piled bracken of the bed-place. And the woman's outflung hair was flame red in the dying firelight, and the naked sword lying ready to the man's hand had a small piece broken out of the blade.

The Chief Huntsman turned away and went back to his horse and set out towards the hunting camp; and before he had gone three bowshots on his way, there was a rustling in the undergrowth and the lost hound came bounding out to follow at his horse's heels.

The camp was still asleep when he reached it, but he roused the King's squire, and went in to the King and told him what he had seen.

The King was silent a long moment when he had done; and then he said, 'Bid them fetch my horse, for I would see this man and this woman.'

So the King's horse was brought, and he and his huntsman set out. It was dawn when they came to the foot of the stream, and the King bade his huntsman wait with the horses, and went on alone up the stream side, his sword naked in his hand.

He came to the hut and looked in, and saw the two sleeping there in the grey dawn light. And he knew that he had only to step over the threshold and quickly use his sword, for they were completely at his mercy. He stood unmoving, looking in; and it seemed to him that he had never seen Iseult so beautiful, and his old love for her and for his kinsman knotted in his belly.

Then he stooped and took up Tristan's sword and laid his own in its place, and he stripped off one of his hunting gloves and laid it lightly on Iseult's breast; and he turned and went his way, sheathing the notched sword in place of his own.

When Tristan and Iseult awoke, they found the King's sword and his glove, and knew that they were discovered. And Iseult would have fled again, leaving a sign for Gorvenal to follow. But Tristan said, 'If we do that, now that he knows we are together, the King will surely hunt us down. And yet he found us here and could have slain us and did not.'

'What does it mean?' said Iseult.

And Tristan remembered how, on the day he brought Iseult to Tintagel, the King had taken her hands and said that they were cold but that his were large enough to warm them. And he said, 'For you, it means a way back, and forgiveness, Iseult.'

'And for you?'

'The sword for me – it means that I must put myself at the King's mercy.'

'And will there be mercy?'

'He would surely have slain me, else.'

'We have been happy here – for a while,' Iseult said.

And in a little, Gorvenal appeared, and flung down the buck that he had killed. And when Tristan told him what had happened, he too said that it was time to be returning to Tintagel.

So they went back.

'You read my message,' said the King, sitting in the High Seat in his Great Hall, when they stood before him.

'We read your message,' Tristan said, 'and we came.'

'That is well,' said King Marc. 'Listen now. I will take the Queen back into my Hall and into my heart. But to you, Tristan, I say that the world is wide. I give you three days to leave Cornwall behind you. *Never come back!*'

Tristan said, 'In three days I will be gone from Cornwall. But if ever hurt or sorrow comes to Iseult at your hands, and I hear of it, *I shall come back!*'

Then Iseult spoke for the first time. 'If I am to be your wife again, I must end what has been between my Lord Tristan and me, not leave it flying like a torn sleeve. Grant us a little time to take leave of each other.'

The King pointed to a log on the fire, already crumbling into white ash. 'I give you until that log burns through.' And he rose and went into an inner chamber. But they knew that from there he would hear when the log burned through and fell.

Then Iseult slipped from her finger a ring of heavy gold, curiously serpent-twined and twisted. 'If ever you are in sore enough need of me,' she said, 'send me back this ring, and I will come to you. But beware how you send it, for if you do, then I will surely come, though it be the death of both of us.'

And Tristan took the ring and kissed it, and pushed it on to his finger.

And the burning log collapsed with a slipping and rustling and a last shower of sparks into the red heart of the fire.

*   *   *

In the Great Hall at Camelot, also, a log slipped on the hearth and fell with a shower of red sparks. And the voice of the harper fell silent; and even the dark wing-beating of the storm died away.

The High King sat gazing into the fire. Sir Lancelot stared at his own bony hands clenched on his knees, while one tear trickled down unheeded beside his ugly nose.

'Is that the end of the story?' asked the Queen, pitifully.

'It seems so.'

'What became of Sir Tristan?'

'There was war in Lothian soon after, and his father was slain, and when he had driven out the enemy and avenged his father, he left Gorvenal to rule the kingdom. And now he wanders the world with his sword and his harp, and the heartspace empty within him, for Iseult's sake.' The harper moved to return his harp to its embroidered bag. And as he did so, the light jinked on the ring he wore; a heavy gold ring curiously twisted like a serpent.

'Thank you for your harp-tale,' said the King gently, 'and welcome to Camelot and to our fellowship, Sir Tristan.'

A murmuring ran round the Hall, and then Sir Bedivere cried, 'Look!' and pointed. And when they followed the direction of his outstretched finger, they saw on the back of one of the empty seats Sir Tristan's name glimmering in the torchlight in letters of new and burnished gold.

So Sir Tristan became one of the knights of Arthur's Round Table. And for a while he came every year to the gathering at Pentecost, and other knights would bring back stories of his deeds up and down Britain and in Less Britain across the Narrow Seas.

And then one year he did not come, and all the stories

ceased.

Nothing more was heard of Tristan, until one day Sir Lional, returning from a quest that had taken him into Cornwall and back to his native Benwick in Less Britain, said, blunt and heavy with sorrow, 'Sirs, I have seen Tristan's grave.'

All faces in the Hall turned to him. 'How did he die?' said the king. 'Is it known to you?'

Lional bent his head. 'I gathered the story, a little here and a little there. It seems that in his wanderings in Less Britain, he came to the castle of King Hoel, who was sore besieged by one Duke Jovelin, because he would not give him his daughter, against her will. Tristan aided the King and his son Karherdin against Duke Jovelin, and when they had the victory over him, the King offered his daughter to Tristan in gratitude. He could not shame her in her father's Hall, and they say she is very fair – she is an Iseult, too; Iseult of the White Hands, and – maybe he hoped for a little happiness . . .'

'So he married her?' said Guenever, half under her breath.

'He married her, and he was a true and loyal lord to her, though he could not love her as she loved him . . . The old King died, and Karherdin was the new King; and there was deep friendship between him and Tristan. And in the end – there was some feud; something to do with a maiden Karherdin loved and who had been torn away from him; and in the feuding Karherdin was killed, and fighting at his shoulder Tristan was sore wounded.

'And for all his wife's tending, and the physicians whom she summoned from far and wide, the wound sickened and he grew weaker day by day.

'He knew that his death was upon him, and that only one person in the world might save him. But whether she could heal him or no, he longed to see her face before he died. At last he sent for his squire and gave him Iseult's ring, and bade him go to the Queen of Cornwall in secret and show it to her, and beg her to come if she would save his life. "And when you return," said he, "if she be with you, cause your ship to show white sails; and if she will not come, then let the sails be black, for it will be time to put on mourning for me."

'So the squire went, disguised as a merchant, and gained speech with the Queen in private, and gave her the ring and Tristan's message, and she gathered up her salves and healing herbs and went with him without a backward glance.

'But the voyage was a slow one, for the ship was becalmed in the Narrow Seas; and all the while Tristan grew weaker, as the fever of the wound burned him up; and all that held him to life was his longing for Iseult and his waiting for the ship that would surely bring her to him.

'And Iseult of the White Hands had always known that his heart was left in Cornwall, and she saw when the ring was gone from his hand. And she heard his fevered mutterings while she tended him in the long nights, and so she knew of the ship, and the signal of the black or white sails. And jealousy tore at her, though she never let him see it, even when he begged her a score of times a day to look from the window and tell him if she saw a ship putting in from the sea.

'And then one morning as she looked from the chamber window, she did see a ship heading in for the harbour, and the sails of it as white as a swan's wings. She told Tristan what she saw, but when he asked her with seemingly the last breath that was in him as to the colour of the sails, for one fatal moment the bitter jealousy flared up in her, and she told him that they were black.

'So for Tristan there was nothing left to hold on to his life for, and he turned his face to the wall and let it go out of him on a great sigh.

'Then she cried out that they were white, white as swans' feathers, but she was too late.

'So the first thing that Iseult of Cornwall heard when she came to shore was the sound of bells tolling. And Tristan lay in the great church with candles burning at his head and feet; and the other Iseult standing beside his bier.

'When she came into the church and saw this, Iseult of Cornwall said, "Lady, stand further off from him, I pray you, for I loved him more than you." And she laid herself down on the bier beside him, and took him in her arms and kissed him. And they say that with the kiss her heart broke.

'When word of all this was brought to King Marc, he took ship for Less Britain, and brought their bodies back to Cornwall. They say he spoke no word of grief or forgiveness, but he had them laid together in one grave.

'And when I stood beside it, a hazel sapling had begun to grow from Tristan's side of the grave, and from Iseult's honeysuckle, and they were already reaching out to intertwine with each other.'

'And that truly is the end of the story,' said Queen Guenever, very softly.

11

GERAINT AND ENID

And the years went by and the years went by, and every
Pentecost the High King's knights, new-made or old,
gathered still to Camelot, where the Round Table stood
in the Great Hall. But at other times of year, Arthur
would hold his court in other parts of his realm, at
Carlisle or London or Caerleon, that he might keep
close touch with all parts of the kingdom.

One Easter he held his court at Caerleon, and on
Easter Day as he and the knights who were with him
were sitting down to dinner, there strode into the Hall a
tall young man who carried his red-gold head as high as
though it were a torch; and he was clad in silk, with fine
dyed leather boots upon his feet, and a gold-hilted

sword hanging at his side. He strode up the length of the Hall to kneel at the King's feet, but still without lowering his head, and said, 'Greetings, my Lord King.'

'Greetings to you also, and God's welcome,' said the King. 'I seem to know your face, and yet I do not know your name.'

'I am Geraint, son of Erbin whose borders march with King Marc of Cornwall. You saw me once when I was a child and my father fought in your wars.'

'And what brings you to me now, Geraint, son of Erbin?'

'I have been biding this while past in the Forest of Dean,' said the young man, 'and this morning in the forest ways I saw a stag such as I never saw before, pure white, and proud-going above any other stag in the forest. Therefore I marked where the beast harboured, and came swiftly to bring you tidings of it.'

'That was well done,' said the King. 'Tomorrow at the young of the day, we will go and hunt this wondrous stag.' And he sent orders to the huntsmen and grooms.

And the Queen said, 'My lord, give me leave tomorrow to ride out to watch this hunting.'

'Gladly I give you leave,' said Arthur, 'and any of your maidens who care to ride with you.'

So the matter was agreed, and the feasting went forward with harp-song and merriment, until it was time to sleep.

But when morning came and the hounds were brought round from their kennels, there was no sign of Geraint, and Guenever lay sleeping late in her bed. 'Let them sleep,' said the King. 'They may follow when they wake, if they are so minded.'

And with Kay and Gawain and others of his knights for hunting companions, he mounted and rode away into the forest in search of the white stag.

Soon after, Queen Guenever awoke. She called to her maidens, and while some of them helped her to dress, she sent a page to the stables to see what horses were left that were suitable for ladies to ride. But the hunting party had taken all the palfreys save for the Queen's own mare and one other. So the Queen, half laughing and half out of humour, chose one of her maidens, and said, 'What selfish creatures are men! You and I will ride after them together.'

So the horses were brought, and the Queen and her maiden rode away, out through the castle gate, and following the broad trail of men and hounds and horses, towards the forest. And presently as they rode, they heard the sound of horses' hooves coming hard behind them, and as they looked round, Geraint ranged up beside them riding a tall willow-grey horse. He was clad as he had been last night, in a damasked silken tunic, and a cloak of blue-purple worked with gold apples at the corners, that blew out behind him on the wind of his going.

'God's greeting to you, lady,' he said, 'I slept late, and so missed the hunting party.'

'I also,' said the Queen, 'but it will not be long before we find them – for if we take our stand up yonder on the ridge, we shall hear the horns when they sound, and the music of the hounds.'

So together they crested the ridge, and found open country beyond. They checked on the woodshore to listen for sounds of the hunt. And while they waited, they heard hoofbeats again, and three riders came by along the track below them.

And first there came a dwarf riding a tall prancing horse and carrying a long wicked looking whip in his hand. And then there came a lady clad all in blue and golden silk, and mounted on a fine cream-coloured palfrey of proud and even pace; and behind her came a

213

tall knight, fully armed and riding a big roan warhorse.

'Geraint,' said the Queen, 'do you know who that knight may be?'

'Not I,' said Geraint, 'for he rides with his vizor closed, and the badge on his shield is strange to me.'

'Angharad,' said the Queen to her maiden. 'Do you go down and ask of the dwarf who his master may be.'

So the maiden rode down to meet the dwarf, and asked him in all courtesy the name of the stranger knight.

'I will not tell you,' said the dwarf.

'Then I will ask him myself; maybe his manners are better than yours.'

'That you will not, by my faith!' said the dwarf.

'And why?' said the maiden.

'Because you are not worthy to speak with such as my master.'

But none the less, she turned her horse's head towards the knight; and at that, the dwarf struck her savagely across the face with his whip, so that the bright blood sprang out.

Sobbing, the maiden returned to Queen Guenever and told her what had passed.

'That dwarf shall tell *me* who his master is,' said Geraint, firing up on the maiden's behalf, and he touched spur to his horse's flank, and went full tilt down the grass slope to the dwarf, and demanded the name of the knight who rode behind him.

'I will not tell you,' said the dwarf, and made to ride by.

'Then I will ask it of your lord himself.'

'That you shall not,' said the dwarf.

'And wherefore shall I not?' demanded Geraint.

'Because you are not worthy to speak with such as my lord!'

'I have spoken with greater men than your lord,' said

Geraint, wrenching his horse round and heading towards the knight.

But the dwarf also flung round and came after him with a shrill cry; and the long whiplash cracked across his face, drawing blood as it had done from the maiden's.

Geraint's temper was as swift to flare even as Gawain's, and his hand flew to his golden sword-hilt. But there remained a cool grain of common sense in him; and he thought, It will be but a poor vengeance if I slay this atomy, and then, being without armour, am slain myself by his knight.

And he rode back to Queen Guenever.

'Lady, with your leave, I will ride after that knight until we come to some place where I can borrow armour and a spear. He *shall* tell me who he is, and make amends for the insult done to you and your maiden.'

'Go,' said the Queen, 'but I shall be sorely anxious until I have tidings of you.'

'If I live,' said Geraint, 'tidings you shall have within two days.'

So Geraint followed the dwarf and the knight and the lady; all day, through steep valleys and over high moors, and along woodshores where the wild cherry trees were in Easter bloom, until towards evening they came to a walled town by a river, and in the heart of the town stood a strong and proud fortress. And as they rode through the narrow streets towards the fortress, the people came thronging to greet them; and it seemed that in every house and courtyard were men and horses, shields being polished and armour furbished and horses shod. And everywhere it seemed to Geraint that amid all the uproar he heard men exclaiming to each other over and over again, 'The sparrowhawk! The sparrowhawk!' And when they came to the castle, the gates were open wide; and the dwarf and the knight and the lady rode in.

But there was no friendly face turned towards Geraint, no one that he knew in all the town, and despite all the armour that he saw, he found no likely place to borrow any. And so, with the day already thickening to dusk, he came to the far side of the town. And there across the open meadow land, almost where the forest closed in again, he saw an ancient manor house, half in ruins, with the long-stranded ivy clothing roofless towers; and only one part of the building that seemed to be weatherproof and still lived in, for a gleam of light shone from it. And as he drew near, thinking that here at least was none of the bustle of the town, and maybe he would find someone to advise him where he could borrow armour and a spear, he saw an old man, grey haired and clad in garments that were faded and tattered but must once have been as rich as his own, sitting at the foot of a broken marble staircase that led to the upper chamber.

Geraint reined in his horse, and sat for a few moments looking down at him; and then the old man looked up and smiled. 'You seem heavily thoughtful, young sir?'

'I am thoughtful.' Geraint returned the smile. 'Because I am a stranger here, and do not know where to go this night; and yours is the first kind look that has come my way since I entered the town.'

'Come in with me, and you shall have the best that I can offer – both you and your horse.'

'God be good to you for your kindness,' Geraint said, and slid wearily from the saddle and, leading his horse, followed where the old man led, first into the half-ruined Hall, and then, leaving his horse there, up the stairway to the chamber from which the light shone.

The chamber must once have been fair, but now, in the light of the fire on the hearth and a few tallow dips, it showed shabby and smoke-darkened, with damp patches on the once gaily painted walls. And beside the fire, in a tall upright chair, sat an old gentlewoman in the threadbare remains of a silk gown that had once, like the old man's, been fine. And looking at her, Geraint thought that when she was young and before sorrow touched her, she must have been as fair as a wayside rose. And beside her on a cushion on the floor sat a maiden in an old tattered smock and mantle; and it seemed to Geraint, looking at her face in the firelight between the soft curtains of her hair, that she was fairer even than the old gentlewoman must have been.

'Daughter,' said the grey-haired man, 'there is no squire but you to tend upon this stranger whom I have brought home, and no other groom to see to his horse.'

'The best tending that I can,' said the maiden, rising, 'I will give to him and to his horse.'

And when Geraint sat down where she bade him on a bench beside the table, she pulled off his boots of fine leather. And then she went down to the Hall to water the horse and give him straw and a measure of corn. Then she returned and set the table for a meal, and put before them boiled meat and plain dark bread, with a little white manchet loaf that Geraint guessed was in his honour, and a flask of thin wine.

And as they ate, the maiden waiting upon them, Geraint asked the old man with all courtesy how he and his ladies came to be living in that half-ruined place with no one to tend upon them. 'Surely,' said he, 'it has not always been so?'

'Indeed no,' replied his host, 'once I owned the town and the castle yonder, and a great dukedom beside.'

'And how in God's name did you come to lose it?'

'Through pride of heart,' said the old man. 'I have a nephew, my brother's son, whose dukedom I held with my own while he was a child. But when he came to strength and manhood and laid claim to his own dukedom, I would not believe him yet ready for so great a charge, and refused him. Then he made war on me, and indeed he proved himself the stronger of us two, and seized not only his own dukedom but mine as well, leaving me nothing but this half-ruined house in which to shelter my wife and my daughter who was then but a child.'

'That is a grievous story,' said Geraint, 'and sorry I am to hear it. But now, pray you tell me the meaning of the great uproar and ready-making of arms in the town as I rode through, and the coming of the knight and the lady and the dwarf, who rode into the castle and were made gladly welcome?'

'The ready-making was for a great joust to be held tomorrow. Every year on the second day after Easter, the young duke my nephew sets up a silver rod between two hazel forks in the meadow below the town, and a fine sparrowhawk fastened to the rod by its jesses, and from all parts, knights flock in to joust for the sparrowhawk, that the victor may give to the lady he loves best. The knight you speak of has won the sparrowhawk for two years, and if he wins it this year also, then he will gain great honour, and be called the Knight of the Sparrowhawk henceforth.'

'Then I would fain joust with him, if I had the armour and spears – indeed it was for that purpose that I followed him here, before ever I heard of the sparrowhawk,' said Geraint, touching his gashed cheek. And he told his host, Duke Ynwl, of the injury done to the Queen and her maiden, and to himself.

'My own armour you should have most willingly,' said the old Duke, shaking his head. 'It is old-fashioned now, and battered, and maybe rusty, for it is long since I had the heart to look at it; but before age and sorrow bowed me, I was about your size. But alas! That will not help us, for you have no maiden with you, and you will not be admitted to the lists unless your lady-love ride with you, and you proclaim her the fairest lady in the world, and do battle in her name.'

Geraint was silent a moment; and then he looked up and saw the maiden Enid in her shabby gown in the firelight, and he said, 'Sir, if it pleases her, will you give me leave that your daughter ride with me tomorrow? If I come out of the jousting alive, then my love and loyalty shall be to her as long as I live; and if I come not out alive, then she will be in no worse case than she was before.'

'Enid?' said the Duke.

And the old Duchess looked at her daughter with a small questioning smile.

And the Lady Enid blushed as pink as a foxglove, and said speaking to Geraint directly, for the first time, 'Gladly will I come with you tomorrow.'

So the old Duke brought his armour from the worm-eaten chest where it was kept; and before they slept, he and his daughter and Geraint burnished off the worst of the rust and replaced here and there a worn strap. And Geraint thought that indeed if she had not been a maiden, Enid would have made a good squire to some knight; and when their hands met on the battered armour, they glanced up and smiled at each other.

Next morning they rose early, and with the help of the old Duke, Geraint put on the armour while the maiden groomed his horse and the aged palfrey that was the only mount they possessed. And while the shadows were still long, they came to the broad meadow below the castle, which was already crowded with knights and their ladies, and pages walking tall warhorses up and down; and the silk-hung stands below the castle walls were filled with onlookers; and at the far end of the meadow the sparrowhawk already sat with her leash made fast to the silver rod between the hazel forks.

Trumpets sounded golden upon the morning air, and

the tall knight on the roan horse whom Geraint had followed yesterday came forward to where his lady sat beneath a silken canopy, and cried in a great voice for all to hear, 'Lady, will you come with me and take the sparrowhawk which awaits you, for it is yours by right of your beauty which outshines the beauty of all other ladies. If any knight shall say you nay, then let him do battle with me!'

'Wait!' Geraint shouted, taking up the challenge. 'Do not touch the sparrowhawk, for my lady here with me is yet more fair than yours, and in her name I lay claim to it!'

Then the knight laughed. 'You? Some country churl who has found a suit of battered armour in a ditch? Come then and we will do battle for it, if you wish to have your head broken!'

Then the two drew apart to the furthest ends of the meadow, and wheeled their horses and came thundering down upon each other so strongly and truly that at their meeting both spears were shattered. Then the dwarf brought another spear for his knight, and the old Duke another for Geraint; and they came together again, and again their spears broke, and a third time yet again. But for the fourth encounter, the old Duke came to Geraint with a spear that was not new as the others had been, but old and battered and stained, and said, 'Sir, this spear was put into my hand on the day that I was made knight, and it has never yet failed me in a joust.'

Geraint thanked him, and set the spear in rest; and a fourth time they thundered together from the far ends of the meadow; and this time, though his antagonist's spear shattered as the others had done, the ancient spear in Geraint's hand took him in mid-shield so strongly that his girths broke and he and his saddle together flew over his horse's crupper to the ground.

Geraint too flung himself from his horse, and as the other scrambled to his feet, he drew his golden-hilted sword and was upon him. So they fought up and down the meadow, blade against blade, until their armour was hacked and hanging loose, and the blood and sweat ran from them, and the light began to fade from their eyes. And at last it seemed that the defender of the sparrow-hawk was gaining on Geraint, and the old Duke cried to him, 'Remember the insults done to you and to Queen Guenever!'

And the red flame of his rage sprang up bright and fierce again and the darkness fell from his eyes, and summoning up the last of his strength, he swung up his sword and brought it crashing down upon the other's head in a blow that cut through crest and helm, and mail coif and flesh, and bit to the very bone.

The knight crashed to the ground, his sword spinning from his hand; and there on his knees he cried quarter, and asked mercy of Geraint.

'Mercy you shall have,' said Geraint, standing over him, 'on this condition, that you go to Guenever the Queen, and make amends to her for the injury done to her maiden by your dwarf; and tell her that Geraint, son of Erbin, sent you. For the injury done to myself – ' he smiled grimly inside his battered helmet – 'I have taken enough payment. Yet I demand one thing more, that now you tell me your name, which at the first I asked in all courtesy.'

'I will go to the Queen as you bid me,' groaned the knight. 'And as for my name, Geraint, son of Erbin, I am Edern, son of Nudd.'

Then came squires to help him away to have his wounds tended; and after, he was put back upon his horse, and drooping in his saddle, with his dwarf and his lady, he set out for Caerleon.

Meanwhile, Geraint said to the maiden Enid, 'Go

now and take up the sparrowhawk on its silver rod, for it is rightfully yours.'

Then came the young Duke with his people, and greeted Geraint and bade him to come back with him to the castle. 'My thanks to you,' said Geraint, 'but where I spent last night, there will I spend this night also.'

'That must be as you wish; but at least you shall have more comfort there than you had last night, and my uncle and his ladies also.'

And when Geraint with the old Duke Ynwl and his wife and daughter came again to the ancient manor house, they found the young Duke's servants had come there before them by a shorter way and were making ready the living chamber as though for a feast, and water was heating on a blazing fire for Geraint to wash off the blood and sweat of his fighting.

And when he came from his bath, the young Duke was there with his household knights and guests from the jousting for the sparrowhawk. And the old Duke in a new furred gown was looking about him as one in a dream, at the fine food and drink upon the table and the fresh water-mint strewn upon the floor, and the rich stuffs being spread over the poor furniture, and everywhere the glint of gold that had been his long ago. But of the old Duchess and the maiden Enid there was no sign, and when he asked where they were, the chamberlain told him, 'They are in the upper chamber, putting on the new gowns that the Duke has brought for them.'

And Geraint said, 'Pray you send and ask the maiden to wear her old gown until she comes to Arthur's court, that the Queen may dress her in gowns of her choosing.'

So Enid came down to the great chamber in her old threadbare gown; but in that, she looked as fair to Geraint as the other ladies in their brilliant silks and damasks.

They all sat down to supper. And over the table that

night, peace was made between the old Duke and the young Duke; and the young Duke restored to the old one all the lands and riches that were his aforetime.

And next day the Lady Enid bade goodbye to her father and her mother; and still in her threadbare gown, but riding a sweet-paced bay palfrey which the young Duke had had brought for her from his own stables, and carrying the sparrowhawk on her gloved fist, she rode out with Geraint upon the long road back to Caerleon.

Meanwhile, the King and his knights had had good hunting and slain the white stag; and on the morrow, the Queen had look-outs set on the ramparts to watch for Geraint's return. Some while after noon they saw coming across the bridge of Usk a dwarf on a tall horse, and behind him a maiden on a palfrey, and last of all a knight in hacked and battered armour, who sat slumped in the saddle of his warhorse with his head hanging down between his shoulders.

And one of the watchers went and told Guenever what he had seen; a dwarf and a lady and a sorry and battered knight. 'But I know not who they may be.'

'But I know,' said the Queen. 'Bring the knight and the lady to me when they have entered the gate.'

So Edern the son of Nudd and his lady-love were brought to the Queen in the Great Chamber. And kneeling at her feet, Edern told her all that had passed. And how Geraint had overcome him and sent him to her to make amends for the injury done to her and her maiden; and he humbly asked her pardon.

And the Queen granted it, and ordered that he be taken to the chief guest-chamber, and Morgan Tudd who was Arthur's own physician summoned to tend his many hurts. And she greeted his lady kindly, and gave her into the keeping of her maidens.

And she bade the look-outs on the ramparts continue their watch for Geraint.

On the edge of dusk, Geraint came riding, and the Lady Enid with him in her threadbare gown, drooping a little with weariness, but the sparrowhawk still on her fist.

And when word of this was brought to the Queen, she gathered all her maidens and went to greet them in the inner courtyard. 'Now welcome and God's greeting to you,' she said, 'and to the maiden who rides with you, for whom you won the sparrowhawk.'

And by her knowing so much of the story, Geraint knew that Edern, son of Nudd, must have kept his promise and reached Caerleon ahead of him. And he dismounted and lifted the maiden down, and while squires took their horses and the sparrowhawk, he took her by the hand and led her to the Queen; and as she sank low before the Queen, Guenever stooped and took her in her arms.

'Lady,' said Geraint, 'I have kept my promise, and the name of the knight is Edern, son of Nudd; but I am thinking that you know that already.'

'Surely,' said the Queen, 'for not many hours since, he rode in, asking my pardon and saying that you had sent him to make amends for the injury his dwarf did my maiden. And he told us all the story of the jousting for the sparrowhawk, so far as he knew it.'

'Is it well with him? He was a good fighter,' said Geraint.

And the Queen smiled. 'As well as may be. He is in the guest chamber while the many wounds you gave him are tended to; and his lady is with him now.'

Then came Arthur with his knights; and Geraint presented the maiden Enid to him, and told the rest of the story, and asked the King's leave that they should be married the next day.

'Assuredly you have my leave,' said the King, 'and seldom saw I a fairer maiden than this duke's daughter, even though she is so poorly clad.'

But the Queen said, 'I am thinking that my Lord Geraint brought her to me in her old gown, that I might have the joy of finding her gowns from among my own, that are more fitting to her beauty.'

And she swept Enid away with her to her own apartments, while Geraint went with the King and his knights to the feasting in the Great Hall. And that evening it was decided that the head of the white stag should be awarded as a bride-piece to Geraint's lady.

Next day, in a gown of golden damask, Enid went to the castle chapel, and there the High King himself gave her hand into Geraint's before the high altar, and so they were wed. And after the marriage there were three days of rejoicing; jousting and hunting by day, and feasting with harpsong and dancing in the Great Hall by night.

But on the fourth morning Geraint went to the King and said, 'My Lord Arthur, now it is time that I was away into Cornwall, to my own place, to bring my Lady Enid before my father, that the sight of her may gladden his autumn days.'

Then the King was sad, and the Queen and her maidens grieved for the loss of the Lady Enid, for in those three days her sweetness and gentleness had made her dear to all of them. But they knew that it was right that Geraint should take her back to his own people and his own place.

So all things were made ready, and the next morning after they had heard Mass, they rode out, with a knot of the King's best knights headed by Sir Lancelot and Sir Gawain to company them on their way. They crossed the Severn by the flat-bottomed barges that always lay there ready to ferry travellers and their horses to the other side, and they turned their horses' heads towards Upper Cornwall, and rode until in two more days they came to the castle of Erbin, Geraint's father.

The old lord greeted his son and his wife with great joy; and for three days there was hunting and hawking and jousting by day, and feasting and harping in the Great Hall at night, just as there had been at Caerleon; and then Arthur's knights took their leave and went back to their own lord.

And Geraint set himself to strengthen his borders, which his father, being old, had allowed to grow weak, and set to rights all things that were in need of it, and help his father in the ruling of his domain. And when ever and where ever there was a tournament or jousting or other such trials of skill, there he would be, eager to pit himself against the best knights that could come against him. But the time came when the borders were strong and secure and all was well with his father's lands and people, and he had overcome all the knights who came against him in joust or tournament, so that there seemed nothing to fight for and no one to try his skill against any more. And he began more and more to forsake his old companions and pass his time in his own apartments or in the castle gardens, with Enid, for being with the Lady Enid was the one thing that he never grew weary of.

So he began to lose his people's hearts, and there was a murmuring among his household knights, some saying that Enid had bewitched him, and others that he was no true son of his father after all. And the murmuring came to the ears of the old Lord Erbin, and he sent for Enid to his own chamber and told her of it, and asked her was it by her wish and her doing that Geraint had forsaken his heart-companions and a man's proper way of life, to spend all his time with her.

Grief and shock struck through Enid when she heard this, and she gripped her hands together and raised her face to the old man's, and said, 'Truly, my lord, I am to blame in this, for I have thought only that it was sweet to have your son by me, when I should have found means to send him from my side. I had not thought that he was forsaking his companions and his courage and his proper way of life for love of me. But I swear that never I asked this of him; and it is hateful to me that it should be so, for I would have him the valiant knight I loved and left my home and kin for.'

'Then tell him so,' said the old lord, gently.

But though she tried and tried again, Enid could not tell him so; she could not give him the wound that she knew it would be to him. And she was afraid of him too, a little; afraid of his fiery temper that was hotter even than Gawain's.

And then one summer morning, lying wakeful as she had lain all night, she looked at Geraint lying asleep beside her, the first sunlight lying across his breast, where he had pushed the coverings down; and she raised herself on her arm to look the better, and saw his sleeping face among the tangle of bright hair, and the way his breast rose and fell, and the way, even in his sleep, he had reached out towards her. And suddenly all her love for him seemed to rise into her throat and choke her, and she began to weep.

'Alas and alas!' she whispered. 'If through me you have lost your valour and your strength as men say! Alas and alas that you are no more the knight that first I loved! An ill day for both of us, when I consented to wed with you!'

And her tears fell on Geraint's bare chest and roused him, so that he heard what she said, confusedly between sleeping and waking, and thought both that she accused him of having lost his knightly valour and that she wept for love of some other knight who she would have wed. And he sprang from the bed, blinded by rage and grief, and flung her aside when she would have clung to him, and shouted for his squire to bring him his armour and have his warhorse saddled and made ready.

Then looking down at Enid still crouching where he had flung her to the ground at his feet, he said, 'Lady, have your mare saddled also, for we are going riding. And we shall not return until you have come to know whether or not I have altogether lost my knighthood. Until also, you have decided whether I am not so well worth loving as him you were weeping for just now.'

And he would pay no heed to her weeping nor her protests that she loved no other man. And he strode off to seek his father and tell him that he was setting out upon a quest.

'So suddenly?' said the old lord. 'And who rides with you?'

'Enid my wife,' said Geraint, harsh in his throat, and strode out with no other word, back to the place where his squire waited for him with his armour.

Meanwhile Enid, not summoning any of her maidens for she could not bear anyone with her in her grief and bewilderment, had gone to the small chamber where her clothes-chest was kept. And first she thought, I will put on my finest gown and my golden bracelets for my pride's sake. But then she drew out the old threadbare smock, carefully treasured, and she thought, If he sees me in this gown, maybe he will remember how he first saw and loved me, and how I left my home and parents in it for his sake, and his heart will gentle and turn to me again.

And she put on the shabby gown and went down into the courtyard.

But when Geraint had been armed by his squire, and came down and found her waiting with her mare at a little distance from his own great warhorse, the face he turned to her was as though it had been carved from stone.

'Mount,' he said, 'take the road that leads uphill, from the tower gate, and ride ahead of me – *well* ahead of me. And do not turn back for anything that you see or hear.'

And when she would have spoken one last plea, he cut her short, 'And speak no word to me unless I speak first to you.'

So Enid mounted and rode sadly out through the gate and turned into the track that led northward up on to the high moors.

Presently the road dipped towards a valley choked with forest, and as they came towards the woodshore, Enid saw two armed men sitting their horses in the shadow of the trees, hedge-knights who lived by robbery. And one said to the other, 'Now here comes a fine chance for us! Two horses and a maiden, aye, and a fine suit of armour off that knight who rides with his head so sunk on his breast; for I am thinking that he will not be one to hold his own against us!'

And hearing, Enid thought, He bade me not to turn, nor speak with him; but I must warn him of this! And she turned her horse and rode swiftly back to Geraint and told him what she had heard.

But Geraint only said, 'No need that you come back to me with such warnings, when I know that in your heart you would gladly see me dead at the hands of these men. Only one thing I require of you – that you obey me and keep silent!'

And at that moment the foremost of the hedge-knights came charging towards him. But Geraint wrenched his horse aside at the last instant, so that the other's spear-point passed him by, then turned and with his own spear laid crosswise swept him from the saddle, so that he crashed to the ground head down with his neck broken under him. Then charging to meet the second, he ran him through the throat-mail with his point, and hurled him to the ground as dead as his comrade.

Then Geraint dismounted and stripped the knights of their armour and bound it upon their horses' backs, and knotted up the reins. Then he remounted, saying to Enid, who had sat her mare looking silently on the while, 'Now ride ahead of me once more, driving these horses ahead of you. And whatever you hear or see, do not turn back or speak to me unbidden, for I vow before God that you shall be sorry if you do!'

And the Lady Enid did as she was bid.

Presently they left the forest country, and the road that they followed led out across bleak and open moors. And as they rode, Enid saw, small in the distance, three knights riding towards them through the heather and low thorn-scrub; and the wind was blowing from them towards her, and brought her the words of the foremost rider as they drew near. 'Now this is our well-starred day! Four horses and three suits of armour – and the woman too, for it's little that lack-lustre knight will be able to do against us!'

Then Enid thought, He bade me not to speak to him; but if I do not, it may be his death, and I had rather that it was mine. And again she rode back to Geraint and warned him of what she had heard.

'Truly your warning means less to me than your disobedience to my orders!' said Geraint.

And in the same moment the first of the three hedge-knights came clattering down upon Geraint with levelled spear, but he swung his horse aside so that the spearpoint only glanced off the rim of his shield while his own drove true to its target and flung the man back over his horse's crupper, dead before he hit the ground; and in the same way Geraint served the second man and the third. Then he dismounted and, stripping the dead men of their armour, bound it across their horses' backs, and knotted up the reins, and gave them into Enid's keeping with the same grim orders as before. 'Now ride ahead of me, driving these five horses, and do not again disobey me, for I think that I shall kill you if you do.'

So they rode on, the land growing rough and thickety about them, and it grew more and more difficult for Enid to drive the five horses before her, but she held on, making no complaint. And Geraint saw the trouble she had, and his heart stirred within him for her sake, but he would not listen to the stirring of it, only rode on with his head on his breast.

And presently as they went, Enid became aware of four hedge-knights skulking on the tangled fringes of a blackthorn thicket. And as they drew near, one of them shouted with laughter, and cried out to the rest, 'Now here is a fine chance come our way! Horses and armour – aye, and a maiden, too, and seemingly the knight who rides behind so spent with capturing them all that he'll have little more fight left in him for keeping them!'

And a great cold and a great fear came upon Enid when she heard the words, and she thought, If I disobey him again, my lord will surely kill me. And then she thought, But if I do not warn him assuredly he must be killed. And she turned as best she could with her five driven horses, and rode back to Geraint and told him what she had heard.

'Is there nothing I can say that will make you obey me?' said Geraint. 'I see these men, and their purpose is plain, and I do not fear them.'

And this time he did not wait for them to attack but struck heel to his horse's flank and spurred towards them, his spear in rest; and the foremost of them he took in mid-shield, flinging him from the saddle, and the second in the breast, piercing his armour and driving to the heart. And the third he took in the throat, breaking his neck before ever he touched the ground, and the fourth, by way of an ending flourish, he took by the hardest stroke of all, the crest stroke that tore his helmet from his head and broke his neck in the doing of it.

Then he dismounted, and disarmed the fallen knights and bound their armour upon their horses' backs, and again he handed the horses over to Enid and bade her drive them ahead of her as before.

Night came upon them while they were in forest country, and at last Geraint spoke to Enid of his own accord. 'Turn aside under the trees; it grows too dark for safe riding, and in the morning we will be on our way again.'

'Whatever you will,' said Enid, and they headed in among the trees, where as they went deeper it was already night. Then Geraint dismounted and lifted Enid from the saddle; but there was no gentleness in his hands as he set her down, and none in his voice. 'Here is a wallet with food in it. Eat, and watch the horses, and take care that you do not sleep lest any of them stray.'

And he stretched himself out with his head on his shield to sleep, while Enid, the food wallet untouched beside her, sat watching, and the moon rose and shone silver all about her, and the night sounds of the forest woke and an owl swooped by on furred wings, and somewhere a vixen cried to her mate, and something rustled in the undergrowth. And Geraint lay still, but slept no more than his lady whom he had left on watch. And as the horses stirred, Geraint's helm clanked softly where it hung from his saddlebow.

And the moon-watered darkness warmed to the summer dawn, and the ferns and foxgloves grew out of the shadows and somewhere a crack-voiced cuckoo called.

And Geraint shifted, cramped in his armour; and

speaking no word of greeting to Enid, he set her on her mare again, and said, 'Take the horses and ride on ahead as you did yesterday.'

That day they rode through gentler country, and from time to time passed by meadows where long lines of men with scythes were getting in the hay. And they met with no more adventures. But towards evening they came to a town of many thatched roofs and the slender spire like an iris bud of a church, and at the end of the town a strong castle that looked as though it had grown from the ground on which it stood. And at the castle gate Geraint asked for lodging for the night.

The porter passed them through into the courtyard, looking somewhat aside at the damosel in the thread-bare gown driving nine horses before her, and the knight who rode like a thunder-cloud behind.

And then, while squires and pages came to help them dismount and take the horses, the Earl of the castle and the town came out from his Great Hall to bid them welcome.

Presently they sat down to eat, and at table Geraint and Enid were set close to each other, but as soon as the meal was over and the Earl's household broke up and began to move and mingle about their evening pastimes, the two shifted far apart. First the Earl spoke with Geraint, asking him the purpose of his journey.

'No purpose save to look for adventure and follow any quest that pleases me,' said Geraint, looking down at his hands that hung lax across his knees. And his face was the face of a man who would find little joy in any quest that came his way. And as he talked with Geraint, the Earl looked across the Hall to where Enid sat sadly by herself with her face turned to the fire, and it seemed to him that she was the fairest maiden that ever he had seen. And presently he said, 'Sir, have I your leave to go and speak with yonder maiden who sits sad and alone?'

'If you wish. It is nothing to me,' said Geraint, not looking up from his hands.

So the Earl went, and drew up a cushioned stool, and with a 'By your leave,' sat him down beside Enid. 'Sweet Lady,' he said, speaking to her gently as though she were a falcon that he did not wish to startle into bating from his fist, 'forgive me – I am thinking that you have little pleasure in following yonder knight.'

'His journey is my journey,' said Enid.

'With neither servants nor maidens to accompany you?'

'It is pleasanter to me to ride with my lord than to have servants and maidens.'

'Yet he must be a churl to treat you so,' said the Earl. 'I would not treat you in such a way, if you were to remain with me.'

Enid looked at him as though she were not sure she had truly heard his words. And when she saw that she had, she said simply, 'My troth is pledged to that man, and I have no thought to break faith with him.'

'Think again,' said the Earl. 'If I slay yonder man, I can keep you for myself as long as I will, and when I weary of you I shall turn you away. But if you come to me of your own free will, you shall be my wife and the lady of all my lands, and I will keep faith with you and love you as long as I live.'

Then Enid was silent a long while, her mind scurrying this way and that as she thought what she must do. And it seemed to her that the best thing would be to pretend to come to the Earl's way of thinking. So she said, speaking quick and low, 'Then this must be the way of it. Tomorrow I must ride on with that knight as before, but in a little I shall contrive it so that it seems I am lost; and do you and a few of your men follow quickly to take me while I am parted from my lord, and bring me back here before he can seize me again. Then I shall be yours, and he will never know that it was by my own will.'

And with that, the Earl was satisfied.

So the next day they set out as before, Enid riding ahead and driving the nine captured horses. But as soon as they were well clear of the town and its castle she drew to the side of the road, and waited for Geraint to come up with her. And at first, when he saw her do so, Geraint made to rein back; but in the end, though darkly as ever, he rode on until he came up with her, and she heeled her mare round and rode beside him.

And as she rode, she told him all that had passed between her and the Earl on the night before. 'At any moment he will be after us, and I fear with more armed men than even you can withstand. Therefore, my dear lord, let us turn these captured horses loose, and take to the forest, where we may escape from him.'

And this time, though still with a brooding face, Geraint heard her out, and when she had finished, he spoke less harshly to her than he had done during the two days of their journey. 'Now despite all my orders it seems that you are determined to save my life. But I will not run like a coursed hare from the hounds. If they come after us, here will I wait their coming – but do you make for the forest, and if I should be overcome, get you back to Arthur's court, for you will be safe there.'

'I have disobeyed you often enough to disobey you once more!' said Enid with a sudden flash of spirit that made him look at her for the first time in those two days. And as he looked, he saw her eyes go past him down the road that they had come; and looking the same way, he saw in the distance a rising dust-cloud turned to gold by the morning sun. And as the cloud rolled nearer he could make out at the base of it the forefront of many horsemen coming at full gallop, the sun glinting on crests and spearpoints.

'Give me the horses,' he said, 'and do you at least draw aside from the road to give me fighting room.' And he pulled down his vizor.

'You cannot! Even you, my lord. There must be four score of them and you are but one!' cried Enid.

'Do as I say,' ordered Geraint, hollow behind his vizor. 'There are ways to even the odds a little.'

'What are you going to do?'

'An unknightly thing. Now, into the trees with you!' And Enid did as he bade her.

Geraint remained waiting in the midst of the road, looking towards the nearing dust-cloud out of which began to sound the drum of many hooves. And at the right moment he loosed the captured horses, slashing his spear butt across the rumps of the hindmost so that they sprang forward snorting from the blows and sweeping the rest in panic along with them, so that all nine went bucketing along the road, the armour clattering and ringing on their backs, towards the on-coming knights.

The Earl and his companions cursed and strove to pull their steeds aside, and then the runaways were in their midst, spreading confusion on all sides.

And while his pursuers fought cursing with their startled mounts and all was a snorting and clashing turmoil, Geraint set his spear in rest and charged down upon them. He crashed into their midst and had picked the first man from the saddle on his spearpoint before they knew what was upon them; then reversing his spear, swept three more from their saddles with a broad-side blow before their own points were ready for him. Then as his spear broke in his hand he flung the splintered butt away and drew his sword.

The dust-cloud rose and swirled about the battle, and out of it, to Enid watching on the woodshore, came the clash of weapons and the shouts of men and the neighing and trampling of horses, and the flash of blades in the sunlight, and the blades growing red. And again and again riderless horses broke free of the tumult and fled away; but none of them was Geraint's willow-grey.

Long and desperately he fought, grimly savage as a wild boar brought to bay with the hounds snapping and snarling at its flanks. But they were four score to his one, and there could be but a single end to that fight. He was struck down with many wounds, and lay for dead, save that dead men do not bleed so redly, upon the stained and trampled ground.

Then his attackers stood back from him, and Enid slid from her saddle and came and knelt in the dust at his side, bending over him and seeming not to heed the Earl and his men all around. She gave a low wailing cry, 'Alas! Now the only man I ever loved lies slain, and it is through me that he came to his death!'

'Nay now, what of your promise to me?' said the Earl, lifting her up. 'Come back now to the castle, and we shall soon find means to heal your grieving.'

And he set her again on her mare, and gave orders for the carrying back of the bodies of the knights that Geraint had slain. And Geraint himself he caused to be carried back lying in the hollow of his shield with his sword beside him.

And himself, he took the bridle of Enid's mare, and so led her back to the castle. And all the way she spoke no word, but gazed straight before her as though she looked at some dreadful sight that had struck her dumb.

When they came into the Great Hall, the bearer-knights laid Geraint, still on his shield, on the dais at the upper end of the place. And then the Earl called for a chamber to be made ready and rosewater warmed for washing and fine silks brought out of the clothes-chests, that Enid might change her threadbare and dusty gown that was now stained also with Geraint's blood.

'I have no taste for emerald damasks and rose-scarlet silks when my lord lies dead,' said she.

'Nay, sweet lady, be not so sorrowful,' said the Earl. 'What though yonder knight be dead? Have you not a rich earldom and its lord along with it to replace him? I shall make you happy again if you will but let me.'

'I shall never be happy again in all my life,' said Enid; and she did not change her gown.

'At least come and eat,' said the Earl, when the tables were set for the noonday meal. 'See, your place shall be here by me.' And he took her hand and led her to the table.

'Eat,' he said again, and himself set the best and most delicate morsels of food on the white manchet bread before her.

But Enid said suddenly in a clear cold voice, 'I swear to God that I will not eat until my lord rises from where he lies upon his shield and eats with me.'

'That is an oath you cannot keep,' said the Earl, 'for that man is already dead.'

'Then I shall not eat again in this world,' said Enid in the same cold clear voice.

'Drink, then,' said the Earl, pouring golden wine into the cup beside her. 'Drink at least, and the fire of the wine will warm you to another way of thinking.'

'I will not drink until my lord rise and drink with me.'

At that, the Earl lost his hard-held temper and shouted at her as he would have shouted at a disobedient hound. 'Since fair words are nothing to you, let us be seeing what this will do!' And he struck her across the face, so that the imprint of his hand sprang out crimson on her white skin.

She let out a wild shriek, and sprang up. 'If my lord

were yet living, you would not have dared to strike me so!'

Now a while before this, Geraint had begun to come back to himself, like someone lying in dark water rising slowly towards the light and the world of living men; but though he heard what passed between Enid and the Earl, he did not know whether he lived, or whether everything about him was real or all a dream; and he lay a while unmoving, as though between two worlds. But Enid's shriek when the Earl struck her pierced through to him like a sword-thrust, and he broke surface from the darkness in which he had lain. And at the sound of Enid's weeping the strength rushed into him, and he sprang to his feet, snatching up his sword that lay in the hollow of his shield beside him, and hurled himself upon the Earl and dealt him such a blow that the keen blade split his head in two and was not stopped in its downward sweep until, as he sagged forward among the platters and wine cups, it was stayed by the table edge.

Then a great tumult broke out, and everyone except Enid fled from the Hall, not fearing one living man with a sword, but believing that a dead man had risen up to slay them by some wizardry.

And alone in the empty Hall, Geraint stood cleaning his blade on the white linen, and looking at Enid who stood unmoving and white as the linen, her eyes clinging to his face. And suddenly his heart smote him with a pang of love for her that was sharper than the pain of his wounds. But there was no time for soft words now; all that must wait.

'Enid,' he said, and the tone of his voice was all the soft words that she needed. 'Do you know where the stables are?'

'Yes,' she said, and then, 'Will you have me go and fetch the horses?'

'We will go together,' said Geraint, 'and swiftly

before the Earl's men find their courage again and return, for I am in no state now for another fight.'

So they went swiftly to the stables, found their horses and saddled them and, mounting, rode out from the castle whose gates stood wide, and not a soul to stand in their path or question their going.

They took the road towards the forest which lay dark as a cloud shadow across the distance; and in the open country the midsummer heat was great, and Geraint's armour stuck to him with blood and sweat, and the heat of it seared his wounds and his head swam and there was a darkness before his eyes. And when they had reached the forest and ridden a short way further, they turned aside under the trees and struggled on further yet, until they judged that the Earl's men would be hard put to it to find them. Then, under a great oak tree, they dismounted and hitched their horses to a low-hanging branch, and the Lady Enid set herself to help Geraint unarm. And she could not hold herself from weeping as she saw the wounds upon him. And while she was helping him with the laces and buckles, they heard hunting horns among the trees.

The meaning of the horns was this: King Arthur and his company had ridden out from Camelot, hunting far into the south-western hills; and their hunting camp was pitched close by in a pleasant clearing of the forest. And it was the horn of the King's huntsman gathering in his hounds that Geraint and Enid had heard. And almost in the same breath of time they heard the sound of a rider brushing through the trees, and out on to the deer path that led beside the oak tree rode Sir Kay the King's Seneschal.

And Geraint knew him, but he did not know Geraint without his shield which he had left in the Earl's Hall, for even though his helm was off and his face bare, he was so battered and blood-stained and like a man half dead that scarce anyone save Enid would have known him. And Enid had turned away to gather up his armour, so that her face was hidden.

So Sir Kay demanded of him to know what he did, standing there so close to the King's hunting camp.

'I am standing here in the shade of a tree out of the sun,' said Geraint, swaying a little on his feet.

'Who are you? And on what journey are you bound?'

'As to who I am, that is my own concern, as for my journey, I am bound wherever adventure leads me.'

'And by the look of you, it has led you into some unchancy places,' said Sir Kay. 'So now leave off your adventuring a while, and come you to King Arthur, whose pavilion is pitched nearby.'

'That I will not, unless I choose,' said Geraint, who was in no mood to be taking Kay's orders.

'It is not for you to choose!' shouted Kay. 'By God, you shall come when I say so!' And he rode at Geraint with his drawn sword. But Geraint reached for his own sword which leaned against the tree-trunk, and with the flat of it, not even drawn from its sheath, caught him a buffet under the chin that tipped him from the saddle all flailing arms and legs on to the carpet of last year's oak leaves.

And at that moment Lancelot, who had been riding close behind him, also came out into the deer path. The sunspots through the leaves dappled on his grey hair, and his one black brow was grave and level while the other flew even more wildly than usual, as he reined in and looked at the scene before him. 'Ah, Sir Kay, Sir Kay,' he said as the King's Seneschal scrambled to his feet, 'will you never learn to judge your man?' And then to Geraint he said, 'Forgive me, Sir Knight, you are somewhat battered – though I judge that there are others in worse case somewhere in these parts this day – but are you not Geraint, son of Erbin?'

'I am,' said Geraint.

'And Enid your lady with you. In a glad day you are returned to us. Now pray you come with me to the King, that he too may be made glad by your return.'

'Right joyfully will we come,' said Geraint, 'since you ask in courtesy.'

By now other knights and squires had appeared; and they took the two weary horses, and would have gone to help Geraint who was almost beyond walking; but he shook them off, and took Enid's hand in his. And together, with the rest about them, they walked into the King's hunting camp, to the big striped pavilion set up in the midst of the clearing, close to the cooking pits where the carcass of a deer they had slain that day was roasting over the flames. Arthur sat on a pile of fern before the entrance, leaning against his saddle, and Cabal, the latest of his hounds to bear the well-loved name, lying at his feet.

Lancelot said, 'Sir, we have had noble hunting this evening, for see, we have found the Lord Geraint and his lady come back to us again.'

Then the King made them joyfully welcome, and Geraint, trying to kneel at his feet, almost fell, but that Enid had her arms round him on the instant and supported him against herself.

'Later,' said the King, 'I shall ask for the story of this adventuring; but it seems that there are other things that must be seen to first.'

And he called for Morgan Tudd, and had Geraint taken to a tent where he could rest and be alone with only Enid and the physician to tend him. And the King and his companions remained in the hunting camp until Geraint was well enough to ride; and then, all together and as blithe as linnets in a hawthorn tree, they rode back to Camelot. And Enid no longer rode ahead of Geraint, nor yet behind, but side by side with him among all the rest.

And when they reached Camelot, and Queen Guenever came out to greet them – for they had sent messengers ahead, and she knew of their coming – she said to the High King, 'My Lord Arthur, now let you and all this company come into the Great Hall, to the Round Table, for there is a thing that you must see.'

And when they came into the Great Hall, there on the high back of one of the Round Table seats that had been empty since the last knight to sit there had died, was Geraint's name in letters of fair bright gold.

So Geraint became a knight of the Round Table; and when he had gone back to his own place and people, and became a strong and wise ruler after his father's time, he never failed to return to the gatherings at Pentecost, so long as he lived, and so long as the Round Table lasted.

12

GAWAIN AND THE
LOATHELY LADY

One year, when there had been Saxon raiding, and a
joining of spears between them and the Old People from
the North, and when the barbarians had been driven
back and the North was quiet again, the High King and
his companion knights kept their Christmas at Carlisle,
and Guenever and her ladies with them.

And on Christmas night when they were all gathered
in the Great Hall, and the squires and pages were
bringing in the feast, the boar's head wreathed in bay
leaves before all, there came a clatter of hooves and a
beating on the door. And when the door was opened,
into the Hall, her hair pulled down and her cloak mired
with her wild winter riding, ran a damosel who flung
herself down at Arthur's feet. 'My Lord King!' she

244

cried. 'Give me your help and save my lover from the black fate that has come upon him!'

'What I can do, that I will,' said the King. 'Tell me quickly what it is, this fate, which has caused you so much weeping.' And he stooped to raise her, but she would not rise, only crouched the more closely.

'I was betrothed to a knight who was more dear to me than my own heart. But yesterday as we rode out making plans for our marriage, through the deep ways of the Forest of Inglewood, we came upon a place where the trees fell back, and in the midst of it a dark lake all jagged with rocks along the shore, and on an islet in the lake, a castle, with black banners flying above the keep and the drawbridge down. And as we lingered there, wondering, for we had never come upon the place before, a terrible creature in full armour, twice the size of a mortal man and mounted on a horse twice the size of a mortal horse, came full gallop across the bridge towards us, and called upon my love to leave me to him and ride on his way alone. My love drew his sword to defend me, but some evil magic lies in that place, and in that moment the spell of it fell upon him so that the sword dropped from his hand and he was powerless against the wicked knight. And the knight hurled him from his saddle and took and bound him and flung him across his horse's back, while I must look on powerless. I tried to fight him, and got this in payment.' She touched her bruised face and torn garments and showed her hands cut and bruised. 'But he only laughed his terrible laughter and dragged my love's horse round to ride away. I called after him that I would go to Arthur's court and tell my wrongs and beg for a champion to save my love – or avenge him – maybe even the King himself. But he only laughed the more, and shouted at me, "Tell your cowardly king that here at Tarn Wathelan he may find me when he will; but much I doubt that even he will find the courage to come against me!" And so he went, driving my dear love on his horse before him. And so do I come to you, my Lord Arthur, kneeling at your feet and praying for your aid!'

Then an angry murmur ran round the Hall, and men looked at each other and their hands moved towards their daggers, and many a one was already half out of his seat.

But the King sprang to his feet and cried in a great voice, 'Now by my knightly honour, I vow that the King indeed shall ride upon this matter, and avenge this maiden's wrongs in full measure!'

And some of the knights, especially the young ones, beat upon the table and gave tongue, applauding the vow. But Gawain said, 'Uncle, let me ride upon this quest; for I smell some evil beyond what the maiden has told, and Britain cannot long be doing without her King!'

But though Lancelot also, and Bedivere and Gareth, and even in a rash moment Sir Kay, offered themselves to go in his stead, the King refused them. 'My thanks to you all, but it is over long since the King himself rode on a quest instead of watching his knights ride out.' And then, looking round on them, on a sudden, he added half in anger and half in something that was like appeal, 'God's truth, my brothers, I am not yet old!'

And there was something in his voice that held them from protesting any more.

Only the Queen was not happy; for like Gawain, it seemed to her that she could catch the smell of some evil that she could give no name to.

Next morning when the King had heard Mass, his squires armed him and buckled on Excalibur and brought him Ron his mighty spear; and his most fiery-hearted warhorse was fetched from the stable. And with the maiden to guide him, he left Carlisle and headed deep into the Forest of Inglewood, the dark fleece of trees that covered all those parts.

Mile after mile they rode, until at last they came out from the trees into the fierce yellow flare of a stormy sunset; and before them spread the waters of a lake giving back its answering fire to the fiery sky; and all around rose the dark rocks of the shore; and set on its islet, a storm-dark castle with its banners streaming crow-black from the turret tops against the sunset light.

'This is the place,' said the damosel. 'Oh, my Lord King, save my love for me and avenge my wrongs!'

Then Arthur took the horn that hung at his saddle-bow, and winded a long-drawn mighty call that echoed back from the rocks of the lake shore and set the ravens whirling on black wings from the crannies and ledges of the castle. Again he sounded his horn; and yet a third time, until the note seemed to fling back from the high sunset clouds above the ramparts, but no other answer came. Then he drew his sword, and cried out in his battle voice, 'Come, Sir Knight of Tarn Wathelan! Your King bides here, and is not used to be kept waiting!'

And as he hurled his challenge, the great drawbridge dropped slowly to span the narrow gap of water between the castle and the shore; and there in the gate arch appeared the Knight of Tarn Wathelan, huge beyond the size of mortal man and armed from crest to toe in black armour, and mounted on a giant red-eyed war-horse the colour of midnight. 'Now welcome, King Arthur!' he shouted. 'For long and long I have wished for your coming, that I may defy you to your face as always I have defied you in my heart!'

Then anger rose in the King, and he spurred his horse full gallop down the track to the water's edge, while the huge knight spurred out as swiftly to meet him. 'Yield you now to me!' shouted back Arthur, above the drum of horse's hooves. 'Yield and make amends for your evil doing, or fight!'

But in the same moment his horse stopped dead, all but flinging him over its head, and stood stock still, neighing in terror; and as the King sought to urge it forward again, he felt it trembling under him. And like an icy shadow, a great fear fell upon him, the more terrible because it was not of the knight or of anything in this world; a black terror of the soul that came between him and the sky, and sucked the strength from him so that sword arm and shield arm sank to his sides and he was powerless to move.

'This is Devil's work!' said something deep within him. 'Devil's work . . .'

And the Knight of Tarn Wathelan reined in his own horse not a spear's throw away, and fell to laughing, until his laughter rang and boomed back from the castle walls. 'Now it is for *you* to yield or fight, my Lord King!'

And Arthur struggled to raise his sword arm until the cold sweat started on him, but could not move a muscle.

'You see!' bellowed the huge knight.

'What – would you – of me?' gasped Arthur.

'As to that, I could kill you now, or fling you into my dungeons to rot among other valiant knights who lie there, and take your realm for my own by means of the magic that is mine to wield. But I am minded to sell you back your life and freedom. How say you to that?'

'What is the price?'

'That you return to me on New Year's Day, bringing me the answer to this question: What is it that all women most desire? Swear on the Holy Rood to return, with or without the answer to the question, for if you have it not, then you will be still my prisoner, your ransom unpaid. And if it pleases me I shall slay you and fling your body into the dark waters of the lake.'

And there was nothing that Arthur could do but

swear, with shame and rage and humiliation battling
with the terrible fear that held him captive like a fly
meshed at the heart of a spider's web.

Then the Knight of Tarn Wathelan made a quick
gesture with his spear; and Arthur's horse reared up and
spun round on its hind hooves, and dashed off at such a
desperate gallop that they were far and far into the trees
before Arthur could rein it to a trembling halt.

It was then that he realised that there had been no
sign of the maiden since they first rode out into the
clearing and saw Tarn Wathelan ahead of them.

With the shame of what had happened eating into
him, the King rode on his way. But not back to Carlisle.
He could not look his companions in the face again until
he had paid his ransom – if indeed his ransom was ever
to be paid.

All that week between Christmas and the New Year,
he rode the forest and moorland ways, North and
South, East and West. And whenever he saw a girl
herding geese, or an ale-wife in the door of a wayside
tavern, a great lady amidst a train of servants, riding by
on a white palfrey whose harness rang with little bells,
or an aged nun by a holy well, telling her beads, he
asked her the question that had been put to him by the
Knight of Tarn Wathelan.

'What thing is it that all women most desire?'

And every one of them gave him a different answer.
Some said riches and some said beauty, some said pomp
and state, some power, some laughter and admiration,
some said love.

And the King thanked each one of them courteously,
and wrote down her answer on a long strip of parchment
which he had obtained from an abbey on the first day of
his quest, that he might forget none of them when he
came again to Tarn Wathelan. But he knew in his heart
that none of them was the right answer. And so at last it

was the morning of New Year's Day, and he set his horse's head once more towards the castle of Tarn Wathelan with a heavy heart. And his thoughts turned back to Merlin, so long asleep under his magic hawthorn tree, for nobody else could help him now.

The hills looked darker than they had done when last he rode that way, and the wind had a keener edge. And the way seemed much longer and rougher than it had done before, and yet it was all too quickly passed.

But when he was not far short of his journey's ending, as he rode chin on breast through a dark thicket, he heard a woman's voice, sweet and soft, calling out to him, 'Now God's greeting to you, my Lord King Arthur. God save and keep you.'

The King turned quickly in the direction from which the voice had come, and saw, close beside the track, a woman in a scarlet gown. She sat upon a turf hummock between an oak sapling and a holly tree; and her gown was as vivid as the holly berries, and her skin as brown and withered as the few winter leaves that still clung to the oak tree. At sight of her shock ran through the King, for in the instant between hearing and seeing, he had expected the owner of the soft voice to be fair. And she was the most hideous creature that ever he had seen, with a piteous nightmare face that he could scarcely bear to look upon. Her nose was long and warty and bent to one side, while her long hairy chin bent to the other. She had only one eye, and that set deep under her jutting brow, and her mouth was no more than a shapeless gash. On either side of her face her hair hung down in grey twisted locks, and the hands that she held folded in her lap were like brown claws, though the jewels that winked upon them were fine enough for the Queen herself.

In his amazement, the King could not at once find his tongue to answer her greeting. And the Loathely Lady raised her head and looked at him, a long full look that seemed to hold grief and anger and an old pride. 'Now by Christ's Cross, my Lord Arthur, you are an ungentle knight, to leave a lady's greeting lying unanswered so! Best remember your manners, for I know on what dark adventure you ride, and proud as you are, it may be that I can help you.'

'Forgive me, lady,' said the High King. 'I was deep in thought, and that, not lack of courtesy, was the reason I did not return your greeting. If you do indeed know the adventure that I ride on, and the question that I must answer, and if you can indeed help me, I shall be grateful to you for all my life.'

'It is more than gratitude that I must have, if I am to help you,' said the Loathely Lady.

'What then?' said the King. 'Whatever you ask, you shall have it.'

'That is a rash promise,' said the Lady, 'and you shall swear it on Christ's Cross, lest later you repent. But first, let you listen to me. You are pledged to tell the Knight of Tarn Wathelan this very day what it is that all women most desire, or else yield yourself up to his mercy. And mercy he has none. That is so?'

'That is so,' said the King.

'You have asked many women, in these past seven days, and all of them have given you answers; and not one of them the right answer. I alone can give you that; the answer that shall pay your ransom. But before I give it to you, you shall swear by the Holy Rood, and by Mary the Mother of God, that whatever boon I ask of you, you will grant it.'

'This oath I take upon me,' said the King, with his hand on the cross of his sword.

'Then bend down to me – closer – closer, that not even the trees may hear,' said the Loathely Lady. And as he did so, she got awkwardly to her feet and

251

whispered the secret in his ear.

Then the King caught his breath in laughter, for it was such a simple answer, after all. But in a little he grew sober again, and asked the Lady what was the boon that she would have in payment. But she said, 'Not yet – when you have given his answer to the Knight of Tarn Wathelan and proved that it is indeed the true one, then come back to me here, where I shall be waiting for you. And now, God go with you on your way.'

So the King rode on towards Tarn Wathelan. And now the hills seemed less dark and the wind less keen, for he was sure that he had the true answer to the Knight's question.

In a while he came to the clearing in the forest, and sitting his horse on the lake shore, he sounded a long note on his horn. This time he did not need to sound more than once, for the master of the place was ready for him, and while the echoes still hung among the rocks, the drawbridge came clanging down, and over it the huge Knight on his huge black horse came riding, and reined up within a spear's length of the King.

'Well, now, little King, do you bring me the answer to my question?'

'I bring you many answers, given to me by many women, and among them must surely be the true one,' said Arthur, and tossed the roll of parchment into the giant's mailed hand.

And sitting his horse there on the lake shore, the huge knight read them from the first to the last. And when he had read them all, he burst into a roar of laughter, and flung the scroll over his shoulder into the deep sky-reflecting waters of the Tarn. 'Here be many answers indeed! Some bad, some good, but none of them the true answer to my question. Your ransom is unpaid and your life and your kingdom are forfeit to me. Bend your neck for the stroke, oh, most lordly Arthur Pendragon, High King of Britain!' And his hand went to the hilt of his sword.

Then Arthur said, 'Give me leave to try one more, before I yield up to you my life and kingdom.'

'One more, then, but be quick,' said the Knight.

'This morning as I rode here,' said King Arthur, 'I met with a lady clad in a scarlet gown and sitting between an oak and a holly tree, and she told me that the thing all women most desire is *their own way*!'

Then the Knight of Tarn Wathelan let out a great bellow of rage. 'It must have been my sister Ragnell who told you this, for none but she knew the true answer. And a curse upon her for the telling! Was she hideous and misshapen?'

'She was indeed the most unlovely lady that ever I saw,' said the King.

'If ever I catch her, I will roast her alive over a slow fire, for she has cheated me of the kingdom of Britain!' roared the Knight. 'Nevertheless, go your way in freedom, for your ransom is paid.'

Back over the moors and through the forest depths rode the King, all at once so weary that he could scarcely even feel relief. And when he came to the place where he had met her before, there between the oak and the holly tree sat the Lady Ragnell, waiting for him.

He reined up beside her, and this time was the first to speak in greeting. 'Lady, your answer was indeed the true one. And I have my life, and kingdom, thanks to you. Now ask your boon, and I will assuredly grant it.'

'Assuredly,' said the Loathely Lady. 'If you are a man of honour as well as a king. So then, this is the boon I ask: That you will bring to me from your court at Carlisle, one of your knights brave and courteous, and good to look upon, to take me for his loving wife.'

At her words, Arthur felt as though he had taken a

blow to the belly. 'Madam,' he said, 'you ask a thing impossible.'

'Then Arthur is not, after all, a man of honour?' said the Lady.

And the King said, 'You shall have your boon, lady.'

And with his head sunk on his breast, he rode away. And never knew how the Lady looked after him with a mingling of hope and fear and desperate pain in her one bleared eye.

On the second day of the New Year the King returned to Carlisle. Wearily he dismounted in the courtyard, and went through into the Great Hall, where his companion knights were gathered and the Queen came to greet him with hands held out and eager questions, for she had been torn with anxiety through the past eight days.

'I have boasted too much of my strength in arms, and I come back to you a beaten man,' said the King heavily.

'My lord, tell us what has come to pass?' said the Queen, her face turning white under the golden circlet that bound her hair.

'The knight whom I rode against was more than a mortal man, and his castle and all the land about it held by black enchantments which suck the courage from a man's heart and the strength from his arm. So I fell into his power and was forced to yield myself to him. And he – bade me go, but return to him on New Year's Day with the answer to a certain question, or forfeit to him my life and kingdom.'

For a moment there was no sound in the Great Hall but the crackle of the logs blazing on the hearth, and a hound under a table scratching for fleas. And then Lancelot said gently, 'But, sir, you are returned to us, so it must be that you gave this wizard knight the true answer that he sought. And therefore you are honourably redeemed.'

'I gave him the true answer, by the help of a lady; but her help was dearly bought, and I cannot pay *that* ransom myself.'

Then Gawain spoke up, 'So – what is it that must be paid to this lady?'

'She asked a boon, to be given her when the question had been answered; and I – I promised her whatever she asked. I swore that I would grant it.' The King groaned. 'And when the question was answered and I was free, and returned to her and bade her ask her boon – she asked that one of my knights should marry her.'

Again there was silence in the Hall; and then Gawain said, 'Och well, that might be none so ill a thing. Is she bonnie?'

'She is the most hideous and misshapen woman that ever I saw,' said the King. 'Crooked of nose and chin, old and withered, and with but one eye. A twisted thorn-tree woman, like something out of an evil dream.'

And for the third time there was silence in the Hall.

'Would to God that I might pay the price myself,' groaned the King. And Guenever reached him her hand like a mother reaching a consoling hand to her child. But she was careful not to look at Sir Lancelot, who was as careful not to look at her.

And a faint breath of relief was running through the knights who already had wives of their own and so were safe from what was coming.

'But you cannot, dear uncle, and so to keep your honour clean, another must pay it for you.' Agravane, always a mischief-maker, leaned forward into the light, his eyes flickering. 'How about you, dear brother Gawain? You are for ever protesting your loyalty to the King, as though it were greater than other men's; protesting yourself the King's champion as Lancelot is the Queen's!'

Lancelot was half out of his seat before the words were well spoken; but even swifter than he, Gawain sprang up, his hot blue eyes blazing and his red hair seeming to lift like the mane of an angry hound. 'Little brother, you speak my very thoughts! My Lord Arthur, I will wed your beldame for you, and quit you of your ransom!'

'My thanks be to you for the offer,' said the King, 'but I shall not – I cannot – accept it until you have first had sight of her.'

'Nay, my lord and uncle, my mind is set to do this in your service, for am I not the King's champion, as my brother Agravane says?' And Gawain caught up his wine-cup from the table beside him, and held it high, thrusting his defiant gaze among his fellow knights. 'Drink, friends, to my bride!' And standing there, he drained the cup and crashed it down upon the table.

Nobody echoed the toast.

'Not without first seeing her,' said the King again, his voice dull and hoarse but with no yielding in it. And Cabal, his huge grey wolfhound, nuzzled into his hand; and he looked down and gently pulled the great hound's ears. Then, abruptly, as a man making up his mind, he raised his head and looked around at the faces turned to him in the torchlight.

'Tomorrow, we ride hunting towards Tarn Wathelan, and Gawain shall see the Lady Ragnell in the cold light of day, with a cooler and clearer head on him than he has at this moment. And all of you who are not yet wed, shall look upon her too, before any of you choose her for his bride!'

So next day, in the first light of the winter morning, the horses were brought from the stables and the hounds from the kennels, and King Arthur and his companions rode hunting. The morning was crisp with frost, and they put up a noble stag and chased him far into the depths of Inglewood Forest, the winding of the horns mingling with the music of the hounds. He led them through dense thickets of holly and yew and bare oak and hazel; and at last, not so far from Tarn Wathelan, they made the kill.

And when the carcass of the deer had been grail-loched and flung across the back of a hunting pony, and they turned back towards Carlisle, they rode merrily along with jest and laughter, though the led palfrey in their midst reminded them all too clearly why they had come hunting that way. And for that very reason they laughed the louder and called to each other under the trees to silence the trouble in their own hearts.

And then suddenly Sir Kay, riding out alone beyond the rest as he often did, caught a glimpse of scarlet among the trees; and ducking under the branches of a great forest yew, he reined back and stayed looking at the woman who sat there in a gown of blazing scarlet, between an oak and a holly tree.

'God's greeting to you, Sir Kay,' said the Lady Ragnell.

But the King's Seneschal was too much astonished to answer. He had heard what the King had said of the Loathely Lady, last night in Carlisle Castle. But he had not imagined anything so terrible as the face he saw turned towards him. He crossed his fingers for fear of witchcraft, and did not even hear her salutation. But by this time most of the other knights had joined him; and in their company Sir Kay felt bolder; and because he had been afraid, his manners were worse than usual, and he began to jibe at her most cruelly. 'See now, here if I mistake not our King's description of her, is the lady we have come to seek. So now, which of us shall woo her to wife? Come, think of the sweetness of her kisses and do not be hanging back!'

And then King Arthur rode up, with Gawain at his

side, and at sight of them Sir Kay fell silent; and the Loathely Lady, who had bowed her face, weeping, into her hands, looked up again, with a kind of pathetic and desperate pride.

'Since one of you must indeed marry her,' said the King, harsh in his throat, 'here is no cause for jesting, Sir Kay!'

'Marry her!' cried Sir Kay. 'Well, it shall not be I! By the boar's head, I had sooner mate with the witch of Cit Coit Caledon!'

'Peace, Sir Kay!' said the King. 'This is churl's treatment of a lady! Mend your speech, or you shall be knight of mine no longer!'

And the other knights watched in silence, sickened and in pity. Some looked away; even Sir Lancelot pretended to be busy with some adjustment to his horse's bridle.

But Sir Gawain looked steadily at the Lady, and something in that pathetic pride and the way she lifted her hideous head made him think of a deer with the hounds about it, and something in the depth of her bleared gaze reached him like a cry for help. And he glared about him at his fellow knights. 'Nay now, why these sideways looks and troubled faces? Kay was ever an ill-mannered hound! The matter was never in doubt, for last night did I not tell the King that I would marry this lady; and marry her I will, if she will have me!'

And so saying, he swung down from his saddle and knelt before her. 'My Lady Ragnell, will you take me for your husband?'

The lady looked at him for a moment out of her one eye, then she said in that voice so surprisingly sweet, 'Not you, too, Sir Gawain. Ah, not you, too.' And as he looked at her in bewilderment, 'Surely you do but jest, like Sir Kay?'

'I was never further from jesting in my life,' said Sir

Gawain, with stiff lips.

'Then think you before it is too late. Will you indeed wed with one as ugly and misshapen and old as I? What sort of wife should I be for the King's own nephew? What will Queen Guenever and her ladies say when you bring such a bride to court?'

'No one will say anything that is not courteous to my wife,' said Gawain. 'I shall know how to guard you from that.'

'Maybe so. But yourself? You will be shamed, and all through me,' said the Lady, and wept again, more bitterly than before, so that her face was wet and blubbered and yet more hideous.

Gawain took her hand. 'Lady, if I can guard you, be very sure that I can guard myself also,' he said, and glared round him at the others with his fighting face upon him. 'Now, lady, come with me back to Carlisle, for this evening is our wedding time.'

'Truly,' said the Loathely Lady, 'though it is a hard thing to believe, you shall not regret this wedding, Sir Gawain.'

And she rose and moved towards the white palfrey they had brought for her, and then they all saw that there was a hump between her shoulders and she was lame in one leg, beside all else. But Sir Gawain helped her into the saddle and mounted his own horse beside her; and the King ranged up on the other side. And so, with the rest of the company strung out behind them the knights on their horses and the huntsmen with the hounds in leash, and the hunting pony with the carcass of the deer across its back, they wended their way back to Carlisle.

Word ran ahead of them from the city gates, and the people came flocking out to see Sir Gawain and his hideous bride go by; and as they passed, the voices of the crowd sank away, and here and there men made the sign of the Cross, or an old woman cried out 'God save us!' in dismay. And so they came to the castle gates and rode inside.

That evening in the castle chapel, Gawain and the Lady Ragnell were married, with the Queen herself to stand beside the bride, and the King to act as groomsman; and after, Sir Lancelot was foremost of the Round Table company to come forward to kiss the Lady's withered brown cheek, followed by Sir Gareth and Sir Gaheris, Sir Ector of the Marsh and Sir Bedivere, Sir Bors and Sir Lional and all the rest; but the words strangled in their throats when they would have wished her and Sir Gawain joy of their marriage, so that they could scarcely speak. And the poor Lady Ragnell looked down upon bent head after bent head, and at the ladies who came forward to touch her fingertips as briefly as might be, but could not bear to kiss her cheek. Only Cabal came and licked her hand with a warm wet tongue and looked up into her face with amber eyes that took no account of her hideous aspect, for the eyes of a hound see differently from the eyes of men.

At the feasting that followed in the Great Hall, the talk and laughter all along the tables was feverish and forced; a hollow pretence at gladness, and through it all Sir Gawain and his bride sat rigidly beside the King and Queen at the High Table. And when at last the feasting was over, the squires set back the tables and began to make the Hall ready for dancing. And then the company thought that now Gawain would be free for a while to leave her side and mingle with his friends. But he said, 'Bride and groom must lead the first dance together,' and offered his hand to the Lady Ragnell.

She took it, with a hideous grimace that was the nearest she could come to a smile, and limped forward to open the dance with him. And throughout the long and stately measure that followed, with the King's eye upon them and Gawain's also, no one in the Hall, not even the youngest page, dared to look as though anything was amiss.

At long last the evening wore to an end. The last measure had been danced, and the minstrels departed, the last wine-cup had been drained, and the bride and groom were escorted to their chamber high in the keep. The great chamber was full of flickering lights and shadows from the fire upon the hearth and the candles that burned in tall sconces either side of the carved and curtained bed, so that the creatures in the woodland scenes upon the walls seemed to move and come and go, and the whole chamber seemed part of some enchanted forest. And when all the company that had brought them there were gone, Gawain flung himself into the deeply cushioned chair beside the fire, and sat gazing into the flames, not looking to see where his bride might be. A sudden draught drove the candleflames sideways and the embroidered creatures on the walls stirred as though on the edge of life. And somewhere very far off, as though from the heart of the enchanted forest, he fancied he heard the faintest echo of a horn.

There was a faint movement at the foot of the bed, and the silken rustle of a woman's skirt; and a low sweet voice said, 'Gawain, my lord and love, have you no word for me? Can you not even bear to look my way?'

Gawain forced himself to turn his head and look at the speaker – and then sprang up in amazement; for there between the candle sconces, still wearing the Lady Ragnell's scarlet gown, and with the Lady Ragnell's jewels on her fingers, stood the most beautiful maiden that he had ever seen. Her skin as white as milk in the candlelight, her hair as darkly gold as corn at harvest time, her huge dark eyes waiting to meet his, and her hands held out to him while a little smile quivered at the corners of her mouth.

'Lady,' he said at half-breath, not sure whether he was awake or dreaming, 'who are you? Where is my wife, the Lady Ragnell?'

'I am your wife, the Lady Ragnell,' said she, 'whom you found between the oak and the holly tree, and wedded this night in settlement of your King's debt – and maybe, a little, in kindness.'

'But – I do not understand,' stammered Gawain, 'you are so changed –'

'Yes,' said the maiden, 'I am changed, am I not? I was under an enchantment, and as yet I am only partly freed from it. But now for a little while I may be with you in my true seeming. Is my lord content with his bride?'

She came a little towards him, and he reached out and caught her into his arms. 'Content? Oh, my most dear love, I am the happiest man in all the world; for I thought to save the honour of the King my uncle, and I have gained my heart's desire. Indeed you spoke truly when you told me I should never regret this marriage, though at the time I could not believe you.' He drew her hard against him and kissed her, while she put her arms round his neck. 'And yet from the first moment I felt something of you reach out to me, and something of me reach back in answer . . .'

In a little, the lady brought her hands down and set them against her breast and gently held him off. 'Listen,' she said, 'for now a hard choice lies before you. I told you that as yet I am only partly free from the enchantment that binds me. Because you have taken me for your wife, it is half broken; but no more than half broken.'

'What is this? I do not understand.'

'Listen,' she said again, 'and you shall understand all too well. I am half free of the spell, half still held by it; for half of each day I may wear my true form as I do now; for the other half I must be as I was when you took me from under my oak and holly tree. And now it is for you to say, whether you will have me fair by day and foul by night, or fair by night and foul by day.'

'That is a hard choice indeed.' said Gawain.

'Think,' said the Lady Ragnell.

And Sir Gawain said in a rush, 'Oh, my dear love, be hideous by day, and fair for me alone!'

'Alas!' said the Lady Ragnell. 'And that is your choice? I must be hideous and misshapen among all the Queen's fair ladies, and abide their scorn and pity, when in truth I am as fair as any of them? Oh, Sir Gawain, is this your love?'

Then Sir Gawain bowed his head. 'Nay, I was thinking only of myself. If it will make you happier, be fair by day and take your rightful place at court. And at night I shall hear your soft voice in the darkness, and that shall be my content.'

'That was indeed a lover's answer,' said the Lady Ragnell. 'But I would be fair for you; not only for the court and the daytime world that means less to me than you do.'

And Gawain said, 'Whichever way it is, it is you who must endure the most suffering; and being a woman, I am thinking that you have more wisdom in such things than I. Make the choice yourself, dear love, and whichever way you choose, I shall be content.'

Then the Lady Ragnell bent her head into the hollow of his neck and wept and laughed together. 'Oh Gawain, my dearest lord, now, by leaving the choice to me, by giving me *my own way* you have broken the spell completely, and I am free of it, to be my true self by night and day. And my brother also –'

'Your brother?' said Gawain, his head whirling.

And seeing his bewilderment, the Lady Ragnell drew him back to the great chair beside the fire, and sank down beside him on to the rushes, her arm across his knees. 'My brother the Knight of Tarn Wathelan,' she said. 'Both of us were spell-drawn from our true seeming by the magic of Morgan La Fay, my brother because she thought to use him in one last attempt against the King her half-brother, me because – I have a little power of my own – I sought to withstand her.'

'But how did you know the way to save the King?' Gawain asked.

'To every spell there is a key, though one that is almost beyond the power of human kind to use.' Gawain was taking down her hair so that it fell in a curtain of harvest-coloured silk about them both. 'I was the key to save the King; and in saving the King, it was given to me also to call to you for aid for myself and my brother. But if you had not answered my call, no one could have saved me, for the name of *that* key is Love.'

Next day there was much bewilderment but even more joy when Sir Gawain led the Lady Ragnell into the Great Hall. And the wedding feast was renewed; a true wedding feast this time, and a fitting end to the Christmas festivities.

For seven years Gawain and Ragnell knew great happiness together, and during all that time Gawain was a gentler and a kinder and a more steadfast man than ever he had been before. But at the end of that time the Lady Ragnell went from him. Some say that she died, some that she had the blood of the Lordly People in her – had she not herself said that she had a little power? – and the Lordly People cannot live for more than seven years with a mortal mate.

In one way or another way, she went; and something of Gawain went with her. He was a valiant knight still, but his old blazing temper returned upon him and he was less steadfast of purpose and less kind that he had been; and he went hollow of heart for her sake, all the remaining days of his life.

13

THE COMING OF PERCIVAL

When King Pellinore was slain, his queen wanted no more to do with the world of men; and she took their young son Percival and disappeared with him into the wilderness. And there among the mountains and forests of Wales, she found an abandoned charcoal-burner's bothie, and made a home for the child, where he might grow up far from wars and feuds and the cruelties of men towards men which are different from the cruelties of the animal kind.

So from that time forward until he was seventeen, the boy grew up never seeing another human face save his mother's, knowing nothing of the outside world or the ways of men and women. At first he remembered his father's court, the ladies smelling of musk and civet and oil of violets, whose fine gowns trailed along the floor behind them, the shine of knights in armour, the strength of his father's arms when he swung him up from the ground to sit upon his shoulder; the old man in the castle armoury who had begun to teach him how to cast a light spear. Above all, the splendid high-stepping horses in the stables, and the great deerhounds in the kennels who had accepted him as a friend. But little by little the memories faded until they were no more than a brightly coloured blur in the back of his head; until they were so faint that he thought they were only the memories of a dream.

The forest and the mountains were his whole world, and the forest creatures were his friends. He knew where every vixen in his home valley had her lair and cubs, and could whistle so like a thrush or a blackbird that the birds would answer to his call. And he grew strong and hardy and brave and simple-hearted. One day he found an old battered spearhead lying where the winter rain had pulled down the earth between the roots of a tree. The shaft was rotten and crumbled at his touch, but when he bore it home and rubbed it up, the spearhead came up bright as new. He showed it to his mother, and a shadow came over her face as she looked, and over her heart as well. But she said nothing, and he honed the blade on a stone until it was keen enough to cut the wind, as the old man in the lost dream had once shown him how to do, and he found a straight ash sapling to make a new spear shaft, and he practised with it until he could make it do whatever he willed. Then he turned hunter; but he never hunted for pleasure, only for food, as the animals of the wild hunted for food themselves.

But as the years went by and he grew towards manhood, Percival began to find something lacking in forest life. He needed other companionship than his mother's and the wildlings', he wanted other sounds than the birdsong and the wind in the trees and the voices of the hill-streams. He did not really know what it was that he wanted, but he wandered further and futher afield in search of it.

And one spring day, wandering further from his home than ever he had been before, he came into a valley down which wound something that was like a deer path, but many times broader and more deeply trodden than any deer path that ever he had seen before.

And as he checked beside it, wondering, he heard sounds that were not any of the forest sounds he knew; and round the bend of the track where it skirted a tangle of elder and wayfaring trees, came four shining figures mounted upon a dun horse and a roan, a grey and a bright chestnut. Percival knew what the horses were, for he had seen the wild Welsh ponies often enough, though these were far bigger and more splendid and high-stepping; and their riders seemed to be shaped like men – or at least, like himself – he had seen himself often enough in the pool under the old willow tree near his home where the bitter dark willow-water was a fine medicine and the wild things came to drink when they were sick; but instead of brown skin and rough yellow hair, and the hides of animals, they each had some kind of hard shining skin – shining like the blade of his beloved spear – and the flash of gold and brilliant colours about them, so that it almost made him blink to look at them. And so with the clopping of their horses' hooves on the beaten ground, and a jingling of chain-mail and harness, they came on towards him along the track.

'God's greeting to you,' said the foremost rider when he drew level with Percival standing at gaze at the side of the track. And he reined in the chestnut, the others behind him, and sat looking down at the boy.

His head was bare, for his helmet hung at his saddlebow, and his mail coif was pushed back on to his shoulders. And Percival saw that his thick hair was grey, though he did not look to be old, and he had a strange crooked face that became all the stranger and more crooked when he smiled, and yet seemed to Percival very beautiful.

'Nay, now,' said the stranger, 'pull your eyes back into your head, I pray you! Have you never seen our like before?'

Percival shook his head. 'That have I not. And truth to tell, I do not know whether you be men from the world of men or angels out of Heaven. My mother has told me about the angels in Heaven; and you are so shining-bright. She said that the angels are shining-bright.'

The others laughed, but not unkindly, and he of the crooked face said, 'No angels we, alas! Though maybe there is something of the angels in all men, aye, and something of the Devil's brood as well.'

'Then if you are men —' Percival began doubtfully. Memory was working in him; the half-lost memories of fine horses, and men who shone like this, that he had seen before. Suddenly the answer came to him. 'Then you must be knights!'

'We are knights indeed, and our fealty is to King Arthur, who made us knights of his Round Table.'

'King Arthur?' said the boy. 'Round Table?'

'Arthur Pendragon, the High King of all Britain,' said the man with the crooked face, gravely now. 'And the Round Table is the order of knighthood which he founded. We who are part of it are vowed always to fight for the right, to defend the weak from oppression, to keep our swords free from tarnish and at the service of Britain, to truly serve the Lord God.'

Percival was silent a long moment, looking up with shining eyes into the ugly face above him. Then he said, 'I would be a knight.'

'Maybe you will, one day,' said the other, kindly.

'What must I do to become a knight?'

'Come to the King at Caerleon, and tell him that I sent you – I, Sir Lancelot of the Lake, who under him hold the Castle of Joyeux Gard beyond the mountains yonder. If you prove worthy, he will make you a knight, when the time comes.'

And bowing his head to Percival with as grave a courtesy as if he had been a duke, he rode on his way, and his companions after him.

And Percival remained standing on the edge of the track, hearing the beat of their horses' hooves and the jingle of harness die away into the distance, with a strange mixture of feelings rising within him.

It was long after dark when he reached the charcoal-burner's bothie that was home to him, and firelight shone from the doorway to meet him, and his mother was tending the supper cooking among the hot ash, fish that he had speared in the shallows of a hill pool. She looked up and saw his face, and a great stillness took her. But Percival had no time for stillness. The news that he carried was blazing within him.

'Mother – I have met with men! At first I thought that they might be angels, for they shone as you have told me the angels shine, but they were knights. The one who seemed to be chief among them – Sir Lancelot of the Lake – told me that they were knights in the service of King Arthur of Britain, and he said that if I went to the King and proved myself worthy, one day he might make me a knight, too.'

'One day,' said his mother. 'There is time enough.'

'No! Mother, you do not understand, I must go tomorrow – I must go to Arthur at Caerleon and show him that I am worthy to be a knight!'

'You?' she said desperately. 'You, a boy out of the woods, clad in deerskins and carrying an old spear?'

And Percival squatted on to his heels beside her and put a big brown hand gently on her knee. 'But that is not all I am, is it, Mother? I used to think that it was only a dream I remembered – shining men and great horses and my father with a golden circlet on his head – but when I saw them, I knew it was no dream.'

And his mother wept in her heart, for she knew that the time had come when she must lose him. But she put her own hand over his, and said, 'No, it was no dream, your father was King Pellinore of Wales. But it is more than ten years since he was killed.'

'Who killed him?' said the boy, turned for a moment from his eagerness to be away after his knighthood and the great world by something that he saw in her face.

'Sir Agravane and Sir Gaheris, in vengeance because he had first killed their father Lot, King of Orkney, though that was done in battle. And after, when your half-brother Lamorack would have avenged your father, they killed him also.'

'When I am a knight,' said Percival, 'I will avenge my father and my half-brother on Agravane and Gaheris.'

But his mother cried out, 'No! Oh, no! It was in part to keep you from the horror of a blood feud that I brought you here and bred you up far from the world of men! And now you would go to the very place where you will find them!'

'Are they also at Caerleon?' asked the boy after a moment.

'They and their brothers Gawain and Gareth are

knights of the Round Table.'

Then it seemed to Percival that the shining world of men, the world beyond the forest was less simple than he had thought it would be. But even in the moment that he realised that, he remembered the strange crooked face of Sir Lancelot smiling down at him, speaking of the honour of knighthood, and knew that he wanted above all things in the world to be one of that company.

And he said, 'Mother, as to the thing between our house and the house of Orkney, it must be as God wills. But I must go to Caerleon and to the High King. I know here –' he put his free hand on his belly – 'that it is the thing that I must do.'

So his mother sighed, and yielded. She had always known that the day would come, and the thing that he must do . . .

So early next morning that the birds were scarcely awake, Percival made ready to set out.

His mother took his face between her hands and kissed him for the last time, knowing that she would not see him again, and said, 'Remember that your father was a true knight as well as a king, remember that I love you, and be worthy of us both. Have a care as to the friends you choose, and in whose company you travel, for you are simple-hearted, and so like to be over trusting. Let no woman ever have cause to cry out against you for your treatment of her. Pray to God daily as I have taught you, that He may be with you in all your ways, and I think that one day you will indeed be a knight, and the knight that you would wish to be.'

Percival promised, and returned his mother's kiss, and picking up his spear from where it leaned against the doorpost, went his way.

He had not forgotten the things that she had told him last night; but the blackthorn was in flower, for it was

Easter time, and as he went, the willow wren who is always the first to feel the coming day, began his faint silvery whisper-song, and then the thrush joined in, and the robin, and the linnets among the gorse in the open places. And the sun at his back sent his shadow streaming out long and eager before him; and Percival went on his way, travelling at the long loose-limbed wolf-lope that eats up distance; tossing up his spear to watch the early sunlight on the blade, and whistling joyously in answer to every bird in all the forests of Wales.

All day he walked; and at dusk he ate the food that his mother had given him, and lay down to sleep in a sheltered hollow between the roots of an ancient ash tree. And next morning before sun-up he was on his way again.

Well before noon on the fifth day he came to the gates of Caerleon. Never having seen such a thing before, he checked for a little, and watched the people coming and going through the archway under the great gatehouse; but nobody seemed to come to any harm, so after a while he walked through, and no harm came to him either. And the crowds in the narrow streets were only men and women like himself and his mother, though they wore garments of coloured cloth instead of skins, and some of them stared as he went by. And so he kept on walking up one street and down another, until he came to another gate arch, and again passed through. One of the men in the gateway asked his business, and he said that he had come to see the High King because he wanted to be a knight, and the men laughed, and one of them tapped his own forehead, but they let him through; and so he came at last to the entrance of the Great Hall.

Arthur and his knights were at their midday meal, and Sir Kay stood beside the King at the High Table, pouring wine into the golden cup in which, though

Percival, watching from the shadows just within the doorway, could not know that, it was Arthur's custom to pledge his knights before it passed from hand to hand among those of the brotherhood present, until all had shared the same cup. It seemed to him that he had never seen anything so brilliant or beautiful as the crowded Hall with the spring sunlight slanting down through the high windows upon the tables where the knights and their ladies sat, with the King, his Queen beside him, under the gold-worked canopy at the high table. He gazed at the splendid distant figure, and thought how wonderful it must be to be one of his knights, and his gaze went up and down the tables in search of the strange face of Sir Lancelot.

But in the same instant, before the King had even taken the goblet from Sir Kay, there came a jingling tramp of mailed feet, and a man all in red-gold armour glistening like a noon-day pheasant, came striding past Percival into the Hall and made for the high table, all men struck with astonishment to see him go by. 'Hai! You wine-bibbing dogs!' he shouted in a great voice. 'If wine-bibbing be a part of knighthood, here stands a better knight than all of you!' And he seized the cup from Sir Kay and drained it at one long gulping draught. Then, bellowing with laughter, he turned and strode out the way he had come, still gripping the precious cup. And they heard his horse's hooves strike sparks from the cobbles outside as he galloped away.

Then the frozen stillness that had seemed to hold the Hall in bonds snapped and Arthur sprang to his feet, and every one of his knights with him. 'Now by my faith!' cried Arthur. 'Here is an insult that shall not go unpaid for! Who will bring me back my drinking cup?'

'I will!' cried a hundred voices. 'Let *me* go!' 'Sir, I claim this quest!'

'No!' said Arthur. 'For none of you, in this quest.

The fellow is a churl, for all his golden armour, and not worthy to fall to a knight's spear. Let one of the squires who seeks for knighthood ride after him. And if he returns with my goblet, and wearing the fellow's game-cock armour, I will make him knight that very hour!'

Then Percival sprang forward from his shadowed corner. 'My lord, King Arthur, send me after your cup! I was needing a suit of armour, and the golden gear that one was wearing will do me finely!'

They all looked at the speaker, seeing a tall, strong young man, brown as an acorn, thatched with shining yellow hair, but wearing only deerskin and carrying a home-made spear. And Sir Kay, with his customary ill manners, let out a thin bark of laughter. 'Here's a fine champion for you, my Lord King! Pah! You stink of goats; get back to your herding, boy.'

'No need for that,' said the King to his Seneschal; and then to Percival, 'Come, if we are to speak together, we cannot well do it with the whole length of the Hall between us!'

And when Percival came and stood before him, he looked into the young face as though he found something suddenly interesting there. 'Pray you, tell me who you are?'

'I am called Percival, and my father was King Pellinore of Wales. But after he was killed, my mother and I lived alone in the forest, until now I come to you, that one day if I am worthy, I may ask you to make me a knight.'

'That's a fine fairy story,' said Sir Kay.

But the King, still looking into Percival's face, said, 'Your father was a friend of mine, and an honourable knight of my Round Table. I thought there was something in your face . . . Very well, the quest is yours. Bring me back my cup, and return flashing in that game-cock armour, and presently you shall take your

275

father's place.'

'I will be the truest knight to you that ever –' Percival began, his blue eyes blazing with eagerness.

'I am sure you will,' said the King. 'But first you must eat.'

Percival shook his head. 'Nay, I'll not wait for that, my Lord King. Pray you give me a horse –'

'There shall be a horse ready for you when you have eaten. Also armour and a spear.'

Percival would have none of the armour and weapons. 'I have my own spear,' he said. 'And armour I can do without, until I can put on the golden beetle-skin of the man who stole your cup.'

But he was hungry and he did eat a little, though in haste, then rose, and bowing to the King and the company, turned to go. But midway down the Hall, a damosel slipped out from among the Queen's maidens at a lower table and stood before him. 'God go with you, Sir Percival, best of knights!' she said.

But Sir Kay, following close behind, struck her across the face, knocking her sideways. 'Out of the way, you witless wench, and hold your peace!'

Percival looked round at him. 'Beware of me, when I return in my golden armour!' he said. 'For I will repay that blow on the maiden's behalf; and you shall not easily forget the repayment!'

And he strode on out of the Hall to the courtyard, where a fine dun horse was waiting for him, and scrambling into the high unfamiliar saddle, he rode away. At the city gate he asked which way the golden knight had gone, and headed in the same direction, giving the horse full rein. He had caught and ridden wild ponies among the Welsh hills, until they bucked him off, but never a tall horse such as this before. But the horse that had been chosen for him by Arthur's order was a wise one, and with no weight of armour to carry, he and his rider made better speed than the churlish knight in his golden harness; and about the time of long shadows they overtook him as he was riding up an open valley.

'Turn! Thief of gold cups!' Percival shouted as he drew nearer. 'Turn and fight!'

The knight checked and looked round, all the light of the westering sun blazing on his red-gold armour. And at sight of the half-naked boy on the warhorse, he laughed. 'And who are you, beggar-brat on a stolen horse, to bid me turn and fight?'

And he swung his horse round on the track and sat watching as the other came up to him.

'No beggar-brat, at least,' said Percival. 'But come from King Arthur's court, on a horse out of King Arthur's stables, to take back the cup that you stole from the King this day.'

'And *you* will take it back?' said the knight. '*You?*' And he rocked with laughter in his high gilded saddle.

'Also you shall yield to me, and strip off, for I've a mind to that fine golden armour that you wear so proudly.' Percival gentled his fidgeting horse with one hand and made ready his spear with the other, and added reasonably, 'Quickly now! Otherwise I shall kill you first and take both the cup and the armour afterwards.'

The golden knight ceased to laugh. He sat silent a moment as though not believing his own ears, and then let out a roar like a wild bull. 'Insolent whelp! You have asked for death, now you shall have it!' And he couched his spear and drove in his spurs and came charging down the steep track upon the half-naked stripling who had dared to stand against him.

But Percival leapt from his horse's back, so that the spear point whistled through the empty air where he had been; and as horse and rider thundered on, he whirled round, shouting after them, 'Coward! Chicken-heart! First you would spear an unarmed man, and then you run away down the hill! Come back and fight!'

Below him the man in the golden armour wrenched his horse round and came charging back, his spear levelled at Percival's breast. Percival waited until the last possible moment, poised lightly on the balls of his feet, then side-ducked, and as the murderous spear again whistled by him, drove in the point of his own weapon between the bars of the knight's vizor, so that it took him between the eyes and pierced through flesh and bone to the brain.

For a moment he swayed in the saddle, then slid over and pitched to the ground, as his horse fled on without him.

Percival, with a strange feeling in him between awe and triumph, knelt down beside the body and pulled out his spear, then took the golden cup from the wallet at the man's waist. Then he set about getting the Golden Knight out of his armour. He contrived to unlace the crested helmet and pull it off; but he could not think how to deal with the rest of the armour, for he did not understand the complicated straps and buckles and laces, and thought that it was all made in one piece. He was trying desperately to pull the Golden Knight bodily through the neck-hole of his harness, when he heard horse's hooves again, and looking up, saw an old man in plain dark armour, his helmet hanging from his saddle bow, sitting his horse and looking down at him, half smiling.

'That was a valiant kill,' said the old man. 'And this robber-knight deserved death if ever a man did; but what is it that you seek to do with him now?'

'I try to get him out of his armour, so that I can wear it myself. For I am sworn to King Arthur to bring him back his cup, which this man stole from him, and return in the robber's golden armour. The King promised me that if I did that, and showed myself worthy, he would make me a knight, by and by.' He gave another tug. 'But the neck-hole is not big enough!'

'Nay, it is not made all in one piece,' said the old knight, the smile deepening in his eyes and in his voice. And he dismounted, and kneeling beside Percival, showed him how to unbuckle and unlace the shining pieces and draw them off one by one.

'And now,' he said, getting to his feet when the task was finished, 'do you tell me your name.'

'I am Percival, son of King Pellinore of Wales.'

'And one day you hope to be Sir Percival, of the Round Table? I am called Gonemanus, and I live close by; so now, come back with me a while, that I may have the training of you in the ways of knighthood, as I would train a son of my own, for more than one skilful man-killing goes to the making of a worthy knight. Then you may go back to Arthur ready for his service.'

So Percival went with Sir Gonemanus to the ancient manor house that was his home, and remained with him all summer. And there he learned to ride, and the proper use of sword, shield and spear, and all the skills of knighthood. There too he learned of gentleness and chivalry and faithkeeping and all those qualities that should be a part of all true knights; though indeed much to that he had learned already from his mother in the charcoal-burner's bothie, just as he had learned from her how to pray.

He was a ready pupil, and by autumn he had learned all that Sir Gonemanus could teach him. So he bade the old man a grateful farewell, and set out, wearing the splendid golden armour and carrying a long spear, for Camelot, where the High King was at that time holding his court.

He rode through a world of gold and brown russet,

the bracken dead and sodden on the high moors, though here and there a strand of honeysuckle still in flower along the bank of some sunken green-way, and the fallen leaves muffled his horse's hoof-beats as he rode. But his heart was as high as springtime within him, and wherever he stopped and asked a night's lodging at some hermitage or lonely steading, or even paused to ask his way of a passing hunter or fellow traveller, always they felt when he had gone by, as though the sun had come out.

At last he came one early morning riding down the aisles of a beech wood, and knew from the forester at whose hut he had spent the night that Camelot was only a few miles ahead of him. It was a misty morning, and on every side the straight trunks of the great beeches rose up so that almost he seemed to be riding down the aisles of some vast many-pillared church. And all the world was quiet, with a solemn quiet as though it were waiting for something.

Presently he came out on to the verge of a broad track that showed signs of much coming and going of horses and men. The forester had told him that he would find such a track hereabouts, and that it led down to Camelot. Here, where there was open sky, he could see that the mist was thinning and faint blurs of blue beginning to show through the milky greyness of it. And so near his journey's end, he reined in his horse and pulled King Arthur's cup from its pouch, wondering suddenly whether he should have taken it back at once, and not kept it all this summer while he learned to be a knight; suddenly anxious lest there should be some dent or scratch on its bright surface. And as he sat turning it over in his hands, the first gleam of early sunshine struck through the mist and caught the cup, so that it flashed into his eyes with a radiance that was almost blinding; and in the same instant, from somewhere a

lark leapt up singing towards Heaven, heralding the
new day. And something pierced Percival as with a
spear of light. A memory? A message? It was gone
before he could lay hold of it to discover what it was.
Only he knew that it was to do with another cup, and
another sunbeam . . . And like the lark, there was
something that he heralded, some word that he had to
bring . . . something beautiful and terrible . . . Then
the mist drifted back again and the lark fell silent, and
he was left looking down at the King's golden cup, and
trying to lay hold of the memory that was already lost,
like the memory of a dream that fades on waking.

Scarcely aware of it, he put the cup back in its pouch.
But he made no move to urge his horse forward, but sat
on by the side of the track, still trying to find again the
lost and lovely moment . . .

He was not even aware of the four knights who came
riding up the track towards him, just as the four had
come on that spring day that now seemed so long ago.
Sir Kay and Sir Gawain and Sir Lancelot, and one who
bore on his shield a blood-red dragon on a golden
ground.

'Ride forward,' said the King to Sir Kay, 'and ask
yonder knight with the plain shield his name and why
he sits thus lost in thought by the side of the road.'

So Sir Kay pricked forward ahead of the rest, and
when he drew near to Percival, shouted with his usual
lack of courtesy, 'Ho! Sir Knight! What is your name
and what brings you on this road?'

But Percival, still seeking his lost moment, did not
even hear him.

'Are you dumb?' demanded Sir Kay, and ranging
alongside he struck Percival in the face with the back of
his mailed hand.

Percival came back to himself with the crash and pain
of the blow, and jerked his head back inside his helmet.

'No one strikes me such a coward's blow and rides away unscathed!' he told the angry knight he saw beside him. Then, recognising him, 'Aye, and there is a blow I promised you for another matter, too,' and wheeled his horse away, closing his vizor and setting his spear in rest. 'Defend yourself, Sir Kay!'

Sir Kay had also pulled his horse back, and for a moment they sat facing each other, then struck in their spurs and came thundering together. But Sir Kay checked a little at the final moment, which was a fault of his in jousting, while Percival pressed in his charge unhesitating; and so Kay's spear had lost force and was turned by the other's shield, while Percival, travelling like a thunderbolt, took him in the shoulder, and carried him clean over his horse's crupper and hurled him to the ground.

Then reining in his horse, he sat with lance in rest once more, defiantly confronting the other three. 'If any more of you would joust with me, come on!' he shouted. 'I am ready to defend my right to sit my horse by the roadside and think my own thoughts, without insults or blows from such a churlish knight as that one.'

Gawain said suddenly, 'That is Percival, I'll swear, and wearing the armour of that other churlish knight who stole your cup at Easter!'

'Go forward, and ask him to come and speak with us, nephew Gawain,' said the King, and added with a flicker of laughter in his tone, 'and ask it in all courtesy!'

So Gawain rode forward, with spear reversed in token of friendship. 'Gentle Sir Knight,' said he, 'yonder is our Lord the High King, and he is wishful to speak with you.'

And looking, Percival saw for the first time the red dragon on the golden ground, and knew that the bearer of that shield must be the King. 'I will beg the King's pardon that I have felled one of his knights,' he said.

'But I am not sorry that I did it, for I owed him that blow he gave to the damosel on the day I first came to Caerleon.'

'As to Sir Kay,' said Gawain, scarcely looking at the battered Seneschal, who was just getting back his wind and clambering slowly to his feet, 'he rides through life asking for what he gets, and often enough he gets it.'

'Then I am glad,' said Percival, 'for now I have kept both my promise to him, and my promise to the King that I would return to him with his golden cup and wearing the golden armour of the knight who stole it.'

And he rode back with Sir Gawain to where the King waited, and dismounted and knelt at his stirrup. 'Sir, my Lord King Arthur, here is your cup again. Now pray you make me one of your knights.'

Sir Gawain spoke, not unkindly, but quickly jealous to guard what he valued, 'It takes more than the slaying of one robber and the unhorsing of the King's Seneschal to make a man worthy of knighthood, let alone the Company of the Round Table!'

But the King said, 'Gawain, I know what I do. His name is already on his waiting place at the Table; it is so that I rode out to meet him.' And to Percival he said, 'Take off your helmet.'

An when that was done, he leaned down from the saddle and gave the kneeling young man in the golden armour a light blow between neck and shoulder. 'Rise, Sir Percival of Wales.'

So they returned to Camelot, with Sir Kay bringing up the rear and nursing his bruises. And when Percival had told his story to the rest of the assembled knights, and the five of them had been unarmed, and all went to take their places, there indeed was Sir Percival's name shining in fair new gold on the tall back of his waiting seat, the seat between Sir Gawain's and the Seat Perilous.

Sir Percival looked at the name, and then at Sir Gawain; and a stiffness came over his face. Gawain saw it, and said steadily, 'Aye, I am Gawain of Orkney, and yonder are my brothers Gaheris and Agravane and Gareth.'

Sir Percival looked at the other three, with the stiffness still in his face; and the other three looked back. And the talk about the Table drifted into silence. All knew that it was for Sir Percival to take up the old feud or leave it lying. And for a long moment Sir Percival himself did not know which he was going to do. He had told his mother that it must be as God willed; but now it seemed that God was leaving the choice to him. And after three slow heartbeats of time, he made it. 'God's greeting to you, sirs – I pray you grant me your friendship.'

'That will I,' said Sir Gareth warmly. 'God's welcome to our midst.'

'And I,' said Sir Gawain. 'And here's my hand on it.'

'And I,' said Sir Gaheris, bringing his own hand down with an open-palmed crash upon the table.

Even Sir Agravane smiled thinly.

And on the surface, that was all. But all those about the Table knew well enough what lay beneath. That what their youngest knight had really said was, 'My father killed yours and you killed mine; and nothing can change that. Therefore let us leave the old feud sleeping.'

And that the Orkney brothers had said, 'We understand, and we accept the peace-making.'

Later that day, the King said to the captain of his knights, 'Gawain was right when he said that it took more than the slaying of one robber and the unhorsing of the King's Seneschal to make a knight. But now I think the boy has proved his worth in a more difficult way.'

'It cannot have been easy to leave the old feud lying,' Lancelot agreed.

They were walking together in the narrow orchard below the western walls of the castle, the autumn sunset making a bonfire blaze beyond the distant hills. There were fallen apples lying in the grass, and a few still clinging to the trees that were almost bare of leaves. When they had first come out through the postern gate, the broad loop of the river below had been flashing back the singing gold of the westering sun. But now the mist was rising . . .

Arthur said suddenly, 'Do you remember Merlin?'

Lancelot thought. 'Yes,' he said at last, 'but not well. I only saw him once, when I was a boy in Less Britain before ever I became your man. It was he that sent me to you.'

'He said once – it was when Guenever came to me and brought the Round Table for her dowry, and when we first gathered to it as a brotherhood – he said then, that when Percival came to join us, it would be as though he were a herald.'

'A herald?'

'A sign, then. For by his coming we should know that within less than a year the Mystery of the Holy Grail would come – will come, upon us here at Camelot, bringing the final flowering and fruiting time of Logres; and the knights will leave the Round Table and ride out upon the greatest quest of all.'

'We shall come together again,' said Lancelot, trying to console him.

'Some of us,' said the King. 'But it will not be the same; never the same again.' He narrowed his eyes into the blazing sky over the western hills. 'We shall have done all that is in us to do. For Britain, for the kingdom of Logres. For all that we have fought and built for and tried to make secure . . . We shall have served our purpose; made a shining time between the Dark and the Dark. Merlin said that it would be as though all things drew on to the golden glory of the sunset. But then it will all be over.'

Lancelot said, 'We shall have made such a blaze, that men will remember us on the other side of the Dark.'

And the mist was rising, rising now all round the orchard, creeping almost among the feet of the apple trees and shutting out all things beyond, so that they might have been on an enchanted island.

Merlin's remembered voice, clear across twenty years and more, was in Arthur's memory, and it was the day that he received Excalibur. 'Away over yonder – away to the West – there lies Ynys Witrin, the Glass Island; Avalon of the Apple Trees, that is the threshold between the world of men and the Land of the Living . . .' Merlin's voice seemed actually in his head. 'And not far off is Camlann, the place of the last battle . . . Nay, but that is another story, for another day as yet far off . . .'

The voice faded, and he was back in the orchard below Camelot, and it was not Merlin with him, but Lancelot. And the voice in his ears was his own. 'It grows late,' he said, 'let us be going in to the feasting, to make welcome our newest-come knight of the Round Table.'

If you have enjoyed this book you may like to read the following Rosemary Sutcliff titles, also published by Knight Books.

SONG FOR A DARK QUEEN

A magnificent and haunting novel of Boudicca, or Boadicea, Queen of the Iceni, and of her battle against the Roman invaders.

'All Rosemary Sutcliff's well-known skills are here . . . brilliant . . . assured . . . superbly exciting.'

Times Literary Supplement

KNIGHT BOOKS

SUN HORSE, MOON HORSE

The world of the Early Iron Age people is powerfully recreated in this compelling interpretation of how the White Horse of Uffington might have been made.

'I found her interpretation both strong with poetic logic and bright with imaginative truth. Miss Sutcliff's best book for a long time.'
Leon Garfield, *The Guardian*

KNIGHT BOOKS

THE LIGHT BEYOND THE FOREST

A beautifully written and dramatic retelling of the legend of the Knights of the Round Table and the quest for the Holy Grail.

'A magnificent poetic retelling of some of the world's greatest legends by one of the best-known historical novelists in the world.'
The Paperback Buyer

KNIGHT BOOKS

MORE ROSEMARY SUTCLIFF TITLES AVAILABLE FROM KNIGHT BOOKS